Hands-On Python Natural Language Processing

Explore tools and techniques to analyze and process text with a view to building real-world NLP applications

Aman Kedia
Mayank Rasu

BIRMINGHAM - MUMBAI

Hands-On Python Natural Language Processing

Commissioning Editor: Sunith Shetty
Acquisition Editor: Siddharth Mandal
Content Development Editor: Sean Lobo
Senior Editor: Ayaan Hoda
Technical Editor: Manikandan Kurup
Copy Editor: Safis Editing
Project Coordinator: Aishwarya Mohan
Proofreader: Safis Editing
Indexer: Tejal Daruwale Soni
Production Designer: Shankar Kalbhor

First published: June 2020

Production reference: 1250620

Published by Packt Publishing Ltd.
Livery Place
35 Livery Street
Birmingham
B3 2PB, UK.

ISBN 978-1-83898-959-0

www.packt.com

Subscribe to our online digital library for full access to over 7,000 books and videos, as well as industry leading tools to help you plan your personal development and advance your career. For more information, please visit our website.

Why subscribe?

- Spend less time learning and more time coding with practical eBooks and Videos from over 4,000 industry professionals

- Improve your learning with Skill Plans built especially for you

- Get a free eBook or video every month

- Fully searchable for easy access to vital information

- Copy and paste, print, and bookmark content

Did you know that Packt offers eBook versions of every book published, with PDF and ePub files available? You can upgrade to the eBook version at www.packt.com and as a print book customer, you are entitled to a discount on the eBook copy. Get in touch with us at customercare@packtpub.com for more details.

At www.packt.com, you can also read a collection of free technical articles, sign up for a range of free newsletters, and receive exclusive discounts and offers on Packt books and eBooks.

About the authors

Aman Kedia is a data enthusiast and lifelong learner. He is an avid believer in **Artificial Intelligence (AI)** and the algorithms supporting it. He has worked on state-of-the-art problems in **Natural Language Processing (NLP)**, encompassing resume matching and digital assistants, among others. He has worked at Oracle and SAP, trying to solve problems leveraging advancements in AI. He has four published research papers in the domain of AI.

Mayank Rasu has more than 12 years of global experience as a data scientist and quantitative analyst in the investment banking industry. He has worked at the intersection of finance and technology and has developed and deployed AI-based applications within the finance domain. His experience includes building sentiment analyzers, robotics, and deep learning-based document review, among many others areas.

About the reviewers

Dr. Deepti Chopra has a Ph.D. in computer science and engineering from Banasthali Vidyapith. She has taught for 4 years as an assistant professor in the Department of Computer Science at Banasthali Vidyapith. Currently, she is working as an assistant professor (IT) at Lal Bahadur Shastri Institute of Management. Her areas of interest include AI, NLP, and computational linguistics. She has written several research papers for various international conferences and journals. Also, she is the author of three books and one MOOC.

Dr. Dhirendra Pratap Singh is a passionate NLP research scholar who strongly believes deep learning techniques can resolve any NLP research problem. His Ph.D. is focused on semantics and information extraction and retrieval using deep learning techniques. He has a good demonstrating background in his academic and industrial research. He has been invited by many prestigious universities for academic talks, including IIT Bombay, Guwahati, JNU, SRM Engineering University, University of Tokyo, and so on. He has publications at top NLP conferences including NAACL, GWC, ICON, LREC, and LSI. Currently, he is associated with two NLP-AI companies (Lionbridge Technologies and Appen) for opening up new ideas for research projects in computational linguistics.

Packt is searching for authors like you

If you're interested in becoming an author for Packt, please visit authors.packtpub.com and apply today. We have worked with thousands of developers and tech professionals, just like you, to help them share their insight with the global tech community. You can make a general application, apply for a specific hot topic that we are recruiting an author for, or submit your own idea.

Table of Contents

Preface

This book provides a blend of both the theoretical and practical aspects of **Natural Language Processing** (**NLP**). It covers the concepts essential to develop a thorough understanding of NLP and also delves into a detailed discussion on NLP-based use cases such as language translation, sentiment analysis, chatbots, and many more. The book also goes into the details of the application of machine learning and deep learning in improving the efficiency of NLP applications and introduces readers to the recent developments in this field. Every module covers real-world examples that can be replicated and built upon.

Who this book is for

This book is for anyone interested in NLP who is seeking to learn about its theoretical and practical aspects alike. The book starts from the basics and gradually progresses to more advanced concepts, making it suitable for an audience with varying levels of prior NLP proficiency, and for those who want to develop a thorough understanding of NLP methodologies to build linguistic applications. However, a working knowledge of the Python programming language and high-school-level mathematics is expected.

What this book covers

Chapter 1, *Understanding the Basics of NLP*, will introduce you to the past, present, and future of NLP research and applications.

Chapter 2, *NLP Using Python*, will gently introduce you to the Python libraries that are used frequently in NLP and that we will use later in the book.

Chapter 3, *Building Your NLP Vocabulary*, will introduce you to methodologies for natural language data cleaning and vocabulary building.

Chapter 4, *Transforming Text into Data Structures*, will discuss basic syntactical techniques for representing text using numbers and building a chatbot.

Chapter 5, *Word Embeddings and Distance Measurements for Text*, will introduce you to word-level semantic embedding creation and establishing the similarity between documents.

Chapter 6, *Exploring Sentence-, Document-, and Character-Level Embeddings*, will dive deeper into techniques for embedding creation at character, sentence, and document level, along with building a spellchecker.

Chapter 7, *Identifying Patterns in Text Using Machine Learning*, will use machine learning algorithms to build a sentiment analyzer.

Chapter 8, *From Human Neurons to Artificial Neurons for Understanding Text*, will introduce you to the concepts of deep learning and how they are used for NLP tasks such as question classification.

Chapter 9, *Applying Convolutions to Text*, will discuss how convolutions can be used to extract patterns in text data for solving NLP problems such as sarcasm detection.

Chapter 10, *Capturing Temporal Relationships in Text*, will explain how to extract sequential relationships prevalent in text data and build a text generator using them.

Chapter 11, *State of the Art in NLP*, will discuss recent concepts, including Seq2Seq modeling, attention, transformers, BERT, and will also see us building a language translator.

To get the most out of this book

You will need Python 3 installed on your system. You can use any IDE to practice the code samples provided in the book, but since the code samples are provided as Jupyter notebooks, we recommend installing the Jupyter IDE. All code examples have been tested on the Windows OS. However, the programs are platform agnostic and should work with other 32/64-bit OSes as well. Other system requirements include RAM of 4 GB or higher, and at least 6 GB of free disk space.

We recommend installing the Python libraries discussed in this book using pip or conda. The code snippets in the book mention the relevant command to install a given library on the Windows OS. Please refer to the source page of the library for installation instructions for other OSes.

Software/hardware covered in the book	OS requirements
pandas	Windows 7 or later, macOS, Linux
NumPy	Windows 7 or later, macOS, Linux
Jupyter	Windows 7 or later, macOS, Linux
beautifulsoup4	Windows 7 or later, macOS, Linux
scikit-learn	Windows 7 or later, macOS, Linux
Keras	Windows 7 or later, macOS, Linux
NLTK	Windows 7 or later, macOS, Linux

The last project covered in this book requires a higher-spec machine. However, you can run the program on the Google Colab GPU machine if needs be.

If you are using the digital version of this book, we advise you to type the code yourself or access the code via the GitHub repository (link available in the next section). Doing so will help you avoid any potential errors related to the copying and pasting of code.

Download the example code files

You can download the example code files for this book from your account at `www.packt.com`. If you purchased this book elsewhere, you can visit `www.packtpub.com/support` and register to have the files emailed directly to you.

You can download the code files by following these steps:

1. Log in or register at `www.packt.com`.
2. Select the **Support** tab.
3. Click on **Code Downloads**.
4. Enter the name of the book in the **Search** box and follow the onscreen instructions.

Once the file is downloaded, please make sure that you unzip or extract the folder using the latest version of:

- WinRAR/7-Zip for Windows
- Zipeg/iZip/UnRarX for Mac
- 7-Zip/PeaZip for Linux

The code bundle for the book is also hosted on GitHub at `https://github.com/PacktPublishing/Hands-On-Python-Natural-Language-Processing`. In case there's an update to the code, it will be updated on the existing GitHub repository.

We also have other code bundles from our rich catalog of books and videos available at `https://github.com/PacktPublishing/`. Check them out!

Download the color images

We also provide a PDF file that has color images of the screenshots/diagrams used in this book. You can download it here: `https://static.packt-cdn.com/downloads/9781838989590_ColorImages.pdf`.

Conventions used

There are a number of text conventions used throughout this book.

`CodeInText`: Indicates code words in text, database table names, folder names, filenames, file extensions, pathnames, dummy URLs, user input, and Twitter handles. Here is an example: "We will be performing preprocessing on the `Tips` dataset, which comes with the `seaborn` Python package."

A block of code is set as follows:

```
import pandas as pd
data = pd.read_csv("amazon_cells_labelled.txt", sep='\t', header=None)

X = data.iloc[:,0] # extract column with review
y = data.iloc[:,-1] # extract column with sentiment

# tokenize the news text and convert data in matrix format
from sklearn.feature_extraction.text import CountVectorizer
vectorizer = CountVectorizer(stop_words='english')
X_vec = vectorizer.fit_transform(X)
X_vec = X_vec.todense() # convert sparse matrix into dense matrix

# Transform data by applying term frequency inverse document frequency
(TFIDF)
from sklearn.feature_extraction.text import TfidfTransformer
tfidf = TfidfTransformer()
X_tfidf = tfidf.fit_transform(X_vec)
X_tfidf = X_tfidf.todense()
```

Any command-line input or output is written as follows:

```
pip install requests
pip install beautifulsoup4
```

Bold: Indicates a new term, an important word, or words that you see on screen. For example, words in menus or dialog boxes appear in the text like this. Here is an example: "This is called **cross-validation** and is an important part of ML model training. "

 Warnings or important notes appear like this.

Tips and tricks appear like this.

Get in touch

Feedback from our readers is always welcome.

General feedback: If you have questions about any aspect of this book, mention the book title in the subject of your message and email us at customercare@packtpub.com.

Errata: Although we have taken every care to ensure the accuracy of our content, mistakes do happen. If you have found a mistake in this book, we would be grateful if you would report this to us. Please visit www.packtpub.com/support/errata, selecting your book, clicking on the Errata Submission Form link, and entering the details.

Piracy: If you come across any illegal copies of our works in any form on the internet, we would be grateful if you would provide us with the location address or website name. Please contact us at copyright@packt.com with a link to the material.

If you are interested in becoming an author: If there is a topic that you have expertise in, and you are interested in either writing or contributing to a book, please visit authors.packtpub.com.

Reviews

Please leave a review. Once you have read and used this book, why not leave a review on the site that you purchased it from? Potential readers can then see and use your unbiased opinion to make purchase decisions, we at Packt can understand what you think about our products, and our authors can see your feedback on their book. Thank you!

For more information about Packt, please visit packt.com.

Section 1: Introduction

This section introduces the field of **Natural Language Processing** (**NLP**) and its applications. It also provides you with an overview of the ongoing research in this area and what future applications could be expected.

This section comprises the following chapters:

- Chapter 1, *Understanding the Basics of NLP*
- Chapter 2, *NLP Using Python*

Understanding the Basics of NLP

1

Natural Language Processing (**NLP**) is an interdisciplinary area of research aimed at making machines understand and process human languages. It is an evolving field, with a rapid increase in its acceptability and adoption in industry, and its growth is projected to continue. NLP-based applications are everywhere, and chances are that you already interact with an NLP-enabled application regularly (Alexa, Google Translate, chatbots, and so on). The objective of this book is to provide a hands-on learning experience and help you build NLP applications by understanding key NLP concepts. The book lays particular emphasis on **Machine Learning** (**ML**)- and **Deep Learning** (**DL**)-based applications and also delves into recent advances such as **Bidirectional Encoder Representations from Transformers** (**BERT**). We start this journey by providing a brief context of NLP and introduce you to some existing and evolving applications of NLP.

In this chapter, we'll cover the following topics:

- Programming languages versus natural languages
- Why should I learn NLP?
- Current applications of NLP

Programming languages versus natural languages

Language has played a critical role in the evolution of our species and was arguably the key competitive advantage for our hunter-gatherer ancestors over other species. Naturally evolved languages, also called natural languages, allowed our ancestors to communicate more efficiently with their flock. The development of language scripts further accelerated their growth, as important information could now be documented and reproduced, obviating the need for memorizing. Needless to say, we humans have a deep affinity toward our languages, and we cherish the ability to communicate with fellow humans.

A new class of languages called programming languages surfaced around the mid-20th century, with the objective of communicating with machines to get the desired output. With the explosive growth of computers, gaining familiarity with programming languages assumed great significance in order to harness the computational power of these machines. You will come across various profiles on LinkedIn in which people refer to themselves as polyglots, implying that they are proficient in multiple programming languages. While there are similarities between natural languages and programming languages, in that they are used to communicate and have rules and syntax, there are some major differences. The most important difference is that natural languages are ambiguous, and therefore cannot be comprehended by machines. For example, refer to the following statement: *Pick an integer and divide it by two; if the remainder is zero, then it is an even number.*

For those who are presumably proficient in Math and English, the preceding statement may make complete sense. However, for someone who is new to deciphering human languages, *it* may refer to either the *integer*, *two*, or the *remainder*. Likewise, natural languages encompass many other elements, such as sarcasm, double negation, rhetorical expressions, and so on, which increases complexity and requires a monumental effort to code every inherent rule of the language for the machine to understand. These factors make natural languages unfit to be used as programming languages.

How, then, do we communicate with computers humanly?

Understanding NLP

Scientists have been working on this precise question since the turn of the last century and, as of today, we have attained reasonable success in this area. The research on how to make computers understand and manipulate natural languages draws from several fields, including computer science, math, linguistics, and neuroscience, and the resulting interdisciplinary area of research is called NLP. Take a look at the following diagram, which illustrates this:

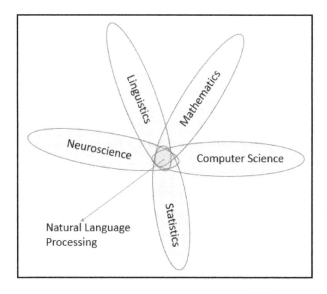

NLP is categorized as a subfield of the broader **Artificial Intelligence (AI)** discipline, which delves into simulating human intelligence in machines. English scientist Alan Turing, who is considered one of the pioneers of AI, developed a set of criteria (called the Turing test), which tested whether a machine could display intelligent behavior indistinguishable from that of a human. The machine's ability to understand and process natural languages is a prominent criterion of the Turing test.

Most early research in the field of NLP relied on fixed complex rules and mapping-based systems. These systems, although moderately successful, were difficult to scale. Another issue with the rule-based approach is that it does not mimic human learning of language very well. For example, if you are from Asia and are traveling to the USA, you will come across people who greet you by saying, *How's it going?* or *How are you doing?* A fixed rule-based language processing system would signal that the person cares about you and is genuinely interested to know about your wellbeing. However, before you prepare to give your long-winded response of how you are actually doing, you will see that the person has already walked by. When you see this pattern reoccurring and observe how other people respond to the same question, your brain overwrites the pre-existing rule and replaces it with a new contextual understanding, which was derived by some form of data analysis.

This data-driven approach is the cornerstone of most modern-day NLP research. With the advent of ML algorithms and the data deluge propelled by the internet and significantly increased computational capacity, NLP solutions have become way more scalable and reliable. The most exciting thing about this NLP revolution is that most of this is driven by open source technology, meaning these solutions are freely available to anyone who wants to consume or contribute to these projects.

We have covered many of these algorithms and tools in this book, including the following:

- ML algorithms (**Naive Bayes**; **Support Vector Machine (SVM)**)
- DL algorithms (**Convolutional Neural Network (CNN)**; **Recurrent Neural Network (RNN)**)
- Similarity/dissimilarity measures
- **Long Short-Term Memory (LSTM)** network; **Gated Recurrent Unit (GRU)**
- BERT
- Building chatbots; sentiment analyzer
- Predictive analytics on text data
- Machine translation system

We hope that by the end of this book, you will be able to build reasonably sophisticated NLP applications on your desktop PC.

Why should I learn NLP?

AI is rapidly penetrating various facets of our lives, from being our home assistant to fielding our queries as automated tech support. Various industry outlook reports project that AI will create millions of jobs (projection range between 200 and 500 million) worldwide by the year 2030. The majority of these jobs will require ML and NLP skills, and therefore it is imperative for engineers and technologists to upskill and prepare for the impending AI revolution and the rapidly evolving tech landscape.

NLP consistently features as the fastest-growing skill in demand by Upwork (largest freelancing platform), and the job listings with an NLP tag continue to feature prominently on various job boards. Since NLP is a subfield of ML, organizations typically hire candidates as ML engineers to work on NLP projects. You could be working on the most cutting-edge ideas in large technology firms or implementing NLP technology-based applications in banks, e-commerce organizations, and so on. The exact work performed by NLP engineers can vary from project to project. However, working with large volumes of unstructured data, preprocessing data, reading research papers on the new development in the field, tuning model parameters, continuous improvement, and so on are some of the tasks that are commonly performed. The authors, having worked on several NLP projects and having followed the latest industry trends closely, can safely state that it's a very exciting time to work in the field of NLP.

You can benefit from learning about NLP even if you are simply a tech enthusiast and not particularly looking for a job as an NLP engineer. You can expect to build reasonably sophisticated NLP applications and tools on your MacBook or PC, on a shoestring budget. It is not surprising, therefore, that there has been a surge of start-ups providing NLP-based solutions to enterprises and retail clients.

A few of the exciting start-ups in this area are listed as follows:

- **Luminance:** Legal tech start-up aimed at analyzing legal documents
- **NetBase:** Real-time social media feed analytics
- **Agolo:** Summarizes large bodies of text at scale
- **Idibon:** Converts unstructured data to structured data

This area is also witnessing brisk acquisition activities with larger tech companies acquiring start-ups (Samsung acquired Kngine; Reliance Communications acquired chatbot start-up Haptik; and so on). Given the low barriers for entry and easily accessible open source technologies, this trend is expected to continue.

Now that we have familiarized ourselves with NLP and the benefits of gaining proficiency in this area, we will discuss the current and evolving applications of NLP.

Current applications of NLP

NLP applications are everywhere, and it is highly unlikely that you have not interacted with any such application over the past few days. The current applications include virtual assistants (Alexa, Siri, Cortana, and so on), customer support tools (chatbots, email routers/classifiers, and so on), sentiment analyzers, translators, and document ranking systems. The adoption of these tools is quickly growing, since the speed and accuracy of these applications have increased manifold over the years. It should be noted that many popular NLP applications such as, Alexa and conversational bots, need to process audio data, which can be quantified by capturing the frequency of the underlying sound waves of the audio. For these applications, the data preprocessing steps are different from those for a text-based application, but the core principles of analyzing the data remain the same and will be discussed in detail in this book.

The following are examples of some widely used NLP tools. These tools could be web applications or desktop applications with which you can interact via the user interface. We will be covering the models powering these tools in detail in the subsequent chapters.

Chatbots

Chatbots are AI-based software that can conduct conversations with humans in natural languages. Chatbots are used extensively as the first point of customer support and have been very effective in resolving simple user queries. As per industry estimates, the size of the global chatbot market is expected to grow to $102 billion by 2025, compared to the market size of $17 billion in 2019 (source: `https://www.mordorintelligence.com/industry-reports/chatbot-market`). The significant savings generated by these chatbots for organizations is the major driver for the increase in the uptake of this technology.

Chatbots can be simple and rule-based, or highly sophisticated, depending on business requirements. Most chatbots deployed in the industry today are trained to direct users to the appropriate source of information or respond to queries pertaining to a specific subject. It is highly unlikely to have a **generalist** chatbot capable of fielding questions pertaining to a number of areas. This is because training a chatbot on a given topic requires a copious amount of data, and training on a number of topics could result in performance issues.

The next screenshots are from my conversation with one of the smartest chatbots available, named Mitsuku (`https://www.pandorabots.com/mitsuku/`). The Mitsuku chatbot was created by Steve Worswick and it has the distinction of winning the Loebner Prize multiple times due to it being adjudged the most human-like AI application.

The application was created using **Artificial Intelligence Markup Language (AIML)** and is mostly a rule-based application. Have a look at the following screenshots:

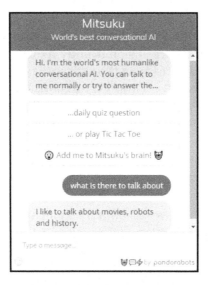

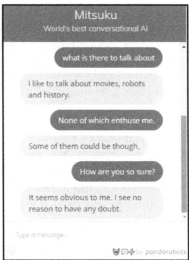

As you can see, this bot is able to hold simple conversations, just like a human. However, once you start asking technical questions or delve deeper into a topic, the quality of the responses deteriorates. This is expected, though, and we are still some time away from full human-like chatbots. You are encouraged to try engaging with Mitsuku in both simple and technical conversations and judge the accuracy yourself.

Sentiment analysis

Sentiment analysis is a set of algorithms and techniques used to detect the sentiment (positive, negative, or neutral) of a given text. This is a very powerful application of NLP and finds usage in a number of industries. Sentiment analysis has allowed entities to mine opinions from a much wider audience at significantly reduced costs. The traditional way of garnering feedback for companies has been through surveys, closed user group testing, and so on, which could be quite expensive. However, organizations can reduce costs by scraping data (from social media platforms or review-gathering sites) and using sentiment analysis to come up with an overall sentiment index of their products.

Here are some other examples of use cases of sentiment analysis:

- A stock investor scanning news about a company to assess overall market sentiment
- An individual scanning tweets about the launch of a new phone to decide the prevailing sentiment
- A political party analyzing social media feeds to assess the sentiment regarding their candidate

Sentiment analyzing systems can be simple lexicon-based (akin to a dictionary lookup) or ML-/DL-based. The choice of the method is dictated by business requirements, the respective pros and cons of each approach, and other development constraints. We will be covering the ML/DL based methods in detail in this book.

A simple Google search will yield numerous online sentiment analyzing sources such as *paralleldots.com* (`https://www.paralleldots.com/sentiment-analysis`).

You are encouraged to try submitting sentences or paragraphs to the tool and analyze the response. These tools will most likely do a reasonably good analysis of simple sentences or articles. However, the output for sentences with complex structures (double negation, rhetorical questions, qualifiers, and so on) will likely not be accurate. It should also be noted that before using a prebuilt sentiment analyzer, it is very important to understand the methodology and training dataset used to build that analyzer. You do not want to use a sentiment analyzer trained on movie review data to predict the sentiment of text from a different area (such as financial news articles or restaurant reviews), as words that carry a positive or negative context for one area may have a neutral or opposite polarity context for another area. For example, some words signifying a positive sentiment in financial news articles are *bullish*, *green*, *expansion*, and *growth*. However, these words, if used in a movie review context, would not be polarity-influencing words. Therefore, it is important to use suitable training data in order to build a sentiment analyzer.

We will delve deeper into sentiment analysis in `Chapter 7`, *Identifying Patterns in Text Using Machine Learning*, and will build a sentiment analyzer using product review data.

Machine translation

Language translation was one of the early problems NLP techniques tried to solve. At the height of the Cold War, there was a pressing need for American researchers to translate Russian documents into English using AI techniques. In 1964, the US government even created a multidisciplinary committee of leading scientists, linguists, and researchers to explore the feasibility of machine translation, and called the committee the **Automatic Language Processing Advisory Committee (ALPAC)**. However, ALPAC was unable to make any significant breakthrough, which caused major skepticism around the feasibility of AI technology, leading to massive funding cuts and a reduced interest in AI research throughout the 1970s. This period is often called the **AI Winter** due to the significant drop in research output pertaining to AI. Although the efforts of ALPAC did not yield promising results back then, today, we have translators with a very high level of accuracy.

The high market value of the translation industry in the present era of highly interconnected communities and global businesses is self-evident. Although businesses still rely mostly on human translators to translate important documents such as legal contracts, the use of NLP techniques to translate conversations has been increasing.

The modern NLP approach toward document translation is rooted in DL and pattern detection, which has significantly increased the accuracy of translations. Google Translate (`https://translate.google.co.in/`) supposedly uses an **Artificial Neural Network (ANN)**-based system that predicts the possible sequence of the translated words.

We wanted to conduct a quick test of Google Translate's accuracy in translating a text from English to Hindi.

Here is a screenshot, showing the result:

For readers who can read Hindi, the first sentence was translated perfectly. However, the second translated sentence is nonsensical. This could be because the usage of the word **wonder** in the sentence is not a wide one, and the training data possibly had all instances of **wonder** in a different context.

We thought it may be a good idea to see how other popular translators would translate the same sentence. The following screenshot shows the result derived from the Bing translator (`https://www.bing.com/translator`):

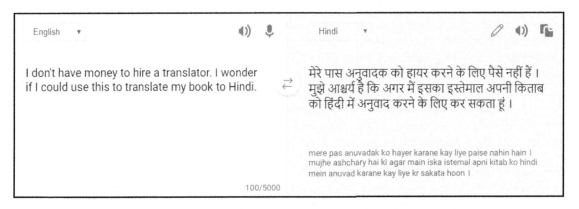

We found that the Bing translator's translation for our sentence was slightly inferior to that provided by Google Translate as, in addition to getting the context of the word **wonder** wrong, it was also unable to translate the word **hire** and simply transliterated it.

Finally, we tried the Babylon translator (`https://translation.babylon-software.com/`) with the same sentence. The following screenshot shows the result:

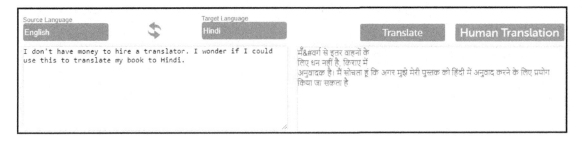

We found that the Babylon translator was unable to translate the sentence, as the output was gibberish.

It should be noted that the translation was instant in all three translators, meaning that the execution time for machine translation has greatly reduced. Based on our very unscientific testing, it is clear that while we have made huge strides in machine translation efficacy, there is still scope for improvement, and research in this area is still ongoing.

Named-entity recognition

When we read and process sentences, we tend to first identify the key players in the sentence (for example, people, places, and organizations). This classification helps us break down the sentence into **entities** and make sense of the semantics of the sentence. **Named-entity recognition** (**NER**) mimics the same behavior and is used to classify the named entities (or proper nouns) in a given text. The applications of this seemingly facile categorization are profound and are used extensively in the industry. Here are some real-world applications of NER:

- **Text summarization:** Scanning text documents and summarizing them by identifying key entities in the document. A popular use case is resume categorization, wherein the NER processes a large number of resumes and highlights key entities such as name, institution, and skills, which facilitates quick evaluation.
- **Automatic indexing:** Indexing is the method of organizing data for efficient retrieval. Using NER, documents are indexed based on underlying entities, which facilitates faster retrieval.
- **Information extraction:** Extracting relevant information (entities) from a document for faster processing. A use case is customer feedback processing, wherein key entities from feedback, such as product name and location are extracted for further processing. Typically, customer feedback processing also involves a sentiment analyzer that detects the tone of the feedback (positive or negative), and the NER then identifies the product, location, and so on, which is covered in the feedback. Such systems allow organizations to quickly process large volumes of customer feedback data and gain precision insights.

Stanford Named Entity Tagger (`https://nlp.stanford.edu/software/CRF-NER.html`) is a popular open source NER tool that comes with a default trained model that classifies entities such as **Person, Location**, and **Organization**. However, users can train their own models on the Stanford NER tool using a labeled dataset. The application is built on a linear chain **Conditional Random Field (CRF)** sequence model, which is a class of statistical modeling methods often used for pattern recognition. The software is written in Java and is available to download for free.

In addition, the trained model can also be accessed through a web interface. The following screenshot shows a sample sentence being processed by the Stanford NER web interface:

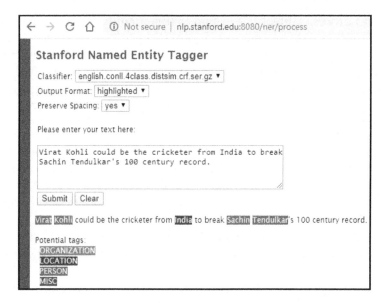

In this example, the NER tool did a decent job and correctly categorized the two persons (**Virat Kohli** and **Sachin Tendulkar**) and one location (**India**) mentioned in the sentence. It should be noted that there are other entities as well in the sentence shown in the preceding screenshot (for example, number and profession). However, the Stanford NER tool only recognizes four entities. The choice of the number of entities to be recognized depends on the training data and the model design.

Now, let's look at some promising future applications of NLP as well.

Future applications of NLP

Although we have made huge strides in improving NLP technologies, ongoing research continues to strive for improved accuracy and more optimized algorithms (for reduced response time). The objective continues to be moving toward more human-like applications. Here are some examples of technological advances and potential future applications in the area of NLP:

- **BERT:** BERT is a path-breaking technique for NLP research and development. It is being developed by Google and is a very clever amalgamation of a number of algorithms and techniques used in NLP (Transformer, ELMo, Semi-Supervised Sequence Learning, and so on). The paper, published by Google researchers, explaining this model can be accessed at `https://arxiv.org/abs/1810.04805`. At a high level, BERT tries to understand the context of a word by taking into account all surrounding words rather than an ordered sequence of words. For example, if the sentence *Are you game for a cup of coffee?* is analyzed by traditional NLP algorithms, they will analyze the word *game* by either looking at *Are you game* or at *game for a cup of coffee*. However, since BERT is bidirectional, it considers the entire sentence to decide the context of the word. BERT is open source and comes with rigorous pre trained models. BERT has significantly improved the efficiency and accuracy of building NLP models. We will get into the details of BERT in `Chapter 11`, *State of the Art in NLP*.

- **Legal tech:** The possibility of applying NLP technology to the legal profession is a very promising and lucrative prospect, and a lot of research is being conducted in this area. Given the vast number of legal documents lawyers need to pore through in order to retrieve required information for a case or the repetitive nature of perusing through legal contracts to ensure that they are correct, NLP can play a significant role in this field. However, most solutions to date remain in the **Proof of Concept (PoC)** phase, and adoption is minimal. However, many legal, tech-focused start-ups are springing up, trying to get a piece of a very lucrative developing market.

- **Unstructured data:** Most NLP tools rely on clean input data to be provided as input. However, the real world has a lot of unstructured data that needs analyzing. For example, a financial analyst may need to go through a company's annual financial filings, emails, call records, chat transcripts, news reports, complaint logs, and so on to prepare their report. Extracting relevant information from these unstructured data sources is a promising area of NLP application, and some exciting research in this area is ongoing.

- **Text summarization:** Research is underway around building applications that have the ability to read through a document, understand the context, and present a summary in a coherent way.

Summary

In this chapter, we discussed the foundational aspects of NLP and highlighted the importance of this evolving field of research. We also introduced some existing and upcoming applications of NLP, which we will build upon in the subsequent chapters.

In the next chapter, we will discuss Python and how it is playing a pivotal role in the development of NLP. We will gain familiarity with key Python libraries used in NLP and also delve into web scraping.

2
NLP Using Python

Natural Language Processing (**NLP**) research and development is occurring concurrently in many programming languages. Some very popular NLP libraries are written in various programming languages, such as Java, Python, and C++. However, we have chosen to write this book in Python and, in this chapter, we'll discuss the merits of using Python to delve into NLP. We'll also introduce the important Python libraries and tools that we will be using throughout this book.

In the chapter, we'll cover the following topics:

- Understanding Python with NLP
- Important Python libraries
- Web scraping libraries and methodology
- Overview of Jupyter Notebook

Let's get started!

Technical requirements

The code files for this chapter can be found at the following GitHub link: `https://github.com/PacktPublishing/Hands-On-Python-Natural-Language-Processing/tree/master/Chapter02`.

Understanding Python with NLP

Python is a high-level, object-oriented programming language that has experienced a meteoric rise in popularity. It is an open source programming language, meaning anyone with a functioning computer can download and start using Python. Python's syntax is simple and aids in code readability, ease of use in terms of debugging, and supports Python modules, thereby encouraging modularity and scalability.

In addition, it has many other features that contribute to its halo and make it an extremely popular language in the developer community. A prominent drawback often attributed to Python is its relatively slower execution speed compared to compiled languages. However, Python's performance is shown to be comparable to other languages and it can be vastly improved by employing clever programming techniques or using libraries built using compiled languages.

If you are a Python beginner, you may consider downloading the Python Anaconda distribution (https://www.anaconda.com/products/individual), which is a free and open source distribution for scientific computing and data science. Anaconda has a number of very useful libraries and it allows very convenient package management (installing/uninstalling applications). It also ships with multiple **Interactive Development Environments (IDEs)** such as Spyder and Jupyter Notebook, which are some of the most widely used IDEs due to their versatility and ease of use. Once downloaded, the Anaconda suite can be installed easily. You can refer to the installation documentation for this (https://docs.anaconda.com/anaconda/install/).

After installing Anaconda, you can use the Anaconda Prompt (this is similar to Command Prompt, but it lets you run Anaconda commands) to install any Python library using any of the Anaconda's package managers. pip and conda are the two most popular package managers and you can use either to install libraries.

The following is a screenshot of the Anaconda Prompt with the command to install the pandas library using pip:

Now that we know how to install libraries, let's explore the simplicity of Python in terms of carrying out reasonably complex tasks.

We have a CSV file with flight arrival and departure data from major US airports from July 2019. The data has been sourced from the US Department of Transportation website (https://www.transtats.bts.gov/DL_SelectFields.asp?Table_ID=236).

The file extends to more than half a million rows. The following is a partial snapshot of the dataset:

YEAR	MONTH	DAY	CARRIER	ORIGIN	DEST	SCHED_DEP_TIME	ACT_DEP_TIME	DEP_DELAY	SCHED_ARR_TIME	ACT_ARR_TIME	ARR_DELAY
2019	7	24	G4	PIE	AVL	1511	1533	22	1644	1659	15
2019	7	29	G4	AUS	SFB	2002	2010	8	2335	2344	9
2019	7	7	G4	GRI	LAS	1118	1118	0	1144	1139	-5
2019	7	7	G4	AUS	MEM	1643	1726	43	1827	1922	55
2019	7	8	G4	IND	PIE	858	905	7	1107	1119	12
2019	7	20	G4	PBG	FLL	1139	1135	-4	1457	1436	-21
2019	7	25	G4	GRR	AZA	1233	1240	7	1315	1314	-1
2019	7	31	G4	BNA	CID	1529	1528	-1	1701	1654	-7
2019	7	2	G4	SFB	LIT	1800	1907	67	1911	2016	65
2019	7	2	G4	SFB	DSM	1141	1136	-5	1330	1327	-3
2019	7	4	G4	PSC	LAX	1842	1854	12	2104	2125	21
2019	7	18	G4	RFD	PGD	1639	1652	13	2019	2035	16
2019	7	19	G4	TUS	PVU	1528	1527	-1	1808	1756	-12
2019	7	19	G4	PIE	FWA	1817	1813	-4	2034	2023	-11
2019	7	21	G4	BLV	LAS	1242	1231	-11	1405	1340	-25
2019	7	2	G4	LCK	PIE	1021	1014	-7	1231	1218	-13
2019	7	15	G4	TYS	BWI	1348	1344	-4	1516	1519	3
2019	7	12	G4	PGD	BNA	1036	1028	-8	1132	1109	-23
2019	7	16	G4	CID	PIE	1720	1835	75	2056	2213	77
2019	7	17	G4	AZA	LAS	930	1018	48	1036	1121	45

We are interested to know about which airport has the longest average delay in terms of flight departure. This task was completed using the following three lines of code. The pandas library can be installed using pip, as discussed previously:

```
import pandas as pd

data = pd.read_csv("flight_data.csv")
data.groupby("ORIGIN").mean()["DEP_DELAY"].idxmax()
```

Here's the output:

```
Out[15]: 'PPG'
```

So, it turns out that a remote airport (Pago Pago international airport) somewhere in the American Samoa had the longest average departure delays recorded in July 2019. As you can see, a relatively complex task was completed using only three lines of code. The simple-looking, almost English-like code helped us read a large dataset and perform quantitative analysis in a fraction of a second. This sample code also showcases the power of Python's modular programming.

In the first line of the code, we imported the pandas library, which is one of the most important libraries of the Python data science stack. Please refer pandas' documentation page (https://pandas.pydata.org/docs/) for more information, which is quite helpful and easy to follow. By importing the pandas library, we were able to avoid writing the code for reading a CSV file line by line and parsing the data. It also helped us utilize pre-coded pandas functions such as idxmax(), which returns the index of the maximum value of a row or column in a data frame (a pandas object that stores data in tabular format). Using these functions significantly reduced our effort in getting the required information.

Other programming languages have powerful libraries too, but the difference is that Python libraries tend to be very easy to install, import, and deploy. In addition, the large, open source developer community of Python translates to a vast number of very useful libraries being made available regularly. It's no surprise, then, that Python is particularly popular in the data science and machine learning domain and that the most widely used **Machine Learning (ML)** and DS libraries are either Python-based or are Python wrappers. Since NLP draws a lot from data science, ML, and **Deep Learning (DL)** disciplines, Python is very much becoming the lingua franca for NLP as well.

Python's utility in NLP

Learning a new language is not easy. For an average person, it can take months or even years to attain intermediate level fluency in a new language. It requires an understanding of the language's syntax (grammar), memorizing its vocabulary, and so on, to gain confidence in that language. Likewise, it is also quite challenging for computers to learn natural language since it is impractical to code every single rule of that language.

Let's assume we want to build a virtual assistant that reads queries submitted by a website's users and then directs them to the appropriate section of the website. Let's say the virtual assistant receives a request stating, *How do we change the payment method and payment frequency?*

If we want to train our virtual assistant the human way, then we will need to upload an English dictionary in its memory (the easy part), find a way to teach it English grammar (speech, clause, sentence structure, and so on), and logical interpretation. Needless to say, this approach is going to require a herculean effort. However, what if we could transform the sentence into mathematical objects so that the computer can apply mathematical or logical operations and make some sense out of it? That mathematical construct can be a vector, matrix, and so on.

For example, what if we assume an N-dimensional space where each dimension (axis) of the space corresponds to a word from the English vocabulary? With this, we can represent the preceding statement as a vector in that space, with its coordinate along each axis being the count of the word representing that axis. So, in the given sentence, the sentence vector's magnitude along the `payment` axes will be 2, the `frequency` axes will be 1, and so on. The following is some sample code we can use to achieve this **vectorization** in Python. We will use the `scikit-learn` library to perform vectorization, which can be installed by running the following command in the Anaconda Prompt:

```
pip install scikit-learn
```

Using the `CountVectorizer` module of Python's scikit-learn library, we have vectorized the preceding sentence and generated the output matrix with the vector (we will go into the details of this in subsequent chapters):

```
from sklearn.feature_extraction.text import CountVectorizer

sentence = ["How to change payment method and payment frequency"]
vectorizer = CountVectorizer(stop_words='english')
vectorizer.fit_transform(sentence).todense()
```

Here is the output:

```
matrix([[1, 1, 1, 2]]), dtype=int64)
```

This vector can now be compared with other sentence vectors in the same *N*-dimensional space and we can derive some sort of meaning or relationship between these sentences by applying vector principles and properties. This is an example of how a sentence comprehension task could be transformed into a linear algebra problem. However, as you may have already noticed, this approach is computationally intensive as we need to transform sentences into vectors, apply vector principles, and perform calculations. While this approach may not yield a perfectly accurate outcome, it opens an avenue for us to explore by leveraging mathematical theorems and established bodies of research.

Expecting humans to use this approach for sentence comprehension may be impractical, but computers can do these tasks fairly easily, and that's where programming languages such as Python become very useful in NLP research. Please note that the example in this section is just one example of transforming an NLP problem into a mathematical construct in order to facilitate processing. There are many other methods that will be discussed in detail in this book.

Important Python libraries

We will now discuss some of the most important Python libraries for NLP. We will delve deeper into some of these libraries in subsequent chapters.

NLTK

The **Natural Language Toolkit library (NLTK)** is one of the most popular Python libraries for natural language processing. It was developed by Steven Bird and Edward Loper of the University of Pennsylvania. Developed by academics and researchers, this library is intended to support research in NLP and comes with a suite of pedagogical resources that provide us with an excellent way to learn NLP. We will be using NLTK throughout this book, but first, let's explore some of the features of NLTK.

However, before we do anything, we need to install the library by running the following command in the Anaconda Prompt:

```
pip install nltk
```

NLTK corpora

A corpus is a large body of text or linguistic data and is very important in NLP research for application development and testing. NLTK allows users to access over 50 corpora and lexical resources (many of them mapped to ML-based applications). We can import any of the available corpora into our program and use NLTK functions to analyze the text in the imported corpus. More details about each corpus could be found here: http://www.nltk. org/book/ch02.html

Text processing

As discussed previously, a key part of NLP is transforming text into mathematical objects. NLTK provides various functions that help us transform the text into vectors. The most basic NLTK function for this purpose is tokenization, which splits a document into a list of units. These units could be words, alphabets, or sentences.

Refer to the following code snippet to perform tokenization using the NLTK library:

```
import nltk

text = "Who would have thought that computer programs would be analyzing
human sentiments"

from nltk.tokenize import word_tokenize

tokens = word_tokenize(text)
print(tokens)
```

Here's the output:

```
['Who', 'would', 'have', 'thought', 'that', 'computer', 'programs',
'would', 'be', 'analyzing', 'human', 'sentiments']
```

We have tokenized the preceding sentence using the `word_tokenize()` function of NLTK, which is simply splitting the sentence by white space. The output is a list, which is the first step toward vectorization.

In our earlier discussion, we touched upon the computationally intensive nature of the vectorization approach due to the sheer size of the vectors. More words in a vector mean more dimensions that we need to work with. Therefore, we should strive to rationalize our vectors, and we can do that using some of the other useful NLTK functions such as stopwords, lemmatization, and stemming.

The following is a partial list of English stop words in NLTK. Stop words are mostly connector words that do not contribute much to the meaning of the sentence:

```
import nltk

stopwords = nltk.corpus.stopwords.words('english')
print(stopwords)
```

Here's the output:

```
['i', 'me', 'my', 'myself', 'we', 'our', 'ours', 'ourselves', 'you',
"you're", "you've", "you'll", "you'd", 'your', 'yours', 'yourself',
'yourselves', 'he', 'him', 'his', 'himself', 'she', "she's", 'her', 'hers',
'herself', 'it', "it's", 'its', 'itself', 'they', 'them', 'their',
'theirs', 'themselves', 'what', 'which', 'who', 'whom', 'this', 'that',
"that'll", 'these', 'those', 'am', 'is', 'are', 'was', 'were', 'be',
'been', 'being', 'have', 'has', 'had', 'having', 'do', 'does', 'did',
'doing', 'a', 'an', 'the', 'and', 'but', 'if', 'or', 'because', 'as',
'until', 'while', 'of', 'at', 'by', 'for', 'with', 'about', 'against',
'between', 'into', 'through', 'during', 'before', 'after', 'above',
'below', 'to', 'from', 'up', 'down', 'in', 'out', 'on', 'off', 'over',
'under', 'again', 'further', 'then', 'once', 'here', 'there', 'when',
'where', 'why', 'how', 'all', 'any', 'both', 'each', 'few', 'more', 'most',
'other', 'some', 'such', 'no', 'nor', 'not', 'only', 'own', 'same', 'so',
'than', 'too', 'very', 's', 't', 'can', 'will', 'just', 'don', "don't",
'should', "should've", 'now', 'd', 'll', 'm', 'o', 're', 've', 'y', 'ain',
'aren', "aren't", 'couldn', "couldn't", 'didn', "didn't", 'doesn',
"doesn't", 'hadn', "hadn't", 'hasn', "hasn't", 'haven', "haven't", 'isn',
"isn't", 'ma', 'mightn', "mightn't", 'mustn', "mustn't", 'needn',
"needn't", 'shan', "shan't", 'shouldn', "shouldn't", 'wasn', "wasn't",
'weren', "weren't", 'won', "won't", 'wouldn', "wouldn't"]
```

Since NLTK provides us with a list of stop words, we can simply look up this list and filter out stop words from our word list:

```
newtokens=[word for word in tokens if word not in stopwords]
```

Here's the output:

```
['Who',
 'would',
 'thought',
 'computer',
 'programs',
 'would',
 'analyzing',
 'human',
 'sentiments']
```

We can further modify our vector by using lemmatization and stemming, which are techniques that are used to reduce words to their root form. The rationale behind this step is that the imaginary *n*-dimensional space that we are navigating doesn't need to have separate axes for a word and that word's inflected form (for example, *eat* and *eating* don't need to be two separate axes). Therefore, we should reduce each word's inflected form to its root form. However, this approach has its critics because, in many cases, inflected word forms give a different meaning than the root word. For example, the sentences *My manager promised me promotion* and *He is a promising prospect* use the inflected form of the root word **promise** but in entirely different contexts. Therefore, you must perform stemming and lemmatization after considering its pros and cons.

The following code snippet shows an example of performing lemmatization using the NLTK library's `WordNetlemmatizer` module:

```
from nltk.stem import WordNetLemmatizer

text = "Who would have thought that computer programs would be analyzing
human sentiments"
tokens = word_tokenize(text)
lemmatizer = WordNetLemmatizer()
tokens=[lemmatizer.lemmatize(word) for word in tokens]
print(tokens)
```

Here's the output:

```
['Who', 'would', 'have', 'thought', 'that', 'computer', 'program', 'would',
'be', 'analyzing', 'human', 'sentiment']
```

Lemmatization is performed by looking up a word in WordNet's inbuilt root word map. If the word is not found, it returns the input word unchanged. However, we can see that the performance of the lemmatizer was not good and it was only able to reduce `programs` and `sentiments` from their plural forms. This shows that the lemmatizer is highly dependent on the root word mapping and is highly susceptible to incorrect root word transformation.

Stemming is similar to lemmatization but instead of looking up root words in a pre-built dictionary, it defines some rules based on which words are reduced to their root form. For example, it has a rule that states that any word with **ing** as a suffix will be reduced by removing the suffix.

The following code snippet shows an example of performing stemming using the NLTK library's `PorterStemmer` module:

```
from nltk.stem import PorterStemmer
from nltk.tokenize import word_tokenize

text = "Who would have thought that computer programs would be analyzing
human sentiments"
tokens=word_tokenize(text.lower())
ps = PorterStemmer()
tokens=[ps.stem(word) for word in tokens]
print(tokens)
```

Here's the output:

```
['who', 'would', 'have', 'thought', 'that', 'comput', 'program', 'would',
'be', 'analyz', 'human', 'sentiment']
```

As per the preceding output, stemming was able to transform more words than lemmatizing, but even this is far from perfect. In addition, you will notice that some stemmed words are not even English words. For example, `analyz` was derived from `analyzing` as it blindly applied the rule of removing `ing`.

The preceding examples show the challenges of reducing words correctly to their respective root forms using NLTK tools. Nevertheless, these techniques are quite popular for text preprocessing and vectorization. You can also create more sophisticated solutions by building on these basic functions to create your own lemmatizer and stemmer. In addition to these tools, NLTK has other features that are used for preprocessing, all of which we will discuss in subsequent chapters.

Part of speech tagging

Part of speech tagging (POS tagging) identifies the part of speech (noun, verb, adverb, and so on) of each word in a sentence. It is a crucial step for many NLP applications since, by identifying the POS of a word, we can deduce its contextual meaning. For example, the meaning of the word **ground** is different when it is used as a noun; for example, *The ground was sodden due to rain*, compared to when it is used as an adjective, for example, *The restaurant's ground meat recipe is quite popular*. We will get into the details of POS tagging and its applications, such as **Named Entity Recognizer** (**NER**), in subsequent chapters.

Refer to the following code snippets to perform POS tagging using NLTK:

```
nltk.pos_tag(["your"])
Out[148]: [('your', 'PRP$')]

nltk.pos_tag(["beautiful"])
Out[149]: [('beautiful', 'NN')]

nltk.pos_tag(["eat"])
Out[150]: [('eat', 'NN')]
```

We can pass a word as a list to the `pos_tag()` function, which outputs the word and its part of speech. We can generate POS for each word of a sentence by iterating over the token list and applying the `pos_tag()` function individually. The following code is an example of how POS tagging can be done iteratively:

```
from nltk.tokenize import word_tokenize
text = "Usain Bolt is the fastest runner in the world"
tokens = word_tokenize(text)
[nltk.pos_tag([word]) for word in tokens]
```

Here's the output:

```
[[('Usain', 'NN')],
 [('Bolt', 'NN')],
 [('is', 'VBZ')],
 [('the', 'DT')],
 [('fastest', 'JJS')],
 [('runner', 'NN')],
 [('in', 'IN')],
 [('the', 'DT')],
 [('world', 'NN')]]
```

The exhaustive list of NLTK POS tags can be accessed using the `upenn_tagset()` function of NLTK:

```
import nltk

nltk.download('tagsets') # need to download first time
nltk.help.upenn_tagset()
```

Here is a partial screenshot of the output:

```
NN: noun, common, singular or mass
    common-carrier cabbage knuckle-duster Casino afghan shed thermostat
    investment slide humour falloff slick wind hyena override subhumanity
    machinist ...
NNP: noun, proper, singular
    Motown Venneboerger Czestochwa Ranzer Conchita Trumplane Christos
    Oceanside Escobar Kreisler Sawyer Cougar Yvette Ervin ODI Darryl CTCA
    Shannon A.K.C. Meltex Liverpool ...
NNPS: noun, proper, plural
    Americans Americas Amharas Amityvilles Amusements Anarcho-Syndicalists
    Andalusians Andes Andruses Angels Animals Anthony Antilles Antiques
    Apache Apaches Apocrypha ...
```

Textblob

Textblob is a popular library used for sentiment analysis, part of speech tagging, translation, and so on. It is built on top of other libraries, including NLTK, and provides a very easy-to-use interface, making it a must-have for NLP beginners. In this section, we would like you to dip your toes into this very easy-to-use, yet very versatile library. You can refer to Textblob's documentation, https://textblob.readthedocs.io/en/dev/, or visit its GitHub page, https://github.com/sloria/TextBlob, to get started with this library.

Sentiment analysis

Sentiment analysis is an important area of research within NLP that aims to analyze text and assess its sentiment. The Textblob library allows users to analyze the sentiment of a given piece of text in a very convenient way. Textblob library's documentation (https://textblob.readthedocs.io/en/dev/) is quite detailed, easy to read, and contains tutorials as well.

We can install the `textblob` library and download the associated corpora by running the following commands in the Anaconda Prompt:

```
pip install -U textblob
python -m textblob.download_corpora
```

Refer to the following code snippet to see how conveniently the library can be used to calculate sentiment:

```
from textblob import TextBlob

TextBlob("I love pizza").sentiment
```

Here's the output:

```
Sentiment(polarity=0.5, subjectivity=0.6)
```

Once the `TextBlob` library has been imported, all we need to do to calculate the sentiment is to pass the text that needs to be analyzed and use the sentiment module of the library. The sentiment module outputs a tuple with the polarity score and subjectivity score. The polarity score ranges from -1 to 1, with -1 being the most negative sentiment and 1 being the most positive statement. The subjectivity score ranges from 0 to 1, with a score of 0 implying that the statement is factual, whereas a score of 1 implies a highly subjective statement.

For the preceding statement, I love pizza, we get a polarity score of 0.5, implying a positive sentiment. The subjectivity of the preceding statement is also calculated as high, which seems correct. Let's analyze the sentiment of other sentences using `Textblob`:

```
TextBlob("The weather is excellent").sentiment
```

Here's the output:

```
Sentiment(polarity=1.0, subjectivity=1.0)
```

The polarity of the preceding statement was calculated as 1 due to the word `excellent`.

Now, let's look at an example of a highly negative statement. Here, the polarity score of -1 is due to the word `terrible`:

```
TextBlob("What a terrible thing to say").sentiment
```

Here's the output:

```
Sentiment(polarity=-1.0, subjectivity=1.0)
```

It also appears that polarity and subjectivity have a high correlation.

Machine translation

Textblob uses Google Translator's API to provide a very simple interface for translating text. Simply use the `translate()` function to translate a given text into the desired language (from Google's catalog of languages). The `to` parameter in the `translate()` function determines the language that the text will be translated into. The output of the `translate()` function will be the same as what you will get in Google Translate.

Here, we have translated a piece of text into three languages (French, Mandarin, and Hindi). The list of language codes can be obtained from https://cloud.google.com/translate/docs/basic/translating-text#language-params:

```
from textblob import TextBlob

languages = ['fr','zh-CN','hi']
for language in languages:
    print(TextBlob("Who knew translation could be
fun").translate(to=language))
```

Here's the output:

```
Qui savait que la traduction pouvait être amusante
谁知道翻译会很有趣
कौन जानता था कि अनुवाद मज़ेदार हो सकता है
```

Part of speech tagging

Textblob's POS tagging functionality is built on top of NLTK's tagging function, but with some modifications. You can refer to NLTK's documentation on POS tagging for more details: https://www.nltk.org/book/ch05.html

The `tags` function performs POS tagging like so:

```
TextBlob("The global economy is expected to grow this year").tags
```

Here's the output:

```
[('The', 'DT'),
 ('global', 'JJ'),
 ('economy', 'NN'),
 ('is', 'VBZ'),
```

```
('expected', 'VBN'),
('to', 'TO'),
('grow', 'VB'),
('this', 'DT'),
('year', 'NN')]
```

Since Textblob uses NLTK for POS tagging, the POS tags are the same as NLTK. This list can be accessed using the `upenn_tagset()` function of NLTK:

```
import nltk

nltk.download('tagsets') # need to download first time
nltk.help.upenn_tagset()
```

These are just a few popular applications of Textblob and they demonstrate the ease of use and versatility of the program. There are many other applications of Textblob, and you are encouraged to explore them. A good place to start your Textblob journey and familiarize yourself with other Textblob applications would be the Textblob tutorial, which can be accessed at `https://textblob.readthedocs.io/en/dev/quickstart.html`.

VADER

Valence Aware Dictionary and sEntiment Reasoner (VADER) is a recently developed lexicon-based sentiment analysis tool whose accuracy is shown to be much greater than the existing lexicon-based sentiment analyzers. This model was developed by computer science professors from Georgia Tech and they have published the methodology of building the lexicon in their very easy-to-read paper (`http://comp.social.gatech.edu/papers/icwsm14.vader.hutto.pdf`). It improves on other sentiment analyzers by including colloquial language terms, emoticons, slang, acronyms, and so on, which are used generously in social media. It also factors in the intensity of words rather than classifying them as simply positive or negative.

We can install VADER by running the following command in the Anaconda Prompt:

```
pip install vaderSentiment
```

The following is an example of VADER in action:

```
from vaderSentiment.vaderSentiment import SentimentIntensityAnalyzer
analyser = SentimentIntensityAnalyzer()
```

First, we need to import `SentimentIntensityAnalyzer module` from the
`vaderSentiment` library and create an `analyser` object of
the `SentimentIntensityAnalyzer` class. We can now pass any text into this object and it
will return the sentiment analysis score. Refer to the following example:

```
analyser.polarity_scores("This book is very good")
```

Here's the output:

```
{'neg': 0.0, 'neu': 0.556, 'pos': 0.444, 'compound': 0.4927}
```

Here, we can see that VADER outputs the negative score, neutral score, and positive score
and then aggregates them to calculate the compound score. The compound score is what
we are interested in. Any score greater than 0.05 is considered positive, while less than -0.05
is considered negative:

```
analyser.polarity_scores("OMG! The book is so cool")
```

Here's the output:

```
{'neg': 0.0, 'neu': 0.604, 'pos': 0.396, 'compound': 0.5079}
```

While analyzing the preceding sentence, VADER correctly interpreted the colloquial terms
(`OMG` and `cool`) and was able to quantify the excitement of the statement. The compound
score is greater than the previous statement, which seems reasonable.

Web scraping libraries and methodology

While discussing NLTK, we highlighted the significance of a corpus or large repository of
text for NLP research. While the available corpora are quite useful, NLP researchers may
require the text of a particular subject. For example, someone trying to build a sentiment
analyzer for financial markets may not find the available corpus (presidential speeches,
movie reviews, and so on) particularly useful. Consequently, NLP researchers may have to
get data from other sources. Web scraping is an extremely useful tool in this regard as it lets
users retrieve information from web sources programmatically.

Before we start discussing web scraping, we wish to underscore the importance of
complying with the respective website policies on web scraping. Most websites allow web
scraping for individual non-commercial use, but you must always confirm the policy before
scraping a website.

To perform web scraping, we will be using a test website (`https://webscraper.io/test-sites/e-commerce/allinone`) to implement our web scraping script. The test website is that of a fictitious e-commerce company that sells computers and phones.

Here's a screenshot of the website:

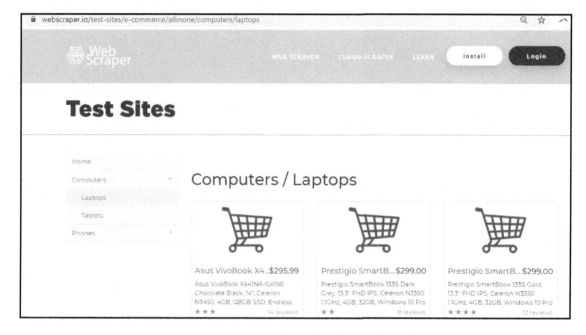

The website lists the products that it sells and each product has price and user rating information. Let's say we want to extract the price and user ratings of every laptop listed on the website. You can do this task manually, but that would be very time-consuming and inefficient. Web scraping helps us perform tasks like this much more efficiently and elegantly.

Now, let's get into how the preceding task could be carried out using web scraping tools in Python. First, we need to install the `Requests` and `BeautifulSoup` libraries, which are the most commonly used Python libraries for web scraping. The documentation for `Requests` can be accessed at `https://requests.readthedocs.io/en/master/`, while the documentation for `BeatifulSoup` can be accessed at `https://www.crummy.com/software/BeautifulSoup/`:

```
pip install requests
pip install beautifulsoup4
```

Once installed, we will import the `Requests` and `BeautifulSoup` libraries. The pandas library will be used to store all the extracted data in a data frame and export data into a CSV file:

```
import requests
from bs4 import BeautifulSoup
import pandas as pd
```

When we type a URL into our web browser and hit *Enter*, a set of events get triggered before the web page gets rendered in our browser. These events include our browser looking up the IP address of the website, our browser sending an HTTP request to the server hosting the website, and the server responding by sending another HTTP response. If everything is agreed to, a handshake between the server and your browser occurs and the data is transferred. The request library helps us perform all these steps using Python scripts.

The following code snippet shows how we can programmatically connect to the website using the `Requests` library:

```
url =
'https://webscraper.io/test-sites/e-commerce/allinone/computers/laptops'
request = requests.get(url)
```

Running the preceding commands establishes a connection with the given website and reads the HTML code of the page. Everything we see on a website (text, images, layouts, links to other web pages, and so on) can be found in the HTML code of the page. Using the `.text` function of `request`, we can output the entire HTML script of the web page, as shown here:

```
request.text
```

Here's the output:

```
Out[146]: '<!DOCTYPE html>\n<html>\n<head>\n\n\t\t\t<!-- Anti-flicker snippet (recommended)
-->\n<style>.async-hide { opacity: 0 !important} </style>
\n<script>(function(a,s,y,n,c,h,i,d,e){s.className+=\' \'+y;h.start=1*new Date;
\nh.end=i=function(){s.className=s.className.replace(RegExp(\' ?\'+y),\'\')};\n(a[n]=a[n]||
[]).hide=h;setTimeout(function(){i();h.end=null},c);h.timeout=c;\n})
(window,document.documentElement,\'async-hide\',\'dataLayer\',4000,\n{\'GTM-NVFPDWB
\':true});</script>\n\t\n    <!-- Google Tag Manager -->\n<script>(function(w,d,s,l,i)
{w[l]=w[l]||[];w[l].push({\'gtm.start\':\n\t\t\tnew Date().getTime(),event:\'gtm.js\'});var
f=d.getElementsByTagName(s)[0],\n\t\tj=d.createElement(s),dl=l!=\'dataLayer\'?\'&l=\'+l:
\'\';j.async=true;j.src=\n\t\t\t'https://www.googletagmanager.com/gtm.js?id=\'+i
+dl;f.parentNode.insertBefore(j,f);\n\t})(window,document,\'script\',\'dataLayer\',\'GTM-
NVFPDWB\');</script>\n<!-- End Google Tag Manager -->    <title>Web Scraper Test Sites</
title>\n    <meta charset="utf-8">\n    <meta http-equiv="X-UA-Compatible"
content="IE=edge,chrome=1">\n\n    <meta name="keywords" content="web scraping,Web
Scraper,Chrome extension,Crawling,Cross platform scraper, "/>\n    <meta name="description"
content="The most popular web scraping extension. Start scraping in minutes. Automate your
```

If you want to see the HTML code of the page on your browser, simply right-click anywhere on the page and select **Inspect**, as shown here:

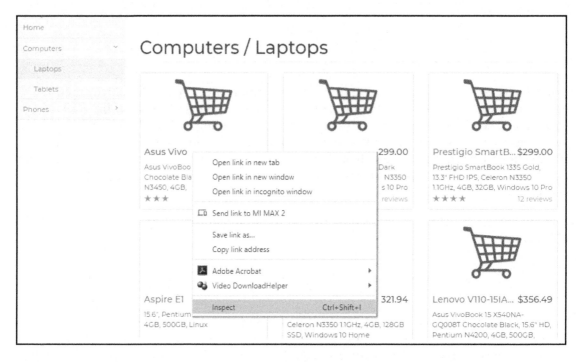

This will open a panel containing the HTML code of the page. If you hover your mouse over any part of the HTML code, the corresponding section on the web page will be highlighted. This tells us that the code for the highlighted portion of the web page's code can be found by expanding that section of the HTML code:

HTML code is generally divided into sections, with a typical page having a header section and a body section. The body section is further divided into elements, with each element having attributes that are represented by a specific tag. In the preceding screenshot, we can see the various elements, classes, and tags of the HTML code. We will need to navigate through this complex-looking code and extract the relevant information (in our case, the product title, price, and rating). This seemingly complex task can be carried out quite conveniently using any of the web scraping libraries available. Beautiful Soup is one of the most popular scrapers out there, so we will see how it can help us parse the intimidating HTML code text. We strongly encourage you to visit Beautiful Soup's documentation page (`https://www.crummy.com/software/BeautifulSoup/bs4/doc/`) and gain a better understanding of this fascinating library.

We use the `BeautifulSoup` module and pass the HTML code (`request.text`) and a parameter called **HTML Parser** to it, which creates a BeautifulSoup HTML parser object. We can now apply many of the versatile `BeautifulSoup` functions to this object and extract the information that we seek. But before we start doing that, we will have to familiarize ourselves with the web page we are trying to scrape and identify where on the web page the elements that we are interested in are to be found. In the e-commerce website's HTML code, we can see that each product's detail is coded within a `<div>` tag (*div* refers to division in HTML) with `col-sm-4 col-lg-4 col-md-4` as the class. If you expand the `<div>` tag by clicking on the arrow, you will see that, within the `<div>` tag, there are other tags and elements as well that store various pieces of information.

To begin with, we are interested in getting the list of product names. To find out where in the HTML code the product names are incorporated, we will have to hover the cursor above any of the product's names, right-click, and then click on **Inspect**.

This will open a panel containing the web page's HTML code, as shown in the following screenshot:

As we can see, the name of the product can be extracted from the `title` element of the `<a>` tag, which is within the `caption` subdivision of the code. Likewise, we can also find price information within the same `caption` subdivision but under the `pull-right price` class. Lastly, rating information can be extracted from the subdivision with the `rating` class:

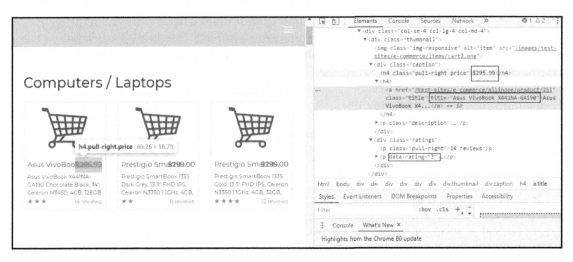

We can now start formulating our web scraping strategy, which will involve iterating over all the code divisions with the `col-sm-4 col-lg-4 col-md-4` class and then extracting the relevant information in each iteration. We'll use Beautiful Soup's `find_all()` function to identify all the `<div>` tags of the `col-sm-4 col-lg-4 col-md-4` class. This function creates an iteratable object and we use a `for` loop to search each subdivision. We can extract the text from a `BeautifulSoup` object by using the `.text` function and can extract the name of an element by using the `.get()` function. Please refer to the following scraping code:

```
titles = []
prices = []
ratings = []
url =
'https://webscraper.io/test-sites/e-commerce/allinone/computers/laptops'
request = requests.get(url)
soup = BeautifulSoup(request.text, "html.parser")
for product in soup.find_all('div', {'class': 'col-sm-4 col-lg-4 col-
md-4'}):
    for pr in product.find_all('div', {'class': 'caption'}):
        for p in pr.find_all('h4', {'class': 'pull-right price'}):
            prices.append(p.text)
        for title in pr.find_all('a' , {'title'}):
            titles.append(title.get('title'))
```

```
for rt in product.find_all('div', {'class': 'ratings'}):
    ratings.append(len(rt.find_all('span', \
                  {'class': 'glyphicon glyphicon-star'})))
```

As the last step, we pass the extracted information to a data frame and export the final result in a CSV file or other file type:

```
product_df = pd.data frame(zip(titles,prices,ratings), columns = \
                  ['Titles','Prices', 'Ratings'])

product_df.to_csv("ecommerce.csv",index=False)
```

The following is a partial screenshot of the file that was created:

Titles	Prices	Ratings
Asus VivoBook X441NA-GA190	$295.99	3
Prestigio SmartBook 133S Dark Grey	$299.00	2
Prestigio SmartBook 133S Gold	$299.00	4
Aspire E1-510	$306.99	3
Lenovo V110-15IAP	$321.94	3
Lenovo V110-15IAP	$356.49	2
Hewlett Packard 250 G6 Dark Ash Silver	$364.46	1
Acer Aspire 3 A315-31 Black	$372.70	2
Acer Aspire A315-31-C33J	$379.94	2
Acer Aspire ES1-572 Black	$379.95	4
Acer Aspire 3 A315-31 Black	$391.48	4
Acer Aspire 3 A315-21	$393.88	3
Asus VivoBook Max	$399.00	1
Asus VivoBook E502NA-GO022T Dark Blue	$399.99	4
Lenovo ThinkPad E31-80	$404.23	1

Likewise, you can extract text information, such as user reviews and product descriptions, for NLP-related projects. Please note that scraped data may require further processing based on requirements.

The preceding steps demonstrate how we can programmatically extract relevant information from web sources using web scraping with relative ease using applicable Python libraries. The more complex the structure of a web page is, the more difficult it is to scrape that page. Websites also keep changing the structure and format of their web pages, which means large-scale changes need to be made to the underlying HTML code. Any change in the HTML code of the page necessitates a review of your scraping code. You are encouraged to practice scraping other websites and gain a better understanding of HTML code structure. We would like to reiterate that it is imperative that you comply with any web scraping restrictions or limits put in place by that website.

Overview of Jupyter Notebook

IDEs are software applications that provide software programmers with a suite of services such as coding interfaces, debugging, and compiling/interpreting. Python programmers are spoilt for choice as there are many open source IDEs for Python, including Jupyter Notebook, spyder, atom, and pycharm, and each IDE comes with its own set of features. We have used Jupyter Notebook for this book. and all the code and exercises discussed in this book can be accessed at `https://github.com/PacktPublishing/Hands-On-Python-Natural-Language-Processing`.

Jupyter Notebook is the IDE of choice for pedagogical purposes as it allows us to weave together code blocks, narrative, multimedia, and graphs in one flowing notebook format. It comes pre-packaged with the Anaconda Python distribution and installing it is quite simple. Please refer to the very nicely written beginner's guide, which should help you gain a basic understanding of Jupyter Notebook: `https://jupyter-notebook-beginner-guide.readthedocs.io/en/latest/execute.html`.

Jupyter Notebook has an `.ipynb` extension. In order to launch a notebook, open the terminal (if you have installed Anaconda, please use the Anaconda Prompt) and `cd` to the directory where the notebook is located. Run the `jupyter notebook` command, which will launch a starter page that lists the files stored in that location. You can either select an existing notebook to open or create a new notebook by clicking on the **New** button and selecting **Python3**, as shown in the following screenshot:

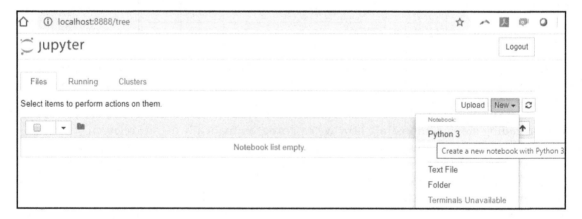

This will create a new notebook with a single cell. By default, this cell is meant for you to type your code into it. However, using the drop-down menu shown in the following screenshot, you can toggle between **Code** and **Markdown** (text):

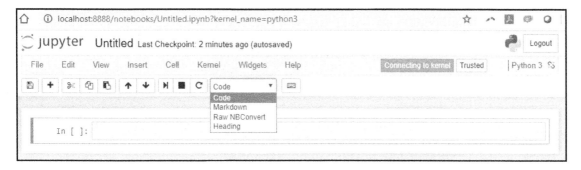

You can either use the icons in the notebook to insert/run cells or use hot keys such as *Shift + Enter* to run the current cell, *Ctrl + Enter* to run multiple selected cells, *A* to insert a cell above, *B* to insert a cell below, and so on. Once you have completed working on the notebook, you can save it in the format of your choice by navigating to **File | Download as**, as shown in the following screenshot. Jupyter provides various options for you to save the file based on the requirement (although you would typically want to save it in Jupyter Notebook (.ipynb) format):

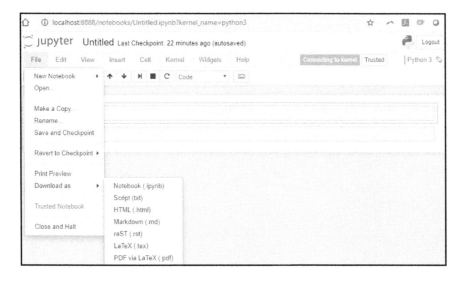

You can also access a finished notebook (a pre-existing `.ipynb` file) by running the `jupyter notebook <filename>` command. This will open the required notebook in a browser. The following are some screenshots of launching and working on a completed notebook.

The following is a screenshot of running a Jupyter Notebook cell with code:

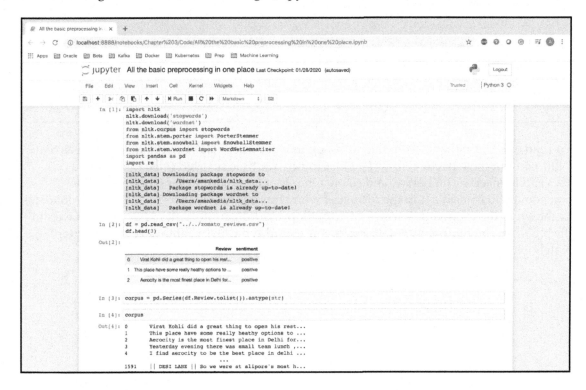

The following screenshot shows how variables can be visualized in Jupyter Notebook inline by running the variable name. You can also see how bar plots can be rendered inline by running the `barplot` command:

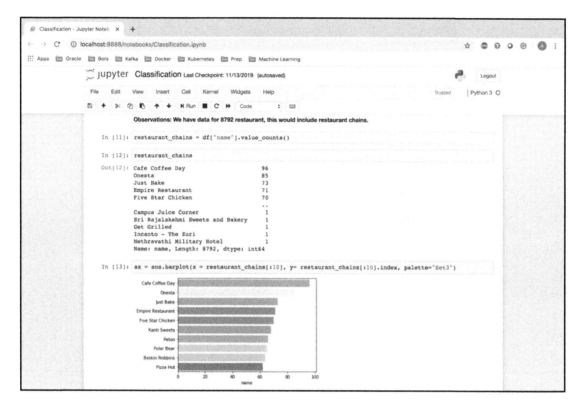

The following screenshot shows how easily you can render a histogram or distribution plot in the Jupyter notebook and how you can add text just below the plot to explain the main points to potential readers:

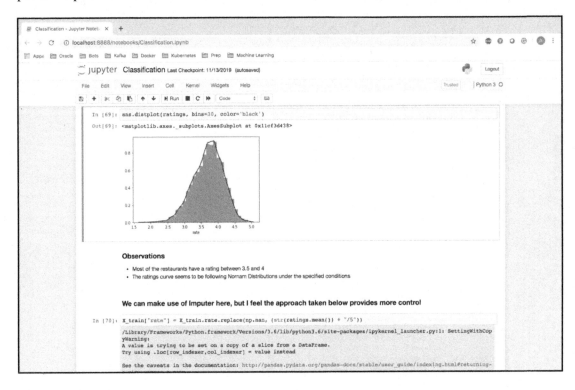

The following screenshot shows how a count plot can be rendered inline and explained using rich text:

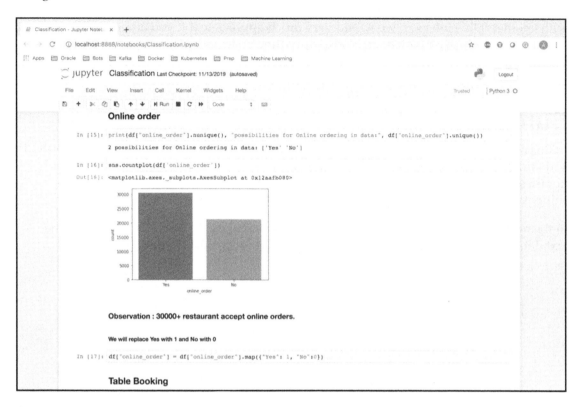

Given its powerful features and ease of use, Jupyter Notebook has become one of the most popular Python IDEs in both academia and industries. Please note that the authors have no intention of persuading you to switch to Jupyter Notebook if you are already comfortable with another IDE. However, we would very much appreciate it if you attain basic familiarity with Jupyter Notebook as the supporting code and exercises in this book have been composed as Notebook.

Summary

In this chapter, we discussed the importance of the Python programming language for NLP and familiarized ourselves with key Python libraries and tools. We will be using these libraries and tools throughout this book, so you are encouraged to practice the code snippets provided and develop some basic level of comfort with these libraries.

In the next chapter, we will get into building the vocabulary for NLP and preprocessing text data, which is arguably the most important step for any NLP-related work.

Section 2: Natural Language Representation and Mathematics

2

This section delves into the preprocessing and text representation aspects of NLP. We will discuss strategies that should be employed as part of natural language data cleaning. After that, we'll deep dive into multiple methodologies that can be used for representing text in the form of numbers capturing syntactical and semantic information.

This section comprises the following chapters:

Building Your NLP Vocabulary

3

In the earlier chapters, you were introduced to why **Natural Language Processing (NLP)** is important especially in today's context, which was followed by a discussion on a few prerequisites and Python libraries that are highly beneficial for NLP tasks. In this chapter, we will take this discussion further and discuss some of the most concrete tasks involved in building a vocabulary for NLP tasks and preprocessing textual data in detail. We will start by learning what a vocabulary is and take the notion forward to actually build a vocabulary. We will do this by applying various methods on text data that are present in most of the NLP pipelines across any organization.

In this chapter, we'll cover the following topics:

- Lexicons
- Phonemes, graphemes, and morphemes
- Tokenization
- Understanding word normalization

Technical requirements

The code files for this chapter can be downloaded from the following GitHub repository: https://github.com/PacktPublishing/Hands-On-Python-Natural-Language-Processing/tree/master/Chapter03.

Lexicons

Lexicons can be defined as the vocabulary of a person, language, or branch of knowledge. In simple terms, a lexicon can be thought of as a dictionary of terms that are called **lexemes**. For instance, the terms used by medical practitioners can be thought of as a lexicon for their profession. As an example, when trying to build an algorithm to convert a physical prescription provided by doctors into an electronic form, the lexicons would be primarily composed of medical terms. Lexicons are used for a wide variety of NLP tasks, where they are provided as a list of words, or vocabulary. Conversations in the concerned field are driven by their respective vocabulary. In this chapter, we will look at the steps and processes involved in building a natural language vocabulary.

Phonemes, graphemes, and morphemes

Before we start looking at the steps for building vocabulary, we need to understand phonemes, graphemes, and morphemes:

- **Phonemes** can be thought of as the speech sounds, made by the mouth or unit of sound, that can differentiate one word from another in a language.
- **Graphemes** are groups of letters of size one or more that can represent these individual sounds or phonemes. The word *spoon* consists of five letters that actually represent four phonemes, identified by the graphemes *s*, *p*, *oo*, and *n*.
- A **morpheme** is the smallest meaningful unit in a language. The word *unbreakable* is composed of three morphemes:
  - *un*—a bound morpheme signifying *not*
  - *break*—the root morpheme
  - *able*—a free morpheme signifying *can be done*

Now, let's delve into some practical aspects that form the base of every NLP-based system.

Tokenization

In order to build up a vocabulary, the first thing to do is to break the documents or sentences into chunks called **tokens**. Each token carries a semantic meaning associated with it. **Tokenization** is one of the fundamental things to do in any text-processing activity. Tokenization can be thought of as a segmentation technique wherein you are trying to break down larger pieces of text chunks into smaller meaningful ones. Tokens generally comprise words and numbers, but they can be extended to include punctuation marks, symbols, and, at times, understandable emoticons.

Let's go through a few examples to understand this better:

```
sentence = "The capital of China is Beijing"
sentence.split()
```

Here's the output.

```
['The', 'capital', 'of', 'China', 'is', 'Beijing']
```

A simple `sentence.split()` method could provide us with all the different tokens in the sentence `The capital of China is Beijing`. Each token in the preceding split carries an intrinsic meaning; however, it is not always as straightforward as this.

Issues with tokenization

Consider the sentence and corresponding split in the following example:

```
sentence = "China's capital is Beijing"
sentence.split()
```

Here's the output:

```
["China's", 'capital', 'is', 'Beijing']
```

In the preceding example, should it be `China`, `Chinas`, or `China's`? A split method does not often know how to deal with situations containing apostrophes.

In the next two examples, how do we deal with `we'll` and `I'm`? `We'll` indicates `we will` and `I'm` indicates `I am`. What should be the tokenized form of `we'll`? Should it be `well` or `we'll` or `we` and `'ll` separately? Similarly, how do we tokenize `I'm`? An ideal tokenizer should be able to process `we'll` into two tokens, `we` and `will`, and *I'm* into two tokens, `I` and `am`. Let's see how our split method would do in this situation.

Here's the first example:

```
sentence = "Beijing is where we'll go"
sentence.split()
```

Here's the output:

```
['Beijing', 'is', 'where', "we'll", 'go']
```

Here's the second example:

```
sentence = "I'm going to travel to Beijing"
sentence.split()
```

Here's the output:

```
["I'm", 'going', 'to', 'travel', 'to', 'Beijing']
```

How do we represent Hong Kong? Should it be two different tokens or should they be one token?

```
sentence = "Let's travel to Hong Kong from Beijing"
sentence.split()
```

Here's the output:

```
["Let's", 'travel', 'to', 'Hong', 'Kong', 'from', 'Beijing']
```

Here, ideally, Hong Kong should be one token, but think of another sentence: *The name of the King is Kong.* In such scenarios, *Kong* should be an individual token. In such situations, context can play a major role in understanding how to treat similar token representations when the context varies. Tokens of size 1, such as Kong, are referred to as **unigrams**, whereas tokens of size 2, such as Hong Kong, are referred to as **bigrams**. These can be generalized under the wing of *n*-**grams**, which we'll discuss towards the end of this chapter.

How do we deal with periods? How do we understand whether they signify the end of a sentence or indicate an abbreviation?

In the following code snippet and subsequent output, the period between M and S is actually indicative of an abbreviation:

```
sentence = "A friend is pursuing his M.S from Beijing"
sentence.split()
```

Here's the output:

```
['A', 'friend', 'is', 'pursuing', 'his', 'M.S', 'from', 'Beijing']
```

In the next example, does a token such as umm carry any meaning? Shouldn't it be removed? Even though a token such as umm is not a part of English vocabulary, it becomes important in use cases where speech synthesis is involved as it indicates that the person is taking a pause here and trying to think of something. Again, as well as the context, the notion of the use case also matters when understanding where something should be tokenized or simply removed as a fragment of text that doesn't convey any meaning:

```
sentence = "Most of the times umm I travel"
sentence.split()
```

Here's the output:

```
['Most', 'of', 'the', 'times', 'umm', 'I', 'travel']
```

The rise of social media platforms has resulted in a massive influx of user data, which is a rich mine of information to understand individuals and communities; however, it has also catered to the rise of a world of emoticons, short forms, new abbreviations (often called the millennial language), and so on. There is a need to understand this ever-growing kind of text, as well those cases where, for instance, a character P used with a colon (:) and hyphen (-) denotes a face with a stuck -out tongue. Hashtags are another very common thing on social media that are mostly indicative of summaries or emotions behind a Facebook post or a tweet on Twitter. An example of this is shown in the following example. Such growth leads to the development of tokenizers such as TweetTokenizer:

```
sentence = "Beijing is a cool place!!! :-P <3 #Awesome"
sentence.split()
```

Here's the output:

```
['Beijing', 'is', 'a', 'cool', 'place!!!', ':-P', '<3', '#Awesome']
```

In the next section, we will look at TweetTokenizer and a few other standard tokenizers available from the nltk library.

Different types of tokenizers

Based on the understanding we have developed so far, let's discuss the different types of tokenizers that are readily available for usage and see how these could be leveraged for the proper tokenization of text.

Regular expressions

Regular expressions are sequences of characters that define a search pattern. They are one of the earliest and are still one of the most effective tools for identifying patterns in text. Imagine searching for email IDs in a corpus of text. These follow the same pattern and are guided by a set of rules, no matter which domain they are hosted upon. Regular expressions are the way to go for identifying such things in text data instead of trying out machine learning-oriented techniques. Other notable examples where regular expressions have been widely employed include the **SUTime** offering from Stanford NLP, wherein tokenization based on regular expressions is used to identify the date, time, duration, and set type entities in text. Look at the following sentence:

```
Last summer, they met every Tuesday afternoon, from 1:00 pm to 3:00 pm.
```

For this sentence, the `SUTime` library would return `TIMEX` expressions where each `TIMEX` expression would indicate the existence of one of the aforementioned entities:

Last summer, they met **every Tuesday afternoon,** from **1:00 pm** to **3:00 pm.**

Last summer	2019-SU	`<TIMEX3 tid="t1" type="DATE" value="2019-SU">Last summer</TIMEX3>`
every Tuesday afternoon	XXXX-WXX-2TAF	`<TIMEX3 periodicity="P1W" quant="every" tid="t2" type="SET" value="XXXX-WXX-2TAF">every Tuesday afternoon</TIMEX3>`
1:00 pm	2020-01-06T13:00	`<TIMEX3 tid="t3" type="TIME" value="2020-01-06T13:00">1:00 pm</TIMEX3>`
3:00 pm	2020-01-06T15:00	`<TIMEX3 tid="t4" type="TIME" value="2020-01-06T15:00">3:00 pm</TIMEX3>`

The `TIMEX` expressions can be parsed to convert them into a user-readable format.

 You can try various phrases at `https://nlp.stanford.edu/software/sutime.shtml`.

Try it out!

Regular expressions-based tokenizers

The `nltk` package in Python provides a **regular expressions-based tokenizers** (`RegexpTokenizer`) functionality. It can be used to tokenize or split a sentence based on a provided regular expression. Take the following sentence:

```
A Rolex watch costs in the range of $3000.0 - $8000.0 in the USA.
```

Here, we would like to have expressions indicating money, alphabetic sequences, and abbreviations together. We can define a regular expression to do this and pass the utterance to the corresponding `tokenizer` object, as shown in the following code block:

```
from nltk.tokenize import RegexpTokenizer
s = "A Rolex watch costs in the range of $3000.0 - $8000.0 in USA."
tokenizer = RegexpTokenizer('\w+|\$[\d\.]+|\S+')
tokenizer.tokenize(s)
```

Here's the output:

```
['A',
 'Rolex',
 'watch',
 'costs',
 'in',
 'the',
 'range',
 'of',
 '$3000.0',
 '-',
 '$8000.0',
 'in',
 'USA',
 '.']
```

Now, how did this work?

The \w+|\$[\d\.]+|\S+ regular expression allows three alternative patterns:

- **First alternative**: \w+ that matches any word character (equal to [a-zA-Z0-9_]). The + is a quantifier and matches between one and unlimited times as many times as possible.
- **Second alternative**: \$[\d\.]+. Here, \$ matches the character $, \d matches a digit between 0 and 9, \. matches the character . (period), and + again acts as a quantifier matching between one and unlimited times.
- **Third alternative**: \S+. Here, \S accepts any non-whitespace character and + again acts the same way as in the preceding two alternatives.

There are other tokenizers built on top of the `RegexpTokenizer`, such as the **BlankLine** tokenizer, which tokenizes a string treating blank lines as delimiters where blank lines are those that contain no characters except spaces or tabs.

The **WordPunct** tokenizer is another implementation on top of `RegexpTokenizer`, which tokenizes a text into a sequence of alphabetic and nonalphabetic characters using the regular expression `\w+|[^\w\s]+`.

Try it out!

Build a regular expression to figure out email IDs from the text. Validate your expression at `https://regex101.com`.

Treebank tokenizer

The **Treebank** tokenizer also uses regular expressions to tokenize text according to the Penn Treebank (`https://catalog.ldc.upenn.edu/docs/LDC95T7/c193.html`). Here, words are mostly split based on punctuation.

The Treebank tokenizer does a great job of splitting contractions such as *doesn't* to *does* and *n't*. It further identifies periods at the ends of lines and eliminates them. Punctuation such as commas is split if followed by whitespaces.

Let's look at the following sentence and tokenize it using the Treebank tokenizer:

```
I'm going to buy a Rolex watch that doesn't cost more than $3000.0
```

The code is as follows:

```
from nltk.tokenize import TreebankWordTokenizer
s = "I'm going to buy a Rolex watch that doesn't cost more than $3000.0"
tokenizer = TreebankWordTokenizer()
tokenizer.tokenize(s)
```

Here's the output:

```
['I',
 "'m",
 'going',
 'to',
 'buy',
 'a',
 'Rolex',
 'watch',
 'which',
```

```
'does',
"n't",
'cost',
'more',
'than',
'$',
'3000.0']
```

As can be seen in the example and corresponding output, this tokenizer primarily helps in analyzing each component in the text separately. The I'm gets split into two components, namely the I, which corresponds to a noun phrase, and the 'm, which corresponds to a verb component. This split allows us to work on individual tokens that carry significant information that would have been difficult to analyze and parse if it was a single token. Similarly, doesn't gets split into does and n't, helping to better parse and understand the inherent semantics associated with the n't, which indicates negation.

TweetTokenizer

As discussed earlier, the rise of social media has given rise to an informal language wherein people tag each other using their social media handles and use a lot of emoticons, hashtags, and abbreviated text to express themselves. We need tokenizers in place that can parse such text and make things more understandable. TweetTokenizer caters to this use case significantly. Let's look at the following sentence/tweet:

```
@amankedia I'm going to buy a Rolexxxxxxx watch!!! :-D #happiness #rolex
<3
```

The tweet contains a social media handle, amankedia, a couple of hashtags in the form of #happiness and #rolex, and :-D and <3 emoticons. The next code snippet and the corresponding output show how all the text gets tokenized using TweetTokenizer to take care of all of these occurrences.

Consider the following example:

```
from nltk.tokenize import TweetTokenizer
s = "@amankedia I'm going to buy a Rolexxxxxxx watch!!! :-D #happiness
#rolex <3"
tokenizer = TweetTokenizer()
tokenizer.tokenize(s)
```

Here's the output:

```
['@amankedia',
 "I'm",
 'going',
```

```
'to',
'buy',
'a',
'Rolexxxxxxx',
'watch',
'!',
'!',
'!',
':-D',
'#happiness',
'#rolex',
'<3']
```

Another common thing with social media writing is the use of expressions such as Rolexxxxxxx. Here, a lot of *x*'s are present in addition to the normal one; it is a very common trend and should be addressed to bring it to a form as close to normal as possible.

The TweetTokenizer provides two additional parameters in the form of reduce_len, which tries to reduce the excessive characters in a token. The word Rolexxxxxxx is actually tokenized as Rolexxx in an attempt to reduce the number of *x*'s present:

```
from nltk.tokenize import TweetTokenizer
s = "@amankedia I'm going to buy a Rolexxxxxxx watch!!! :-D #happiness
#rolex <3"
tokenizer = TweetTokenizer(strip_handles=True, reduce_len=True)
tokenizer.tokenize(s)
```

Here's the output:

```
["I'm",
 'going',
 'to',
 'buy',
 'a',
 'Rolexxx',
 'watch',
 '!',
 '!',
 '!',
 ':-D',
 '#happiness',
 '#rolex',
 '<3']
```

The parameter strip_handles, when set to True, removes the handles mentioned in a post/tweet. As can be seen in the preceding output, @amankedia is stripped, since it is a handle.

One more parameter that is available with `TweetTokenizer` is `preserve_case`, which, when set to `False`, converts everything to lower case in order to normalize the vocabulary. The default value for this parameter is `True`.

Understanding word normalization

Most of the time, we don't want to have every individual word fragment that we have ever encountered in our vocabulary. We could want this for several reasons, one being the need to correctly distinguish (for example) the phrase U.N. (with characters separated by a period) from UN (without any periods). We can also bring words to their root form in the dictionary. For instance, *am*, *are*, and *is* can be identified by their root form, *be*. On another front, we can remove inflections from words to bring them down to the same form. Words *car*, *cars*, and *car's* can all be identified as *car*.

Also, common words that occur very frequently and do not convey much meaning, such as the articles *a*, *an*, and *the*, can be removed. However, all these highly depend on the use cases. *Wh-* words, such as *when*, *why*, *where*, and *who*, do not carry much information in most contexts and are removed as part of a technique called **stopword removal**, which we will see a little later in the *Stopword removal* section; however, in situations such as question classification and question answering, these words become very important and should not be removed. Now, with a basic understanding of these techniques, let's deep dive into them in detail.

Stemming

Imagine bringing all of the words *computer*, *computerization*, and *computerize* into one word, *compute*. What happens here is called **stemming**. As part of stemming, a crude attempt is made to remove the inflectional forms of a word and bring them to a base form called the **stem**. The chopped-off pieces are referred to as **affixes**. In the preceding example, *compute* is the base form and the affixes are *r*, *rization*, and *rize*, respectively. One thing to keep in mind is that the stem need not be a valid word as we know it. For example, the word *traditional* would get stemmed to *tradit*, which is not a valid word in the English dictionary.

The two most common algorithms/methods employed for stemming include the **Porter stemmer** and the **Snowball stemmer**. The Porter stemmer supports the English language, whereas the Snowball stemmer, which is an improvement on the Porter stemmer, supports multiple languages, which can be seen in the following code snippet and its output:

```
from nltk.stem.snowball import SnowballStemmer
print(SnowballStemmer.languages)
```

Here's the output:

```
('arabic', 'danish', 'dutch', 'english', 'finnish', 'french', 'german',
'hungarian', 'italian', 'norwegian', 'porter', 'portuguese', 'romanian',
'russian', 'spanish', 'swedish')
```

One thing to note from the snippet is that the Porter stemmer is one of the offerings provided by the Snowball stemmer. Other stemmers include the Lancaster, Dawson, Krovetz, and Lovins stemmers, among others. We will look at the Porter and Snowball stemmers in detail here.

The Porter stemmer works only with strings, whereas the Snowball stemmer works with both strings and Unicode data. The Snowball stemmer also allows the option to ignore stopwords as an inherent functionality.

Let's now first apply the Porter stemmer to words and see its effects in the following code block:

```
plurals = ['caresses', 'flies', 'dies', 'mules', 'died', 'agreed', 'owned',
'humbled', 'sized', 'meeting', 'stating',
 'siezing', 'itemization', 'traditional', 'reference', 'colonizer',
'plotted', 'having', 'generously']

from nltk.stem.porter import PorterStemmer
stemmer = PorterStemmer()
singles = [stemmer.stem(plural) for plural in plurals]
print(' '.join(singles))
```

Here's the stemmed output from the Porter stemming algorithm:

```
caress fli die mule die agre own humbl size meet state siez item tradit
refer colon plot have gener
```

Next, let's see how the Snowball stemmer would do on the same text:

```
stemmer2 = SnowballStemmer(language='english')
singles = [stemmer2.stem(plural) for plural in plurals]
print(' '.join(singles))
```

Here's the stemmed output of applying the Snowball stemming algorithm:

```
caress fli die mule die agre own humbl size meet state siez item tradit
refer colon plot have generous
```

As can be seen in the preceding code snippets, the Snowball stemmer requires the specification of a language parameter. In most of cases, its output is similar to that of the Porter stemmer, except for `generously`, where the Porter stemmer outputs `gener` and the Snowball stemmer outputs `generous`. The example shows how the Snowball stemmer makes minor changes to the Porter algorithm, achieving improvements in some cases.

Over-stemming and under-stemming

Potential problems with stemming arise in the form of over-stemming and under-stemming. A situation may arise when words that are stemmed to the same root should have been stemmed to different roots. This problem is referred to as **over-stemming**. In contrast, another problem occurs when words that should have been stemmed to the same root aren't stemmed to it. This situation is referred to as **under-stemming**.

 More about stemming can be read at `https://pdfs.semanticscholar.org/1c0c/0fa35d4ff8a2f925eb955e48d655494bd167.pdf`.

Lemmatization

Unlike stemming, wherein a few characters are removed from words using crude methods, **lemmatization** is a process wherein the context is used to convert a word to its meaningful base form. It helps in grouping together words that have a common base form and so can be identified as a single item. The base form is referred to as the lemma of the word and is also sometimes known as the dictionary form.

Lemmatization algorithms try to identify the lemma form of a word by taking into account the neighborhood context of the word, **part-of-speech** (**POS**) tags, the meaning of a word, and so on. The neighborhood can span across words in the vicinity, sentences, or even documents.

Also, the same words can have different lemmas depending on the context. A lemmatizer would try and identify the part-of-speech tags based on the context to identify the appropriate lemma. The most commonly used lemmatizer is the WordNet lemmatizer. Other lemmatizers include the Spacy lemmatizer, TextBlob lemmatizer, and Gensim lemmatizer, and others. In this section, we will explore the WordNet and Spacy lemmatizers.

WordNet lemmatizer

WordNet is a lexical database of English that is freely and publicly available. As part of WordNet, nouns, verbs, adjectives, and adverbs are grouped into sets of cognitive synonyms (synsets), each expressing distinct concepts. These synsets are interlinked using lexical and conceptual semantic relationships. It can be easily downloaded, and the nltk library offers an interface to it that enables you to perform lemmatization.

Let's try and lemmatize the following sentence using the WordNet lemmatizer:

```
We are putting in efforts to enhance our understanding of Lemmatization
```

Here is the code:

```
import nltk
nltk.download('wordnet')
from nltk.stem import WordNetLemmatizer
lemmatizer = WordNetLemmatizer()
s = "We are putting in efforts to enhance our understanding of \
        Lemmatization"
token_list = s.split()
print("The tokens are: ", token_list)
lemmatized_output = ' '.join([lemmatizer.lemmatize(token) for token \
                            in token_list])
print("The lemmatized output is: ", lemmatized_output)
```

Here's the output:

```
The tokens are:  ['We', 'are', 'putting', 'in', 'efforts', 'to', 'enhance',
'our', 'understanding', 'of', 'Lemmatization']
The lemmatized output is:  We are putting in effort to enhance our
understanding of Lemmatization
```

As can be seen, the WordNet lemmatizer did not do much here. Out of are, putting, efforts, and understanding, none were converted to their base form.

What are we lacking here?

The WordNet lemmatizer works well if the POS tags are also provided as inputs.

It is really impossible to manually annotate each word with its POS tag in a text corpus. Now, how do we solve this problem and provide the part-of-speech tags for individual words as input to the WordNet lemmatizer?

Fortunately, the nltk library provides a method for finding POS tags for a list of words using an averaged perceptron tagger, the details of which are out of the scope of this chapter.

The POS tags for the sentence We are trying our best to understand Lemmatization here provided by the POS tagging method can be found in the following code snippet:

```
nltk.download('averaged_perceptron_tagger')
pos_tags = nltk.pos_tag(token_list)
pos_tags
```

Here's the output:

```
[('We', 'PRP'),
 ('are', 'VBP'),
 ('putting', 'VBG'),
 ('in', 'IN'),
 ('efforts', 'NNS'),
 ('to', 'TO'),
 ('enhance', 'VB'),
 ('our', 'PRP$'),
 ('understanding', 'NN'),
 ('of', 'IN'),
 ('Lemmatization', 'NN')]
```

As can be seen, a list of tuples of the form (the token and POS tag) is returned by the POS tagger. Now, the POS tags need to be converted to a form that can be understood by the WordNet lemmatizer and sent in as input along with the tokens.

The code snippet does what's needed by mapping the POS tags to the first character, which is accepted by the lemmatizer in the appropriate format:

```
from nltk.corpus import wordnet
##This is a common method which is widely used across the NLP community of
practitioners and readers
def get_part_of_speech_tags(token):
"""Maps POS tags to first character lemmatize() accepts.
We are focusing on Verbs, Nouns, Adjectives and Adverbs here."""
```

```
tag_dict = {"J": wordnet.ADJ,
            "N": wordnet.NOUN,
            "V": wordnet.VERB,
            "R": wordnet.ADV}
tag = nltk.pos_tag([token])[0][1][0].upper()
return tag_dict.get(tag, wordnet.NOUN)
```

Now, let's see how the WordNet lemmatizer performs when the POS tags are also provided as inputs:

```
lemmatized_output_with_POS_information = [lemmatizer.lemmatize(token,
get_part_of_speech_tags(token)) for token in token_list]
print(' '.join(lemmatized_output_with_POS_information))
```

Here's the output:

```
We be put in effort to enhance our understand of Lemmatization
```

The following conversions happened:

- are to be
- putting to put
- efforts to effort
- understanding to understand

Let's compare this with the Snowball stemmer:

```
stemmer2 = SnowballStemmer(language='english')
stemmed_sentence = [stemmer2.stem(token) for token in token_list]
print(' '.join(stemmed_sentence))
```

The following conversions happened:

```
we are put in effort to enhanc our understand of lemmat
```

As can be seen, the WordNet lemmatizer makes a sensible and context-aware conversion of the token into its base form, unlike the stemmer, which tries to chop the affixes from the token.

Spacy lemmatizer

The **Spacy lemmatizer** comes with pretrained models that can parse text and figure out the various properties of the text, such as POS tags, named-entity tags, and so on, with a simple function call. The prebuilt models identify the POS tags and assign a lemma to each token, unlike the WordNet lemmatizer, where the POS tags need to be explicitly provided.

We can install Spacy and download the en model for the English language by running the following command from the command line:

```
pip install spacy && python -m spacy download en
```

Now that we have installed spacy, let's see how spacy helps with lemmatization using the following code snippet:

```
import spacy
nlp = spacy.load('en')
doc = nlp("We are putting in efforts to enhance our understanding of
Lemmatization")
" ".join([token.lemma_ for token in doc])
```

Here's the output:

```
'-PRON- be put in effort to enhance -PRON- understanding of lemmatization'
```

The spacy lemmatizer performed a decent job without the input information of the POS tags. The advantage here is that there's no need to look out for external dependencies for fetching POS tags as the information is built into the pretrained model.

Another thing to note in the preceding output is the -PRON- lemma. The lemma for Pronouns is returned as -PRON- in Spacy's default behavior. It can act as a feature or, conversely, can be a limitation, since the exact lemma is not being returned.

 Spacy supports multiple languages other than English. You can learn what they are at https://spacy.io/usage/models.

Stopword removal

From time to time in the previous sections, a technique called stopword removal was mentioned. We will finally look at the technique in detail here.

What are stopwords?

Stopwords are words such as *a, an, the, in, at,* and so on that occur frequently in text corpora and do not carry a lot of information in most contexts. These words, in general, are required for the completion of sentences and making them grammatically sound. They are often the most common words in a language and can be filtered out in most NLP tasks, and consequently help in reducing the vocabulary or search space. There is no single list of stopwords that is available universally, and they vary mostly based on use cases; however, a certain list of words is maintained for languages that can be treated as stopwords specific to that language, but they should be modified based on the problem that is being solved.

Let's look at the stopwords available for English in the `nltk` library!

```
nltk.download('stopwords')
from nltk.corpus import stopwords
stop = set(stopwords.words('english'))
", ".join(stop)
```

Here's the output:

```
"it's, yours, an, doing, any, mightn't, you, having, wasn't, themselves,
just, over, below, needn't, a, this, shan't, them, isn't, was, wouldn't,
as, only, his, or, shan, wouldn, don, where, own, were, he, out, do, it,
am, won, isn, there, hers, to, ll, most, for, weren, have, by, while, the,
re, that, down, haven, has, is, here, itself, all, didn, herself, shouldn,
him, ve, who, doesn, m, hadn't, after, further, weren't, at, hadn,
should've, too, because, can, now, same, more, she's, wasn, these,
yourself, himself, being, very, until, myself, few, so, which, ourselves,
they, t, you'd, did, o, aren, but, that'll, such, whom, of, s, you'll,
those, doesn't, my, what, aren't, during, hasn, through, will, couldn, i,
mustn, needn, mustn't, d, had, me, under, won't, haven't, its, with, when,
their, between, if, once, against, before, on, not, you're, each,
yourselves, in, and, are, shouldn't, some, nor, her, does, she, off, how,
both, our, then, why, again, we, no, y, be, other, ma, from, up, theirs,
couldn't, should, into, didn't, ours, about, ain, you've, don't, above,
been, than, your, hasn't, mightn"
```

If you look closely, you'll notice that *Wh-* words such as who, what, when, why, how, which, where, and whom are part of this list of stopwords; however, in one of the previous sections, it was mentioned that these words are very significant in use cases such as question answering and question classification. Measures should be taken to ensure that these words are not filtered out when the text corpus undergoes stopword removal. Let's learn how this can be achieved by running through the following code block:

```
wh_words = ['who', 'what', 'when', 'why', 'how', 'which', 'where', 'whom']
stop = set(stopwords.words('english'))
```

```
sentence = "how are we putting in efforts to enhance our understanding of
Lemmatization"
for word in wh_words:
    stop.remove(word)
sentence_after_stopword_removal = [token for token in sentence.split() if
token not in stop]
" ".join(sentence_after_stopword_removal)
```

Here's the output:

```
'how putting efforts enhance understanding Lemmatization'
```

The preceding code snippet shows that the sentence how are we putting in efforts to enhance our understanding of Lemmatization gets modified to how putting efforts enhance understanding Lemmatization. The stopwords are, we, in, to, our, and of were removed from the sentence. Stopword removal is generally the first step that is taken after tokenization while building a vocabulary or preprocessing text data.

Case folding

Another strategy that helps with normalization is called **case folding**. As part of case folding, all the letters in the text corpus are converted to lowercase. *The* and *the* will be treated the same in a scenario of case folding, whereas they would be treated differently in a non-case folding scenario. This technique helps systems that deal with information retrieval, such as search engines.

Lamborghini, which is a proper noun, will be treated as *lamborghini*; whether the user typed *Lamborghini* or *lamborghini* would not make a difference, and the same results would be returned.

However, in situations where proper nouns are derived from common noun terms, case folding will become a bottleneck as case-based distinction becomes an important feature here. For instance, *General Motors* is composed of common noun terms but is itself a proper noun. Performing case folding here might cause issues. Another problem is when acronyms are converted to lowercase. There is a high chance that they will map to common nouns. An example widely used here is *CAT* which stands for Common Admission Test in India getting converted to *cat*.

A potential solution to this is to build machine learning models that can use features from a sentence to determine which words or tokens in the sentence should be lowercase and which shouldn't be; however, this approach doesn't always help when users mostly type in lowercase. As a result, lowercasing everything becomes a wise solution.

The language here is a major feature; in some languages, such as English, capitalization from point to point in a text carries a lot of information, whereas in some other languages, cases might not be as important.

The following code snippet shows a very straightforward approach that would convert all letters in a sentence to lowercase, making use of the `lower()` method available in Python:

```
s = "We are putting in efforts to enhance our understanding of
Lemmatization"
s = s.lower()
s
```

Here's the output:

```
'we are putting in efforts to enhance our understanding of lemmatization'
```

N-grams

Until now, we have focused on tokens of size 1, which means only one word. Sentences generally contain names of people and places and other open compound terms, such as *living room* and *coffee mug*. These phrases convey a specific meaning when two or more words are used together. When used individually, they carry a different meaning altogether and the inherent meaning behind the compound terms is somewhat lost. The usage of multiple tokens to represent such inherent meaning can be highly beneficial for the NLP tasks being performed. Even though such occurrences are rare, they still carry a lot of information. Techniques should be employed to make sense of these as well.

In general, these are grouped under the umbrella term of *n*-grams. When *n* is equal to 1, these are termed as unigrams. Bigrams, or 2-grams, refer to pairs of words, such as *dinner table*. Phrases such as the *United Arab Emirates* comprising three words are termed as trigrams or 3-grams. This naming system can be extended to larger *n*-grams, but most NLP tasks use only trigrams or lower.

Let's understand how this works for the following sentence:

```
Natural Language Processing is the way to go
```

The phrase `Natural Language Processing` carries an inherent meaning that would be lost if each of the words in the phrase is processed individually; however, when we use trigrams, these phrases can be extracted together and the meaning gets captured. In general, all NLP tasks make use of unigrams, bigrams, and trigrams together to capture all the information.

The following code illustrates an example of capturing bigrams:

```
from nltk.util import ngrams
s = "Natural Language Processing is the way to go"
tokens = s.split()
bigrams = list(ngrams(tokens, 2))
[" ".join(token) for token in bigrams]
```

The output shows the list of bigrams that we captured:

```
['Natural Language',
 'Language Processing',
 'Processing is',
 'is the',
 'the way',
 'way to',
 'to go']
```

Let's try and capture trigrams from the same sentence using the following code:

```
s = "Natural Language Processing is the way to go"
tokens = s.split()
trigrams = list(ngrams(tokens, 3))
[" ".join(token) for token in trigrams]
```

The output shows the trigrams that were captured from the sentence:

```
['Natural Language Processing',
 'Language Processing is',
 'Processing is the',
 'is the way',
 'the way to',
 'way to go']
```

Taking care of HTML tags

Often, data is scraped from online websites for information retrieval. Since these are mostly HTML pages, there needs to be some preprocessing to remove the HTML tags. HTML tags are mostly noise; however, sometimes they can also carry specific information. Let's think of a use case where a website such as Amazon uses specific tags for identifying features of a product—for example, a <price> tag can be custom created to carry price entries for products. In such scenarios, HTML can be highly useful; however, they are noise for most NLP data.

How do we get rid of them?

BeautifulSoup is an amazing library that helps us with handling such data. The following code snippet shows an example of how this can be achieved:

```
html = "<!DOCTYPE html><html><body><h1>My First Heading</h1><p>My first
paragraph.</p></body></html>"
from bs4 import BeautifulSoup
soup = BeautifulSoup(html)
text = soup.get_text()
print(text)
```

Here's the output:

```
My First HeadingMy first paragraph.
```

How does all this fit into my NLP pipeline?

The steps we discussed should be performed as part of preprocessing the text corpora before applying any algorithms to the data; however, which steps to apply and which to ignore depend on the use case.

These tokens can also be put together after the necessary preprocessing steps that we looked at previously to form the vocabulary. A simple example of this can be seen in the following code:

```
s = "Natural Language Processing is the way to go"
tokens = set(s.split())
vocabulary = sorted(tokens)
vocabulary
```

Here's the output:

```
['Language', 'Natural', 'Processing', 'go', 'is', 'the', 'to', 'way']
```

Summary

In this chapter, we looked at the various steps that are needed to build a natural language vocabulary. These play the most critical role in preprocessing any natural language data. Data preprocessing is probably one of the most important aspects of any machine learning application, and the same applies to NLP as well. When performed properly, these steps help with the machine learning aspects that generally occur after preprocessing the data, consequently providing better results most of the time compared with scenarios where no preprocessing is involved.

In the next chapter, we will use the techniques discussed in this chapter to preprocess data and subsequently build mathematical representations of text that can be understood by machine learning algorithms.

4
Transforming Text into Data Structures

Text data offers a very unique proposition by not providing any direct representation available for it in terms of numbers. Computers only understand numbers. Representing text using numbers is a challenge. At the same time, it is an opportunity to invent and try out approaches to represent text so that the maximum information can be captured in the process. In this chapter, we will look at how text and math interface. Let's take baby steps toward transforming text data into mathematical data structures that will provide insights on how to actually represent text using numbers and, consequently, build **Natural Language Processing (NLP)** models.

Pause for a moment here and dwell on how would you try to solve it.

As we progress toward the end of this chapter, we will be better equipped to handle text data as we understand techniques including count vectorization and **term frequency-inverse document frequency (TF-IDF)** vectorization, among others.

Before we proceed and discuss various possible approaches such as count vectors and TF-IDF vectors in this chapter and more approaches such as Word2vec in future chapters, we need to understand two supremely important concepts that validate every language. These are **syntax** and **semantics**. *Syntax* defines the grammatical structures or the set of rules defining a language. It can be thought of as a set of guiding principles that define how words can be put in each other's vicinity to form sentences or phrases. However, syntactically correct sentences may not be meaningful. *Semantics* is the part that takes care of the meanings and defines how to put words together so that they actually make sense when organized based on the available syntactical rules.

In this chapter, we will primarily focus on the syntactical aspects, where we use information such as how many times a word occurred in a document or in a set of documents as potential features to represent documents. Let's see how these approaches pan out in solving the representation problem we have.

The following topics will be covered in this chapter:

- Understanding vectors and matrices
- Exploring the **Bag-of-Words** (**BoW**) architecture
- TF-IDF vectors
- Distance/similarity calculation between document vectors
- One-hot vectorization
- Building a basic chatbot

Technical requirements

The code files for this chapter can be found at the following GitHub link: `https://github.com/PacktPublishing/Hands-On-Python-Natural-Language-Processing/tree/master/Chapter04`.

Understanding vectors and matrices

The introduction to this chapter touched upon the challenge of representing text data in a mathematical form. Two of the most popular data structures used with text data are vectors and matrices. We will now have a look at each one of these in detail.

Vectors

Vectors are a one-dimensional array of numbers in which each number could be identified by its respective indices. They are typically represented as a column enclosed in square brackets, as shown here:

$$x = \begin{bmatrix} x_1 \\ x_2 \\ x_3 \end{bmatrix}$$

In this example, the x vector has three elements, and these three elements store information about the vector. Mathematicians abstract vectors as an object in space, where each element of the vector represents the projection of that vector along a given axis. We often use the term R^n to define a vector, where R is a representation mechanism and n denotes the number of dimensions used to describe the vector. In general, R^n is the set of all n-tuples of real numbers.

In the preceding example, the x vector is in R^3, meaning the vector is in a three-dimensional space and its projection along the three axes is $x1$, $x2$, and $x3$. Once an object is abstracted as a vector, it must satisfy all vector properties, and we can perform any vector operation on it.

For example, let's assume we have height and weight data on two people—Person A and Person B, as shown in the following table:

	Height in cm	Weight in kg
Person A	164	68
Person B	188	81

We can assume a two-dimensional space where these two persons are represented by two vectors, as shown in the following screenshot. The respective height and weight of a person can be thought of as the coordinates that determine their position in the R^2 space:

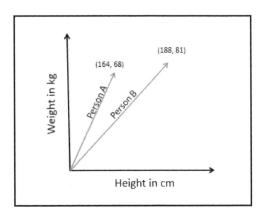

If we also had the body temperature of these people, we could have abstracted this in R^3 space, which would have required a three-dimensional visualization. Vectorization enables us to analyze subjects by using vector properties and operations such as magnitude, similarity, dissimilarity, and so on. Although visualizing vectors in a space greater than R^3 is not humanly possible, all vector properties hold true for any dimensional space, and therefore we are not limited by the number of features of a given subject to transform data into vectors.

All this is great, but how is this going to help us with text analysis?

We have already discussed tokenization in Chapter 3, *Building Your NLP Vocabulary*. A tokenized text document could be abstracted as a vector in an n-dimensional space where each dimension (axis) in the space corresponds to a unique token of that document. The vector's projection along a given axis (coordinate) would be the count of that unique token in the text document. Once *vectorized*, the text document could be analyzed along with other text document vectors, using vector math.

Matrices

Matrices are an extension of arrays. They are a rectangular array of numbers wherein each number is identified by two indices. Like vectors, matrices are also represented using squared brackets, but matrices have both rows and columns, as shown in the following screenshot:

$$A = \begin{bmatrix} x_{11} & z_{12} \\ x_{21} & z_{22} \\ x_{31} & z_{32} \end{bmatrix}$$

A matrix with height m and width n is said to be in $R^{m \times n}$ (the preceding matrix belongs to $R^{3 \times 2}$). In the context of text analysis, matrices are used frequently to represent and analyze text data. Typically, each document vector is represented as a row of a matrix. In the following example, we have read three (small) documents in our system and have used the CountVectorizer module of the sklearn library to represent this data in a matrix format. The CountVectorizer module helps us vectorize each document and then combine each document vector to create the matrix.

The following code block will give you some perspective about building vectors and matrices based on text data. These will be discussed in detail in the later sections of this chapter:

```
from sklearn.feature_extraction.text import CountVectorizer
X = ("Computers can analyze text",
    "They do it using vectors and matrices",
    "Computers can process massive amounts of text data")
vectorizer = CountVectorizer(stop_words='english')
X_vec = vectorizer.fit_transform(X)
print(vectorizer.vocabulary_)
print(X_vec.todense())
```

The following output block from the previous code block shows a matrix, wherein each row corresponds to the document being imported in the same order and each column corresponds to a unique token whose ordering can be obtained using the `.vocabulary_` function of the `CountVectorizer` class:

```
{'computers': 2, 'analyze': 1, 'text': 7, 'using': 8, 'vectors': 9,
'matrices': 5, 'process': 6, 'massive': 4, 'amounts': 0, 'data': 3}
[[0 1 1 0 0 0 0 1 0 0]
 [0 0 0 0 0 1 0 0 1 1]
 [1 0 1 1 1 0 1 1 0 0]]
```

Once text data is converted into a matrix, we can apply any matrix operation to it (vector-matrix multiplication, matrix-matrix multiplication, transpose, and so on).

Now that we have understood vectors and matrices, let's see how can we leverage them to obtain the syntactical representation of text in the next sections.

Exploring the Bag-of-Words architecture

A very intuitive approach to representing a document is to use the frequency of the words in that particular document. This is exactly what is done as part of the BoW approach.

In Chapter 3, *Building Your NLP Vocabulary*, we saw how it is possible to build a vocabulary based on a list of sentences. The vocabulary-building step comes as a prerequisite to the BoW methodology. Once the vocabulary is available, each sentence can be represented as a vector. The length of this vector would be equal to the size of the vocabulary. Each entry in the vector would correspond to a term in the vocabulary, and the number in that particular entry would be the frequency of the term in the sentence under consideration. The lower limit for this number would be 0, indicating that the vocabulary term does not occur in the sentence concerned.

What would be the upper limit for the entry in the vector?

Think!

Well, that could possibly be the frequency of the occurrence of the word in the text corpora. This would indicate that the most frequently occurring word occurs in only one sentence. However, this is an extremely rare situation.

Hey! I understood the BoW approach, but how do I code all this?

Let's begin with importing the various libraries we will be using, as follows:

```
import nltk
nltk.download('stopwords')
nltk.download('wordnet')
from nltk.corpus import stopwords
from nltk.stem.porter import PorterStemmer
from nltk.stem.snowball import SnowballStemmer
from nltk.stem.wordnet import WordNetLemmatizer
import pandas as pd
import re
import numpy as np
```

Now, let's figure that out with the help of the following steps:

1. Take a list of sentences, as illustrated in the following code snippet:

```
sentences = ["We are reading about Natural Language Processing
Here",
"Natural Language Processing making computers comprehend language
data",
"The field of Natural Language Processing is evolving everyday"]
```

2. Create a `pandas` series object from the list of sentences, as follows:

```
corpus = pd.Series(sentences)
corpus
```

Here's the output:

```
0    We are reading about Natural Language Processi...
1    Natural Language Processing making computers c...
2    The field of Natural Language Processing is ev...
dtype: object
```

3. Preprocess the corpus using the NLP pipeline we built in the previous chapter, as follows:

```
preprocessed_corpus = preprocess(corpus, \
    keep_list = common_dot_words, stemming = False, \
    stem_type = None, lemmatization = True, \
    remove_stopwords = True)
preprocessed_corpus
```

This gives the following output:

```
['read natural language process',
 'natural language process make computers comprehend language
data',
 'field natural language process evolve everyday']
```

4. Build your vocabulary, like this:

```
set_of_words = set()
for sentence in preprocessed_corpus:
    for word in sentence.split():
        set_of_words.add(word)
vocab = list(set_of_words)
print(vocab)
```

Here is the output:

```
['read', 'natural', 'language', 'computers', 'everyday', 'data',
'evolve', 'field', 'process', 'comprehend', 'make']
```

5. Fetch the position/index of each token in the vocabulary, like this:

```
position = {}
for i, token in enumerate(vocab):
    position[token] = i
print(position)
```

Here is the output:

```
{'read': 0, 'natural': 1, 'language': 2, 'computers': 3,
'everyday': 4, 'data': 5, 'evolve': 6, 'field': 7, 'process': 8,
'comprehend': 9, 'make': 10}
```

6. Create a placeholder matrix for holding the BoW. Attention: the shape of the matrix is (*number of sentences * length of vocabulary*), as illustrated in the following code snippet:

```
bow_matrix = np.zeros((len(preprocessed_corpus), len(vocab)))
```

7. Increase the positional index of every word by 1 if it appears in a sentence, as illustrated in the following code snippet:

```
for i, preprocessed_sentence in enumerate(preprocessed_corpus):
    for token in preprocessed_sentence.split():
        bow_matrix[i][position[token]] = \
                            bow_matrix[i][position[token]] + 1
```

8. Let's see the final BoW:

```
bow_matrix
```

Here is the output:

```
array([[1., 1., 1., 0., 0., 0., 0., 0., 1., 0., 0.],
       [0., 1., 2., 1., 0., 1., 0., 0., 1., 1., 1.],
       [0., 1., 1., 0., 1., 0., 1., 1., 1., 0., 0.]])
```

If you look at *Step 5*, the index for the `language` token is 2. Column 2 in the BoW matrix has 1, 2, and 1 respectively, which resonates with the fact that the `language` token appeared once, twice, and again once in the sentences 1, 2, and 3 respectively. You can draw more similar conclusions from the matrix.

Try it out!

Here, we only took into account unigrams. This can be easily extended to bigrams, trigrams, and other n-grams. As part of this *Try it out* exercise, include bigrams and trigrams in the BoW model.

Hey! Do I need to code all this up? Doesn't any Python library provide all this as an inbuilt functionality?

Of course it does!! Let's see how can we do that.

Understanding a basic CountVectorizer

`CountVectorizer` is a tool provided by the `sklearn` or `scikit-learn` library in Python that saves all the effort performed in the previous section and provides **application programming interfaces (APIs)** that would conveniently help in building a BoW model.

It converts a list of text documents into a matrix such that each entry in the matrix would correspond to the count of a particular token in the respective sentences. Let's look at how to instantiate `CountVectorizer` and fit data to it in the following code block:

```
vectorizer = CountVectorizer()
bow_matrix = vectorizer.fit_transform(preprocessed_corpus)
```

The results on the preprocessed corpus are as follows. As shown in the following code snippet, the results are the same as what was obtained for the BoW model discussed in the previous section:

```
print(vectorizer.get_feature_names())
print(bow_matrix.toarray())
```

Here is the output:

```
['comprehend', 'computers', 'data', 'everyday', 'evolve', 'field',
'language', 'make', 'natural', 'process', 'read']
[[0 0 0 0 0 0 1 0 1 1 1]
 [1 1 1 0 0 0 2 1 1 1 0]
 [0 0 0 1 1 1 1 0 1 1 0]]
```

Hence, we can conclude that this simple API does wonders in terms of saving efforts. However, that's not all. Let's look into other important features provided by the CountVectorizer tool in the upcoming section.

Out-of-the-box features offered by CountVectorizer

Next, we will explore some necessary features that are offered off the shelf by the CountVectorizer module, eliminating the need to write custom code.

Prebuilt dictionary and support for n-grams

CountVectorizer offers a lot of flexibility in terms of using a prebuilt dictionary of words instead of creating a dictionary based on the data. It provides options to tokenize text as well, along with the removal of stopwords. In the previous *Try it out!* exercise you were asked to build a BoW using bigrams and trigrams. The CountVectorizer module provides the ability to do that without explicitly writing code, using an attribute named ngram_range. Let's explore an example of that in the following code block:

```
vectorizer_ngram_range = CountVectorizer(analyzer='word',
ngram_range=(1,3))
bow_matrix_ngram =
vectorizer_ngram_range.fit_transform(preprocessed_corpus)

print(vectorizer_ngram_range.get_feature_names())
print(bow_matrix_ngram.toarray())
```

Here is the output:

```
['comprehend', 'comprehend language', 'comprehend language data',
'computers', 'computers comprehend', 'computers comprehend language',
'data', 'everyday', 'evolve', 'evolve everyday', 'field', 'field natural',
'field natural language', 'language', 'language data', 'language process',
'language process evolve', 'language process make', 'make', 'make
computers', 'make computers comprehend', 'natural', 'natural language',
'natural language process', 'process', 'process evolve', 'process evolve
everyday', 'process make', 'process make computers', 'read', 'read
natural', 'read natural language']
[[0 0 0 0 0 0 0 0 0 0 0 0 0 1 0 1 0 0 0 0 0 1 1 1 1 0 0 0 0 1 1 1]
 [1 1 1 1 1 1 1 0 0 0 0 0 0 2 1 1 0 1 1 1 1 1 1 1 1 0 0 1 1 0 0 0]
 [0 0 0 0 0 0 0 1 1 1 1 1 1 1 0 1 1 0 0 0 0 1 1 1 1 1 1 0 0 0 0 0]]
```

As can be seen in the preceding example, we modified the `ngram_range` parameter to accommodate unigrams, bigrams, and trigrams. If you observe closely, the ninth phrase from the end is the `natural language process` trigram, and it occurs once in every sentence. Consequently, the column corresponding to it contains values 1, 1, and 1 respectively, as we would have expected.

max_features

An extremely important thing to keep in mind while building a BoW model is to ensure that the vocabulary does not shoot up and become excessively large. This is because this would increase the dimensionality of the model largely, and a very big dimensionality does not convert into a very good model; rather, it can hamper the model's inference ability. This is referred to as the **curse of dimensionality** and it can potentially lead to a condition called **overfitting**, which we will look into in Chapter 8, *From Human Neurons to Artificial Neurons for Understanding Text*. The `CountVectorizer` functionality provides a parameter called `max_features` that will build a vocabulary such that the size of the vocabulary would be less than or equal to `max_features` ordered by the frequency of tokens occurring in a corpus, as illustrated in the following code block:

```
vectorizer_max_features = CountVectorizer(analyzer='word',
ngram_range=(1,3), max_features = 6)
bow_matrix_max_features =
vectorizer_max_features.fit_transform(preprocessed_corpus)

print(vectorizer_max_features.get_feature_names())
print(bow_matrix_max_features.toarray())
```

```
['language', 'language process', 'natural', 'natural language',
 'natural language process', 'process']
[[1 1 1 1 1 1] [2 1 1 1 1 1] [1 1 1 1 1 1]]
```

This example illustrates that only six of the most frequently occurring n-grams among unigrams, bigrams, or trigrams in the corpus were selected since the value of the `max_features` attribute was set to 6.

Min_df and Max_df thresholds

Now that we are clear on how `max_features` help by limiting the vocabulary size, we also need to understand that at the top of this limited vocabulary would be terms or phrases that have occurred very frequently in the text corpus under consideration. These phrases might occur very frequently in an individual document or may be present in almost all documents in the corpus, and may not carry any pattern. One approach we have discussed so far to remove such terms is the removal of stopwords.

Another convenient technique that comes along with `CountVectorizer` is `max_df`, which will ignore terms having a document frequency higher than a provided threshold mentioned as part of the `max_df` parameter. Similarly, we can remove rarely occurring terms that occur fewer times in a document than a given threshold, using a `min_df` parameter. This can potentially have issues as these rarely occurring terms might be very significant for certain documents in the text corpus. We will look into how to capture such information in the *TF-IDF vectors* section.

The following example illustrates how `max_df` and `min_df` can be put into action and consequently provide minimum and maximum thresholds toward the occurrence of a phrase in a corpus:

```
vectorizer_max_features = CountVectorizer(analyzer='word',
ngram_range=(1,3), max_df = 3, min_df = 2)
bow_matrix_max_features =
vectorizer_max_features.fit_transform(preprocessed_corpus)

print(vectorizer_max_features.get_feature_names())
print(bow_matrix_max_features.toarray())
```

Here is the output:

```
['language', 'language process', 'natural', 'natural language', 'natural
language process', 'process']
[[1 1 1 1 1 1]
```

```
[2 1 1 1 1 1]
[1 1 1 1 1 1]]
```

Now that we have developed an understanding of the BoW model, let's see what its limitations are.

Limitations of the BoW representation

The BoW model provides a mechanism for representing text data using numbers. However, there are certain limitations to it. The model only relies on the count of terms in a document. This might work well for certain tasks or use cases with a limited vocabulary, but it would not scale to large vocabularies efficiently.

The BoW model also intrinsically provides possibilities for eliminating or reducing the significance of tokens or phrases that occur very rarely. These phrases might be present in a very small number of documents, but they can be very important in the representation of those documents. The BoW model does not support such possibilities.

These models do not take into account semantics or meanings associated with a token or phrases in a document. It ignores the possibility of capturing features from the neighborhood of a phrase that can hint at the context in which a word or phrase is being used. Therefore, it completely ignores the context involved.

The BoW model can also get extremely huge in terms of the vocabulary for a large text corpus. This can lead to vectors of huge sizes representing every document, which might cause a deterioration in the model's performance.

TF-IDF vectors

In the *Exploring the BoW architecture* section, it was witnessed that the frequency of words across a document was the only pointer for building vectors for documents. The words that occur rarely are either removed or their weights are too low compared to words that occur very frequently. While following this kind of approach, the pattern of information carried across terms that are rarely present but carry a high amount of information for a document or an evident pattern across similar documents is lost. The TF-IDF approach for weighing terms in a text corpus helps mitigate this issue.

The TF-IDF approach is by far the most commonly used approach for weighing terms. It is found in applications, in search engines, information retrieval, and text mining systems, among others. TF-IDF is also an occurrence-based method for vectorizing text and extracting features out of it. It is a composite of two terms, which are described as follows:

- **TF** is similar to the `CountVectorizer` tool. It takes into account how frequently a term occurs in a document. Since most of the documents in a text corpus are of different lengths, it is very likely that a term would appear more frequently in longer documents rather than in smaller ones. This calls for normalizing the frequency of the term by dividing it with the count of the terms in the document. There are multiple variations to calculate TF, but the following is the most common representation:

$$TF(w) = \frac{Number\ of\ times\ the\ word\ w\ occurs\ in\ a\ document}{Total\ number\ of\ words\ in\ the\ document}$$

- **IDF** is what does justice to terms that occur not so frequently across documents but might be more meaningful in representing the document. It measures the importance of a term in a document. The usage of TF only would provide more weightage to terms that occur very frequently. As part of IDF, just the opposite is done, whereby the weights of frequently occurring terms are suppressed and the weights of possibly more meaningful but less frequently occurring terms are scaled up. Similar to TF, there are multiple ways to measure IDF, but the following is the most common representation:

$$IDF(w) = log\frac{Total\ number\ of\ documents}{Number\ of\ documents\ containing\ word\ w}$$

As you can see, the weight of word w in document d is given by the following TF-IDF weighting:

$$weight(w, d) = TF(w, d) \times IDF(w)$$

As can be seen, the weight of word w in document d is a product of the TF of word w in document d and the IDF of word w across the text corpus.

Let's understand how all this pans out in action. We will take the same corpus as the one taken for the `CountVectorizer` model for this example to see the differences. Also, the data underwent the same preprocessing pipeline here as well.

Building a basic TF-IDF vectorizer

A basic TF-IDF vectorizer can be instantiated, as shown in the two steps demonstrated in the following code snippet. The second step allows the data to be fitted to the TF-IDF vectorizer, followed by the transformation of the data into TF-IDF vector forms using the `fit_transform` function:

```
vectorizer = TfidfVectorizer()
tf_idf_matrix = vectorizer.fit_transform(preprocessed_corpus)
```

The results on the preprocessed corpus after TF-IDF vectorization are shown in the following code snippet. The vocabulary is the same as `CountVectorizer`; however, the weights are completely different for the various terms across the documents:

```
print(vectorizer.get_feature_names())
print(tf_idf_matrix.toarray())
print("\nThe shape of the TF-IDF matrix is: ", tf_idf_matrix.shape)
```

Here is the output:

```
['comprehend', 'computers', 'data', 'everyday', 'evolve', 'field',
'language', 'make', 'natural', 'process', 'read']

[[0. 0. 0. 0. 0. 0. 0.41285857 0. 0.41285857 0.41285857 0.69903033]
 [0.40512186 0.40512186 0.40512186 0. 0. 0. 0.478543 0.40512186 0.2392715
0.2392715 0. ] [0. 0. 0. 0.49711994 0.49711994 0.49711994 0.29360705 0.
0.29360705 0.29360705 0. ]]

The shape of the TF-IDF matrix is: (3, 11)
```

If you look carefully, the third column from the end corresponds to the term `natural`. It occurs once in each document; still, the TF-IDF weight for the term is different across the documents because even though the IDF would remain the same across the documents for `natural`, the TF would change since the size of each document is different and the TF component gets normalized based on that. Another reason for this is that each row or vector is normalized to have a unit norm or the length of the vector as 1. The default option, which need not be explicitly specified, has been taken in this example, which is the l2 norm, wherein the **sum of squares of the vector elements is equal to** 1.

Let's see how the TF-IDF matrix would change when the norm is changed to l1 and the rest of the settings are kept the same. The **sum of absolute values of the vector elements is** 1 **with the l1 norm**. The following code block illustrates this:

```
vectorizer_l1_norm = TfidfVectorizer(norm="l1")
tf_idf_matrix_l1_norm =
```

```
vectorizer_l1_norm.fit_transform(preprocessed_corpus)

print(vectorizer_l1_norm.get_feature_names())
print(tf_idf_matrix_l1_norm.toarray())
print("\nThe shape of the TF-IDF matrix is: ", tf_idf_matrix_l1_norm.shape)
```

Here is the output:

```
['comprehend', 'computers', 'data', 'everyday', 'evolve', 'field',
 'language', 'make', 'natural', 'process', 'read']
[[0.          0.          0.          0.          0.          0.
  0.21307663 0.          0.21307663 0.21307663 0.3607701 ]
 [0.1571718   0.1571718   0.1571718   0.          0.          0.
  0.1856564   0.1571718   0.0928282   0.0928282   0.        ]
 [0.          0.          0.          0.2095624   0.2095624   0.2095624
  0.12377093 0.          0.12377093 0.12377093 0.        ]]

The shape of the TF-IDF matrix is:  (3, 11)
```

The TF-IDF matrix changed as we changed the norm to `l1`, as can be seen in the preceding code snippet and the corresponding output.

N-grams and maximum features in the TF-IDF vectorizer

Similar to `CountVectorizer`, the TF-IDF vectorizer offers the capability of using `n-grams` and `max_features` to limit our vocabulary. The following code snippet shows the same:

```
vectorizer_n_gram_max_features = TfidfVectorizer(norm="l2",
analyzer='word', ngram_range=(1,3), max_features = 6)
tf_idf_matrix_n_gram_max_features =
vectorizer_n_gram_max_features.fit_transform(preprocessed_corpus)
print(vectorizer_n_gram_max_features.get_feature_names())
print(tf_idf_matrix_n_gram_max_features.toarray())
print("\nThe shape of the TF-IDF matrix is: ",
tf_idf_matrix_n_gram_max_features.shape)
```

Here is the output:

```
['language', 'language process', 'natural', 'natural language', 'natural
language process', 'process']
[[0.40824829 0.40824829 0.40824829 0.40824829 0.40824829 0.40824829]
 [0.66666667 0.33333333 0.33333333 0.33333333 0.33333333 0.33333333]
 [0.40824829 0.40824829 0.40824829 0.40824829 0.40824829 0.40824829]]

The shape of the TF-IDF matrix is: (3, 6)
```

Here, we took the top six features among unigrams, bigrams, and trigrams, and used them to represent the TF-IDF vectors. The TF-IDF vectorizer provides the `Min_df` and `Max_df` parameters as well, and the usage is exactly the same as `CountVectorizer`. Other features offered by the TF-IDF vectorizer include the usage of a prebuilt vocabulary, tokenization, and the removal of stopwords.

Limitations of the TF-IDF vectorizer's representation

The TF-IDF vectorizer offers an improvement over `CountVectorizer` by scaling the weights of the less frequently occurring terms as well as by using the IDF component. It is also computationally fast. However, it still relies on lexical analysis and does not take into account things such as the co-occurrence of terms, semantics, the context associated with terms, and the position of a term in a document. It is dependent on the vocabulary size, like `CountVectorizer`, and will get really slow with large vocabulary sizes.

Now that we have understood some representation techniques, let's apply them to a real-life problem of computing the distance between text documents using cosine similarity, in the next section.

Distance/similarity calculation between document vectors

We have seen two methods of building vectors to represent text documents. The next question that comes up is:

How can you measure how similar or dissimilar text documents are and how can the vectors built so far be leveraged to have a solution to this problem?

If the words being used in two documents are similar, it indicates that the documents are similar as well. In this section, we will look into cosine similarity and use it to find how similar documents are based on the term vectors.

Cosine similarity

Cosine similarity provides insights into the angle between two vectors. Two vectors would be similar if they are pretty close in terms of both direction and magnitude. We will use techniques developed in the previous sections to build these vectors, and then figure out how close or far they are from each other using cosine similarity.

Cosine similarity helps in measuring the cosine of the angles between two vectors. The value of cosine similarity would lie in the range -1 to +1. The value +1 indicates that the vectors are perfectly similar, and the value -1 indicates that the vectors are perfectly dissimilar or exactly opposite to each other. As you can comprehend, two documents are similar if their cosine similarity values are close to +1. Also, these similarity measures are always between document pairs. Cosine similarity can only be computed for vectors that are of the same size. The formula for cosine similarity for two vectors A and B is as follows:

$$cos(\theta) = \frac{A \cdot B}{||A||||B||}$$

Here, $A.B$ is the scalar product or dot product between the two vectors, and $||A||$ and $||B||$ represent the magnitude of these two vectors respectively. The preceding formula can also be represented as follows:

$$cos(\theta) = \frac{A \cdot B}{\sqrt{\sum_{i=1}^{i=N} w_{iA}^2} \sqrt{\sum_{i=1}^{i=N} w_{iB}^2}}$$

Here, w_{iA} and w_{iB} represent the weight or magnitude of vectors A and B along the ith dimension respectively, in an n-dimensional space.

Solving Cosine math

Let's try to do some math around cosine similarity. We have two documents, *d1* and *d2*, such that the count vectors for them are *d1* = (5, 0, 3, 0, 2, 0, 0, 2, 0, 0) and *d2* = (3, 0, 2, 0, 1, 1, 0, 1, 0, 1).

Therefore, we have the following:

$$cos(d1, d2) = \frac{d1 \cdot d2}{||d1|| ||d2||}$$

Here, the following applies:

- $d1 \cdot d2$ = 5*3+0*0+3*2+0*0+2*1+0*1+0*1+2*1+0*0+0*1 = 25
- $||d1||$ = (5*5+0*0+3*3+0*0+2*2+0*0+0*0+2*2+0*0+0*0)$^{0.5}$ = (42)$^{0.5}$ = 6.481
- $||d2||$ = (3*3+0*0+2*2+0*0+1*1+1*1+0*0+1*1+0*0+1*1)$^{0.5}$ = (17)$^{0.5}$ = 4.12
- cos(*d1*, *d2*) = 0.94

A cosine value of *0.94* indicates that the documents are highly similar. Now that we know what cosine similarity is and we have also done the math behind it, let's see how it works in code.

The following method in Python would help in calculating the cosine similarity between two vectors:

```
def cosine_similarity(vector1, vector2):
    vector1 = np.array(vector1)
    vector2 = np.array(vector2)
    return np.dot(vector1, vector2) / (np.sqrt(np.sum(vector1**2)) * \
                np.sqrt(np.sum(vector2**2)))
```

Now, how can the preceding method be used to calculate the cosine similarity for the document vectors built using a `CountVectorizer` tool and a `TfIdfVectorizer` tool? Let's find out!

Cosine similarity on vectors developed using CountVectorizer

We would use `bow_matrix`, obtained in the `CountVectorizer` section, here to find the document distances. The following code block helps us to do that:

```
for i in range(bow_matrix.shape[0]):
    for j in range(i + 1, bow_matrix.shape[0]):
        print("The cosine similarity between the documents ", i, "and", \
                j, "is: ", cosine_similarity(bow_matrix.toarray()[i], \
                bow_matrix.toarray()[j]))
```

As can be noted from the cosine similarity calculations in the following output block, document 0 and document 1 are the closest or most similar, while document 1 and document 2 are the farthest or least similar:

```
The cosine similarity between the documents  0 and 1 is:
0.6324555320336759
The cosine similarity between the documents  0 and 2 is:
0.6123724356957946
The cosine similarity between the documents  1 and 2 is:
0.5163977794943223
```

Let's see how the values change when `TfIdf` is used instead of `CountVectorizer`.

Cosine similarity on vectors developed using TfIdfVectorizers tool

Next, we will use the `tf-idf` matrix obtained in the `TfIdfVectorizer` section and compute document distances based on that, as follows:

```
for i in range(tf_idf_matrix.shape[0]):
    for j in range(i + 1, tf_idf_matrix.shape[0]):
        print("The cosine similarity between the documents ", i, "and", \
                j, "is: ", cosine_similarity(tf_idf_matrix.toarray()[i], \
                tf_idf_matrix.toarray()[j]))
```

The results are also shown in the following output block, showing that document 0 and document 1 are the closest, and document 1 and document 2 are the farthest. However, the magnitudes here vary from what was obtained with `CountVectorizer` but the relative order of similarity remains the same, as can be seen here:

```
The cosine similarity between the documents  0 and 1 is:
0.39514115766749125
The cosine similarity between the documents  0 and 2 is:
0.36365455673761865
The cosine similarity between the documents  1 and 2 is:
0.2810071916500233
```

In actual systems, though, these values can vary based on the form of vectorization being used. In case you didn't realize already, the cosine similarity is actually helping to measure BoW overlap across documents. In the next section, we will discuss a technique called **one-hot vectorization** for token representation, which is widely used in the deep-learning world, as we will see when we talk about the Word2vec algorithm.

One-hot vectorization

In general, a one-hot vector is used to represent categorical variables that take in values from a predefined list of values. These help in representing tokens as vectors that are required in certain use cases. In such vectors, all values are 0 except the one where the token is present, and this entry is marked 1. As you may have guessed, these are binary vectors.

For example, *weather* can be represented as a categorical variable with the values hot and cold. In this scenario, the one-hot vectors would be as follows:

```
vec(hot)  = <0, 1>
vec(cold) = <1, 0>
```

There are two bits in here—the second bit is 1, to denote hot, and the first bit is 1, to denote cold. The size of the vector is 2 since there are only two possibilities available in terms of *hot* and *cold*.

Hey! Where does this work similarly in NLP?

In NLP, each of the terms present in the vocabulary can be thought of as a category, just as we had two categories to represent weather conditions. Now, whenever there is a need to represent a token in the vocabulary as a vector, it can be one-hot encoded. Only one slot in this vector corresponding to the position of the term in the vocabulary would take the value 1, and the rest would be zeros. The dimensionality of these vectors, as you might have guessed already, is $|V|*1$, where V is the vocabulary and $|V|$ denotes the size of the vocabulary.

These primarily find their place in developing word embedding, which will be discussed in detail in the next chapter.

How do we build one-hot vectors?

Let's try to write some code to figure that out! The steps are as follows:

1. In here, for the demonstration, only one sentence would be taken in the corpus, as follows:

```
sentence = ["We are reading about Natural Language Processing
Here"]
corpus = pd.Series(sentence)
corpus
```

```
0    We are reading about Natural Language Processi...
dtype: object
```

2. The data undergoes the same preprocessing pipeline that we have been using throughout. The following code is for the preprocessed corpus:

```
# Preprocessing with Lemmatization here
preprocessed_corpus = preprocess(corpus, keep_list = [], stemming =
False, stem_type = None,lemmatization = True, remove_stopwords =
True)
preprocessed_corpus
```

Here is the output:

```
['read natural language process']
```

3. In the following code snippet, we are building the vocabulary:

```
set_of_words = set()
for word in preprocessed_corpus[0].split():
    set_of_words.add(word)
vocab = list(set_of_words)
print(vocab)
```

Here is the output:

```
['read', 'process', 'natural', 'language']
```

4. Here is the code for maintaining the position of each token in the vocabulary:

```
position = {}
for i, token in enumerate(vocab):
    position[token] = i
    print(position)
```

Here is the output:

```
{'read': 0, 'process': 1, 'natural': 2, 'language': 3
```

5. In the following code snippet, we are instantiating the one-hot matrix:

```
one_hot_matrix = np.zeros((len(preprocessed_corpus[0].split()),
len(vocab)))
one_hot_matrix.shape
```

Here is the output:

```
(4, 4)
```

The shape here is 4, 4 because there would be one row for the one-hot vector of each token in the preprocessed corpus.

6. Here is the code for building the one-hot vectors:

```
for i, token in enumerate(preprocessed_corpus[0].split()):
    one_hot_matrix[i][position[token]] = 1
```

The preceding code snippet marks the position in the vector where the token is present as 1; other positions remain at 0.

7. Here is the code for visualizing the one-hot matrix:

```
one_hot_matrix
```

Here is the output:

```
array([[1., 0., 0., 0.],
       [0., 0., 1., 0.],
       [0., 0., 0., 1.],
       [0., 1., 0., 0.]])
```

As can be seen in the matrix, only one entry in each row is 1 and the others are 0. The first row corresponds to the one-hot vector of read, the second to natural, the third to language, and the final one to process, based on their respective indices in the vocabulary.

Building a basic chatbot

We discussed chatbots as one of the important real-world applications of NLP in Chapter 1, *Understanding the Basics of NLP*. By now, we know enough to create a basic chatbot that could be trained using a predefined corpus and provide responses to queries using similarity concepts. In this section, we will create a chatbot using the concepts of vectorization and cosine similarity.

The most important requirement for building a chatbot is the corpus or text data on which the chatbot will be trained. The corpus should be relevant and exhaustive. If you are building a chatbot for the **Human Resources (HR)** department of your organization, you would typically need a corpus with all HR policies to train the bot and not a corpus containing presidential speeches. You would also need to ensure that the response time is acceptable and that the bot is not taking an inordinate amount of time to respond. The bot should also ideally seem human-like and have an acceptable accuracy rate.

For the purposes of the chatbot that we will create in this section, we will be using Amazon's Q&A data, which is a repository of questions and answers gathered from Amazon's website for various product categories (`http://jmcauley.ucsd.edu/data/amazon/qa/`). Since the dataset is massive, we will only be using the Q&A data for electronic items. Being trained on Q&A data for electronic items, our chatbot could be deployed as automated Q&A support under the **Electronic Items** section. The following screenshot shows a partial snapshot of the corpus, which is in a **JavaScript Object Notation (JSON)**-like format:

```
1   {'questionType': 'yes/no', 'asin': '0594033926', 'answerTime': 'Dec 27, 2013', 'unixTime': 1388131200, 'question': 'Is this cover the one that fits the old
    nook color? Which I believe is 8x5.', 'answerType': 'Y', 'answer': 'Yes this fits both the nook color and the same-shaped nook tablet'}
2   {'questionType': 'yes/no', 'asin': '0594033926', 'answerTime': 'Jan 5, 2015', 'unixTime': 1420444800, 'question': 'Does it fit Nook GlowLight?', 'answerType':
    'N', 'answer': 'No. The nook color or color tablet'}
3   {'answer': "I don't think so. The nook color is 5 x 8 so not sure anything smaller would stay locked in, but would be close.", 'asin': '0594033926',
    'answerTime': '2 days ago', 'question': 'Would it fit Nook 1st Edition? 4.9in x 7.7in ?', 'questionType': 'open-ended'}
4   {'questionType': 'yes/no', 'asin': '0594033926', 'answerTime': '17 days ago', 'question': "Will this fit a Nook Color that's 5 x 8?", 'answerType': 'Y',
    'answer': 'yes'}
5   {'questionType': 'yes/no', 'asin': '0594033926', 'answerTime': 'Feb 10, 2015', 'unixTime': 1423555200, 'question': 'will this fit the Samsung Galaxy Tab 4
    Nook 10.1', 'answerType': 'N', 'answer': "No, the tab is smaller than the 'color'"}
6   {'questionType': 'yes/no', 'asin': '0594033926', 'answerTime': 'Jan 30, 2015', 'unixTime': 1422604800, 'question': 'does it have a flip stand?', 'answerType':
    'N', 'answer': 'No, there is not a flip stand. It has a pocket in the front flap. It is a very nice cover.'}
7   {'questionType': 'yes/no', 'asin': '0594033926', 'answerTime': 'Jan 30, 2015', 'unixTime': 1422604800, 'question': 'does this have a flip stand', 'answerType'
    : '?', 'answer': "Hi, no it doesn't"}
8   {'questionType': 'open-ended', 'asin': '0594033926', 'answerTime': 'Dec 22, 2014', 'unixTime': 1419235200, 'question': 'also fits the HD+?', 'answer': 'It
    should. They are the same size and the charging port is in the same place.'}
9   {'questionType': 'yes/no', 'asin': '0594033926', 'answerTime': 'Nov 16, 2014', 'unixTime': 1416124800, 'question': 'Does it have 2 positions for the reader?
    Horizontal/vertical Thank You KWOD', 'answerType': 'Z', 'answer': 'Yes'}
10  {'questionType': 'open-ended', 'asin': '0594033926', 'answerTime': 'Aug 7, 2014', 'unixTime': 1407369600, 'question': 'Is there a closure mechanism? Bands,
    magnetic, etc.?', 'answer': "No- it is more like a normal book would be. It doesn't flop open- so it has never wen an issue for me. The nook clips into a
    secure and safe holder inside that is small and convenient. This is the best cover I've ever had for my nook- trim and functional (no magnets or elastic
    needed)."}
```

As we can see, each row of data is in a dictionary format with various key-value pairs. Now that we have familiarized ourselves with the corpus, let's design the architecture of the chatbot, as follows:

1. Store all the questions from the corpus in a list
2. Store all corresponding answers from the corpus in a list
3. Vectorize and preprocess the question data
4. Vectorize and preprocess the user's query
5. Assess the most similar question to the user's query using cosine similarity
6. Return the corresponding answer to the most similar question as a chat response

Now that we have the blueprint of the solution, let's start coding. As the first step, we will need to import the corpus (`qa_Electronics.json`) into Python. We read the file as a text file and then use the `ast` library's `literal_eval` function to convert the rows from a string to a Python dictionary. We then iterate through each dictionary to extract and store questions and answers in separate lists, as shown in the following code block:

```
import ast
questions = []
answers = []
with open('qa_Electronics.json','r') as f:
    for line in f:
        data = ast.literal_eval(line)
        questions.append(data['question'].lower())
        answers.append(data['answer'].lower())
```

While importing, we also perform the preprocessing step of converting all characters to lowercase. Next, using the `CountVectorizer` module of the `sklearn` library, we convert the `questions` list into a sparse matrix and apply TF-IDF transformation, as shown in the following code block:

```
from sklearn.feature_extraction.text import CountVectorizer
vectorizer = CountVectorizer(stop_words='english')
X_vec = vectorizer.fit_transform(questions)
tfidf = TfidfTransformer(norm='l2')
X_tfidf = tfidf.fit_transform(X_vec)
```

`X_tfidf` is the repository matrix that will be searched every time a new question is entered in the chatbot for the most similar question. To implement this, we create a function to calculate the angle between every row of the `X_tfidf` matrix and the new question vector. We use the `sklearn` library's `cosine_similarity` module to calculate the cosine between each row and the vector, and then convert the cosine into degrees. Finally, we search the row that has the maximum cosine (or the minimum angle) with the new question vector and return the corresponding answer to that question as the response. If the smallest angle between the question vector and every row of the matrix is greater than a threshold value, then we consider that question to be different enough to not warrant a response. The implementation of the function is shown in the following code block:

```
def conversation(im):
    global tfidf, answers, X_tfidf
    Y_vec = vectorizer.transform(im)
    Y_tfidf = tfidf.fit_transform(Y_vec)
    angle = np.rad2deg(np.arccos(max(cosine_similarity(Y_tfidf, \
                       X_tfidf)[0])))
    if angle > 60 :
        return "sorry, I did not quite understand that"
```

```
    else:
        return answers[np.argmax(cosine_similarity(Y_tfidf, X_tfidf)[0])]
```

Lastly, we implement the chat, wherein the user enters their username and is then greeted by the chatbot. The chat is initiated with the user asking questions and the bot providing a response based on the preceding functions. The chat continues until the user types bye. The implementation of the chat function is shown in the following code block:

```
def main():
    usr = input("Please enter your username: ")
    print("support: Hi, welcome to Q&A support. How can I help you?")
    while True:
        im = input("{}: ".format(usr))
        if im.lower() == 'bye':
            print("Q&A support: bye!")
            break
        else:
            print("Q&A support: "+conversation([im]))
```

That's it. We have just created a Q&A support chatbot that answers electronics products-related questions based on an existing repository of similar Q&As. The following is a sample conversation performed by the chatbot, which does not seem too bad for such a simple implementation:

```
Please enter your username: mike

support: Hi, welcome to Q&A support. How can I help you?

mike: what is the battery life of my phone?
Q&A support: so far after i charge the battery it will last about 90
minutes. i have not had any issues with the battery.

mike: great. does it have blue tooth?
Q&A support: no

mike: too bad. is there a replacement warranty on my phone?
Q&A support: the guarantee is one month. (the phone must be free of shocks
or manipulated its hardware) the costs paid by the buyer.

mike: what about theft?
Q&A support: have to see if it covers it.

mike: bye
Q&A support: bye!
```

In this section, we used the concepts of vectorization and cosine similarity to create a basic chatbot. Needless to say, there is plenty of room for further improvement in this chatbot and we urge you to explore ways to improve its accuracy. Some areas that can be further refined are preprocessing, the cleaning of raw data, tweaking TF-IDF normalization, and so on. While cosine similarity-based chatbots were the first-generation NLP applications used in industry to automate simple Q&A-based tasks, new-age chatbots have come a long way and are able to handle much more complex and bespoke requirements using deep learning-based models. We will be covering some of these advanced concepts in the later chapters of this book.

Summary

In this chapter, we took baby steps in understanding the math involved in the representation of text data using numbers based on some heuristics. We made an attempt to understand the BoW model and build it using the `CountVectorizer` API provided by the `sklearn` module. After looking into limitations associated with `CountVectorizer`, we tried mitigating those using `TfIdfVectorizer`, which scales the weights of the less frequently occurring terms. We understood that these methods are purely based on lexical analysis and have limitations in terms of not taking into account features such as semantics associated with words, the co-occurrence of words together, and the position of words in a document, among others.

The study of the vectorization methods was followed up by making use of these vectors to find similarity or dissimilarity between documents using cosine similarity as the measure that provides the angle between two vectors in n-dimensional space. Finally, we looked into one-hot vectorization, a mechanism used for building vectors for tokens.

Which vectorization method to use where TD-IDF is concerned, of course, builds on top of the idea of `CountVectorizer` and helps in mitigating the issues involved with it. However, neither of these methods would scale well if the vocabulary is large or keeps on increasing. These would be ideally suited in use cases where the vocabulary size is limited and similar terms occur frequently across documents.

Now that we have understood a few mechanisms of representing text using its syntactical representation, let's take it forward in the next chapter by taking semantics into account as well. On these lines, let's explore techniques such as Word2vec in the next chapter.

5
Word Embeddings and Distance Measurements for Text

In `Chapter 4`, *Transforming Text into Data Structures*, we discussed the bag-of-words and term-frequency and inverse document frequency-based methods to represent text in the form of numbers. These methods mostly rely on the syntactical aspects of a word in terms of its presence or absence in a document or across a text corpus. However, information about the neighborhood of the word, in terms of what words come after or before a word, wasn't taken into account in the approaches we have discussed so far. The neighborhood of a word carries important information in terms of what context the word is carrying in a sentence. The relationship between the word and its neighborhood tends to define the semantics of a word and its overall positioning and presence in a sentence. In this chapter, we will use this idea to build word vectors that will try to capture the meaning of the word based on the context it's been used in.

The following topics will be covered in this chapter:

- Understanding word embeddings
- Demystifying Word2vec
- Training a Word2vec model
- Word mover's distance

Technical requirements

The code files for this chapter can be found at the following GitHub link: `https://github.com/PacktPublishing/Hands-On-Python-Natural-Language-Processing/tree/master/Chapter05`.

Understanding word embeddings

Word embedding is a learned representation of a word wherein each word is represented using a vector in *n*-dimensional space. Words with similar meanings should have similar representations. These representations can also help in identifying synonyms, antonyms, and various other relationships between words. We mentioned that embeddings can be built to correspond to individual words; however, this idea can be extended to develop embeddings for individual sentences, documents, characters, and so on. Word2vec captures relationships in text; consequently, similar words have similar representations. Let's try to understand what type of semantic information Word2vec can actually encapsulate.

We will look at a few examples to understand what relationships and analogies can be captured by a Word2vec model. A very frequently used example deals with the embedding of King, Man, Queen, and Woman. Once a Word2vec model is built properly and the embedding from it is obtained for these words, the following relationship is frequently obtained, provided that these words are actually a part of the vocabulary:

$$vector\ (Man) - vector\ (King) + vector\ (Queen) = vector\ (Woman)$$

This equation boils down to the following relationship:

$$vector\ (Man) + vector\ (Queen) = vector\ (King) + vector\ (Woman)$$

The thought process here is that the relationship of Man:King is the same as Woman:Queen. The Word2vec algorithm is able to capture these semantic relationships when it devises an embedding for each of these words.

Let's take one more example, but this time we will relate countries to capitals. If we build vectors for France, Italy, and Paris using Word2vec, what would be the output of the following equation?

$$vector\ (France) + vector\ (Rome) - vector\ (Italy) = ??$$

The output would be vector (Paris).

Similar to the previous example, the analogy here is that the Italy: Rome relationship is the same as the France: Paris relationship.

All of this seems to be magic!

Now, let's try to understand how exactly we capture all of this information. It all boils down to the Word2vec algorithm. Let's look at Word2vec in detail in the next section.

The values or vectors obtained from the simple mathematics discussed previously are not exactly equal to the actual vector representation of the words, but they are close enough to substantiate that these relationships are obtained using the Word2vec methodology.

Demystifying Word2vec

Word2vec targets exactly what **John Rupert Firth** famously said:

"A word is known by the company it keeps."

It is a model that enables the building of word vectors using contextual information from the neighborhood of a word. For every word whose embedding is developed, it's based on the words around it. Word2vec uses a simple neural network to build this architecture. We'll discuss the details of neural networks in depth in Chapter 8, *From Human Neurons to Artificial Neurons for Text Understanding*, onward.

A paper on Word2vec came out in 2013 and was one of the revolutionary findings in the domain of **Natural Language Processing (NLP)**. It was developed by Thomas Mikolov et al. at Google and was later made open source for the community to use and build on. A link to the paper can be found at https://papers.nips.cc/paper/5021-distributed-representations-of-words-and-phrases-and-their-compositionality.pdf.

Before we get into the details of Word2vec, we will try to define what supervised and unsupervised learning is.

Supervised and unsupervised learning

Supervised and unsupervised learning will be covered in detail in Chapter 7, *Identifying Patterns in Text Using Machine Learning*. In order to just give you a brief heads up on supervised and unsupervised learning, we'll look at a few examples here:

- **Supervised learning**: This includes cases such as breast cancer prediction, where we have labeled data in which each data point either belongs to a person suffering from breast cancer or someone who is not.

- **Unsupervised learning**: Apart from the type of task mentioned in the previous point, there are tasks such as ones where we need to figure out segments or groups of customers based on their spending patterns. These data points do not have any labels, such as high-spending or low-spending, and the aim is to just group users. These tasks come under the scope of unsupervised learning.

Now that we have understood the difference between supervised and unsupervised, let's find out which category Word2vec belongs to.

Word2vec – supervised or unsupervised?

Word2vec is an unsupervised methodology for building word embeddings. In the Word2vec architecture, an attempt is made to do either of the following:

- Predict the target word based on the context word
- Predict the context word based on the target word

Even though words are being predicted, the prediction component or the class attribute itself comes from the text or the corpus. Hence, there is no specific class attribute available, as is the case in a supervised learning scenario. Due to this, Word2vec falls under the class of unsupervised algorithms. All the learning comes from unstructured data in an unsupervised manner.

Pretrained Word2vec

As discussed previously, the Word2vec algorithm tries to capture relationships between words in the text corpus. In this section, we will explore the pretrained implementations available for Word2vec. This will be followed by a deep dive into the Word2vec architecture, where, using that knowledge, we will try to understand how exactly the Word2vec model encapsulates contextual information.

The output of the Word2vec algorithm is a $|V| * D$ matrix, where $|V|$ is the size of the vocabulary we want vector representations for and D is the number of dimensions used to represent each word vector. As you may have guessed, each row in this matrix carries the embedding for an individual word in the vocabulary. The value of D can be changed and played around with depending on several factors, such as the size of the text corpus and the various relationships that need to be captured. Generally, D takes values between 50 and 300 in real-life use cases.

There is a pretrained, globally available Word2vec model that Google trained on Google News dataset. It has a vocabulary size of 3 million words and phrases and each vector has 300 dimensions. This model is 1.5 GB in size and can be downloaded from `https://code.google.com/archive/p/word2vec/`. Python's `gensim` library provides various methods to use the pretrained model directly or to fine-tune it. It also allows the Word2vec model to be built from scratch based on any provided dataset. We will use this model intensively as part of this chapter.

Exploring the pretrained Word2vec model using gensim

Let's go through a few steps in detail that will help us import, explore, and infer from the pretrained model:

1. Install the `genism` library:

   ```
   pip install gensim
   ```

   The preceding statement can be run from the command line.

2. Import the `gensim` library and the `KeyedVectors` component:

   ```
   import gensim
   from gensim.models import KeyedVectors
   ```

3. Load the pretrained vectors from the pretrained Word2vec model file:

   ```
   model=KeyedVectors.load_word2vec_format('/Users/amankedia/Desktop/S
   unday/nlp-book/Chapter5/Code/GoogleNews-vectors-negative300.bin',
   binary=True)
   ```

4. Validate the size of the pretrained Word2vec vocabulary:

   ```
   len(model.wv.vocab)
   ```

   Here is the output:

   ```
   3000000
   ```

   As you can see, the vocabulary size for this model is `3000000`.

5. Explore the size of each Word2vec vector:

   ```
   model.vector_size
   ```

Here is the output:

```
300
```

As you can see, each vector is 300-dimensional.

6. Explore the pretrained Word2vec vocabulary:

```
model.wv.vocab
```

 You can check the output of the preceding command in the Jupyter notebook (code files) for this book as the output is too large to be displayed here.

7. Check the most_similar functionality:

```
model.most_similar('Delhi')
```

Here is the output:

```
[('Kolkata', 0.7663769721984863),
 ('Mumbai', 0.7306068539619446),
 ('Lucknow', 0.7277829051017761),
 ('Patna', 0.7159016728401184),
 ('Guwahati', 0.7072612643241882),
 ('Jaipur', 0.6992814540863037),
 ('Hyderabad', 0.6983195543289185),
 ('Ranchi', 0.6962575912475586),
 ('Bhubaneswar', 0.6959235072135925),
 ('Chandigarh', 0.6940240859985352)]
```

This output shows that the embedding for 'Delhi' is most similar to 'Kolkata'.

8. Let's validate the king, queen, woman, and man examples from earlier, both in terms of the closest word and the second-closest word:

```
result = model.most_similar(positive=['man', 'queen'],
negative=['king'], topn=1)
print(result)
```

Here is the output:

```
[('woman', 0.760943531990513)]
```

9. Let's see what the two closest words are:

```
result = model.most_similar(positive=['man', 'queen'],
negative=['king'], topn=1)
print(result)
```

Here is the output:

```
[('woman', 0.7609435319900513), ('girl', 0.6139994263648987)]
```

This output validates the first equation that we saw earlier, where we had *vector (man) + vector (queen) – vector (king) = vector (woman)*. The second closest entity here is girl.

10. Let's now validate the country and capital example we saw earlier in this chapter:

```
result = model.most_similar(positive=['France', 'Rome'],
negative=['Italy'], topn=1)
print(result)
[('Paris', 0.7190686464309692)]
```

The result is Paris, which is consistent with our expected output.

The Word2vec architecture

In the previous section, *Pretrained Word2vec*, we saw the pretrained Word2vec offering from Google and explored its various associated features. In this section, we will try to understand how Word2vec models are trained and what the architecture for training a Word2vec algorithm is.

As we discussed earlier, Word2vec models can be trained by two approaches, as follows:

- Predicting the context word using the target word as input, which is referred to as the **Skip-gram** method
- Predicting the target word using the context words as input, which is referred to as the **Continuous Bag-of-Words (CBOW)** method

Here, we will discuss the Skip-gram method in detail, but you can use the ideas from our Skip-gram discussion to build the Word2vec model using the CBOW approach.

The Skip-gram method

The Skip-gram method builds a Word2vec model by trying to predict a context word when a target word is taken as input. These words are present in each others' neighborhoods. Each target-context pair will help you build the embeddings of these target words. Let's see how the Skip-gram method works.

How do you define target and context words?

Let's take the following sentence:

```
All that glitters is not gold
```

Here, `glitters` is the target word.

The context words are comprised of the words appearing in the neighborhood of `glitters`. We can define something called `window_size`, which is a configurable parameter that conveys to the model the size of the neighborhood to consider when taking in a word as the target word. For the preceding sentence, let's define a `window_size` value of 5. When the window size is defined as 5, the model takes in two words from the left and two words from the right of the target word as the context words.

In this example, the mapping would be as follows for `glitters`:

Target/Input Word	Context Word
glitters	All
glitters	that
glitters	is
glitters	not

The expectation is that whenever `glitters` is provided as input, the model should be able to predict the correct context word. Based on how it is doing in terms of predicting the correct context word, it learns and, over time, gets better at predicting the right context work.

Now, that we understand what the target word and context word are, let's try to generalize our understanding. We will follow a sliding window approach to generate target and context words for the sentence.

Say we have the sentence `Let us make an effort to understand natural language processing`:

Let	us	make	an	effort	to	understand	Natural	Language	Processing
Let	us	make	an	effort	to	understand	Natural	Language	Processing
Let	us	make	an	effort	to	understand	Natural	Language	Processing
Let	us	make	an	effort	to	understand	Natural	Language	Processing
Let	us	make	an	effort	to	understand	Natural	Language	Processing
Let	us	make	an	effort	to	understand	Natural	Language	Processing
Let	us	make	an	effort	to	understand	Natural	Language	Processing
Let	us	make	an	effort	to	understand	Natural	Language	Processing
Let	us	make	an	effort	to	understand	Natural	Language	Processing
Let	us	make	an	effort	to	understand	Natural	Language	Processing

Every row in the preceding graph has one word shaded in brown. This word represents the target word. Each row also has some words shaded in gray. These words represent the context words for the corresponding target word. As you will have guessed, the `window_size` value used here is 5.

As an example, let's pick up the fourth row. The word `an`, shaded in brown, is the target word and the words `us`, `make`, `effort`, and `to`, shaded in gray, are the context words for the target word, `an`.

Let's now dive into the various components that are required as part of building the Skip-gram model and attain the functionality to predict correct context words based on the target word.

Exploring the components of a Skip-gram model

Let's now understand and explore the various components that are involved in building a Skip-gram model.

Input vector

The input is a one-hot vector with a size of $|V| * 1$, where $|V|$ is the size of the vocabulary. Only one entry in this vector is marked 1, which corresponds to the position of the target word. All other entries are marked 0.

For example, let's assume that our vocabulary contains the words the, Sun, is, and rising. If the words are in the same order, the one-hot vector for each of these words would be as follows:

- For the, we would have the following:

$$1\ 0\ 0\ 0$$

- For sun, we would have the following:

$$0\ 1\ 0\ 0$$

- For is, we would have the following:

$$0\ 0\ 1\ 0$$

- For rising, we would have the following:

$$0\ 0\ 0\ 1$$

The size of each vector is 4, since our vocabulary contains four words. In each of the vectors, only one entry is 1, which corresponds to the index of the word in the vocabulary.

Embedding matrix

The next entry in the Word2vec architecture is the embedding matrix, which has a size of $|V| * N$, where $|V|$ is the size of the vocabulary and N is the number of dimensions we wish to represent each word vector with.

The embedding matrix can be instantiated with random numbers; however, certain initialization methods, such as Xavier initialization, provide better results than random initialization. You can read more about this at http://cs231n.github.io/neural-networks-2/#init.

A dot product is performed between the embedding matrix and the input vector, which yields an intermediate vector. In hindsight, when this dot product is performed, the row corresponding to the target word in the embedding matrix will be activated and come out as the intermediate vector because only that particular word's entry is 1 in the input vector, and the rest are 0.

Context matrix

The next matrix in our architecture is called the context matrix, which also has a size of |V| * N, which is the same dimensionality as the embedding matrix. The dot product of the intermediate vector obtained previously and the context matrix is performed to yield the output vector.

The thinking here is that the target word's embedding obtained as the intermediate vector will be able to activate the context word's entry in the context matrix.

Output vector

The dot product of the intermediate vector and the context matrix yields the output vector, which has a size of |V| * 1, where |V| is the size of the vocabulary. Each entry in this vector has a number that represents the chances of the word corresponding to that index being the context word predicted by the model. The higher the value in a particular position, the higher the model's inclination to predict the word corresponding to that index as the context word.

These entries can take in any real numbers as their values. However, we want normalized values between 0 and 1, and for that, we use something called the softmax function, which is discussed next.

Softmax

The softmax function takes the following form:

$$\frac{e^z}{\sum_{i=1}^{|V|} e^z}$$

Here, z is the predicted value of each word being the context word.

The softmax function returns normalized probabilities for a set of numbers.

Let's look at an example so as to be able to understand softmax.

Assuming we have seven words, the following array shows z, or the predicted value of each word to be the context word:

$$z = [2.0, 3.0, 1.0, 4.0, 2.0, 3.0, 2.0]$$

Now, we want the normalized probabilities such that they sum up to 1.

The normalized probability of 2.0 will be as follows:

$$\frac{exp(2.0)}{exp(2.0) + exp(3.0) + exp(1.0) + exp(4.0) + exp(2.0) + exp(3.0) + exp(2.0)}$$

Let's see how can we achieve this using three lines of code:

```
import numpy as np
z = [2.0, 3.0, 1.0, 4.0, 2.0, 3.0, 2.0]
np.exp(z) / np.sum(np.exp(z))
```

The normalized probabilities outputted by our simple code are as follows:

```
array([0.06175318, 0.16786254, 0.02271772, 0.45629768, 0.06175318,
       0.16786254, 0.06175318])
```

The first value in our output array gives the normalized probability of the first entry in the input array, z. The same is true for other indices as well. So, the normalized probability of 2.0, in this case, is 0.06175318.

Loss calculation and backpropagation

After the normalized probability is obtained for whether something is the context word, this is compared with the actual expected context word, and the loss function or error in prediction is calculated, as in the following diagram. The models predict the **predicted vector**, which contains the normalized probability of each word in the vocabulary being the context word. The **target vector** is a one-hot vector, which indicates which value we expect to be the context word. These two vectors are subtracted to compute the error made in predicting the context word when given the target word as input:

As part of the loss function calculation, we attempt to figure out how close or far the model was to predicting the correct context word. The results of the loss function show how well or badly the model performed in predicting the context word. The computed error is sent back to the model, where the weights or entries in the embedding and context matrices are adjusted based on how much they were responsible for predicting the context word correctly or incorrectly. This methodology is referred to as backpropagation. You can read more about backpropagation and loss functions at http://cs231n.github.io/optimization-2/ and http://cs231n.github.io/neural-networks-2/#losses, respectively.

Inference

The preceding steps are repeated several times or for several epochs (which is a configurable parameter) and, at the end of the training, the *embedding matrix* provides the output we need. It is drawn out of the architecture and each row in this trained matrix contains the word embedding for a word in the vocabulary. The ith row here contains the word vector for the ith word in our vocabulary:

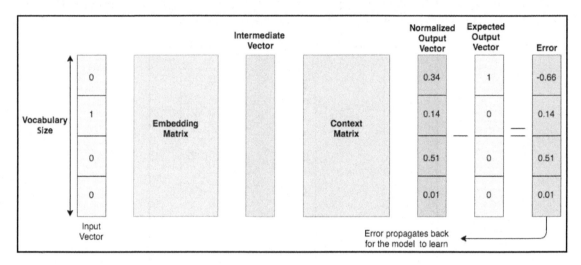

This diagram shows all the components and various interactions involved in building the Word2vec model based on the Skip-gram method.

The CBOW method

The CBOW method works similarly to the Skip-gram method. However, the change here is that the vector corresponding to the context word is sent in as input and the model tries to predict the target word.

Computational limitations of the methods discussed and how to overcome them

The methods we discussed previously are computationally expensive since all the weights or entries in the embedding and context matrix are updated for each `target word, context word` or `context word, target word` pair. Mikolov et al. addressed this problem by employing two strategies—subsampling and negative sampling. We will discuss both of them in the following sections.

Subsampling

There are some situations where certain words, such as `a`, `an` and `the`, don't add much context when they appear in the neighborhood of a target word. Also, these words occur too frequently in any text corpus, so the creators of this method decided to subsample certain words so that these words would be deleted from the text itself. These words would not be used as target words, hence reducing the training data size, and neither would they play a role in being the context word for other target words. Whether a word is sampled depends on a metric called the sampling rate.

The sampling rate or probability of keeping a word is determined by the following formula:

$$P(word_i) = (\sqrt{\frac{f(word_i)}{0.001}} + 1) \times \frac{0.001}{f(word_i)}$$

Here, $f(word_i)$ is the fraction of total words in the corpus, which is $word_i$.

Negative sampling

The other methodology applied to prevent all the weights updating is referred to as negative sampling. As part of negative sampling, a very small subset of negative words, or words that are not expected to appear in the context of a target word, are selected and only their weights are updated, apart from the actual context word. As a result, only a very small fraction of weights in the matrix are updated, instead of all the weights.

How to select negative samples

The negative samples or words whose weights are updated again depend on the frequency of the occurrence of the word relative to other words in the corpus.

The probability of picking a word is given by the following formula:

$$P(word_i) = \frac{freq(word_i)}{\sum_{j=0}^{j=|V|} freq(word_j)}$$

freq(word$_i$) is the number of times the ith word occurs in the corpus.

These two methodologies largely help in reducing the computational efforts required to build Word2vec models.

Training a Word2vec model

Now that we know how the pretrained Word2vec model can be leveraged and we have looked at and understood the Word2vec model architecture, let's try to actually train a Word2vec model. We can create a custom implementation for this; however, for the sake of this exercise, we will leverage the functionalities provided by the `gensim` library.

The `gensim` library provides a convenient interface for building a Word2vec model. We will start by building a very simple model using the fewest possible parameters and then we will build on it.

Building a basic Word2vec model

Let's build a basic Word2vec model by executing the following steps:

1. We will start by importing the Word2vec module from `gensim`, define a few sentences as our data, and then build a model using the following code:

```
from gensim.models import Word2Vec
sentences = [["I", "am", "trying", "to", "understand", "Natural",
              "Language", "Processing"],
```

```
                    ["Natural", "Language", "Processing", "is", "fun",
                    "to", "learn"],
                    ["There", "are", "numerous", "use", "cases", "of",
                    "Natural", "Language", "Processing"]]
        model = Word2Vec(sentences, min_count=1)
```

We can provide the Word2vec module with a list of tokenized sentences as input, as we have done in the preceding example. We can also provide a text corpus as input using the `corpus_file` parameter as the corpus contains a list of sentences where the words in each sentence are separated by whitespace.

The `min_count` parameter helps create custom vocabulary based on the text itself. The value of `min_count` sets a minimum threshold so that vectors are built only for words that occur more often than the value specified in the `min_count` parameter.

Here, we have used a very small list of custom-built sentences to build out the Word2vec model. However, this can be extended to any dataset. In real-life scenarios, the entire dataset is provided as a list of sentences or a corpus a whole.

2. Let's see what the size of each vector that we just built is using the following one-line code:

    ```
    model.vector_size
    ```

    The output for this is as follows:

    ```
    100
    ```

    The default vector size in Word2vec is 100; however, this is a configurable parameter and we will look at changing it in the upcoming sections.

3. Let's find out the size of the vocabulary we built:

    ```
    len(model.wv.vocab)
    ```

    Our vocabulary has a size of 17, as shown in the following output:

    ```
    17
    ```

The size of the vocabulary is equal to the number of unique words in the sentences we have defined.

Now that we have built a basic Word2vec model, let's learn how to modify the `min_count` parameter in the following section.

Modifying the min_count parameter

In order to modify the min_count parameter, we execute the following steps:

1. The `min_count` parameter helps restrict the vocabulary so that word vectors are only built for words that occur at least `min_count` times in the corpus:

```
model = Word2Vec(sentences, min_count=2)
```

2. Let's find out what the vocabulary size is when we set `min_count` to 2 based on the previous code block:

```
len(model.wv.vocab)
```

Here is the output:

```
4
```

The vocabulary size is 4 because only four words occur twice or more in our corpus.

3. Let's see what those words are:

```
model.wv.vocab
```

Here is the output:

```
{'to': <gensim.models.keyedvectors.Vocab at 0x127591a58>,
 'Natural': <gensim.models.keyedvectors.Vocab at 0x127591a90>,
 'Language': <gensim.models.keyedvectors.Vocab at 0x127591ac8>,
 'Processing': <gensim.models.keyedvectors.Vocab at 0x127591b00>}
```

4. The dimension for these vectors would still be `100`. Let's validate that:

```
model.vector_size
```

As expected, the vector size is `100`, as we can see in the following output code block:

```
100
```

Let's move on and try some more interesting things with the Word2vec parameters.

Playing with the vector size

Higher-dimensional vectors capture more information across dimensions, especially when the corpus and vocabulary are big and the data is highly varied.

Let's try to build a model where each vector is 300-dimensional using the following code block:

```
model = Word2Vec(sentences, min_count=2, size = 300)
```

Let's now find out the vector size for the model we just built using the following line of code:

```
model.vector_size
```

Here is our vector size:

```
300
```

As we can see, each of the four words that occur more than once is now represented using 300 dimensions.

Other important configurable parameters

Apart from `min_count` and `size`, some other important parameters are as follows:

- `sg`, whose value when 1 uses the Skip-gram approach and, when 0, uses the CBOW approach
- `negative`, which when greater than 0, indicates that negative sampling should be used and the integer value signifies the number of negative samples to use
- `workers`, which defines the number of threads to use for training:

model = Word2Vec (sentences, min_count=1, size = 300, workers = 2, sg = 1, negative = 1)

Let's find out the vocabulary size and vocabulary for this model:

```
len(model.wv.vocab)
```

Our vocabulary size is as follows:

```
17
```

Let's check the vocabulary using the following code:

```
model.wv.vocab
```

Here's our vocabulary:

```
{'I': <gensim.models.keyedvectors.Vocab at 0x1275ab5c0>,
 'am': <gensim.models.keyedvectors.Vocab at 0x1275ab588>,
 'trying': <gensim.models.keyedvectors.Vocab at 0x1275ab518>,
 'to': <gensim.models.keyedvectors.Vocab at 0x1275ab4e0>,
 'understand': <gensim.models.keyedvectors.Vocab at 0x1275ab4a8>,
 'Natural': <gensim.models.keyedvectors.Vocab at 0x1275ab438>,
 'Language': <gensim.models.keyedvectors.Vocab at 0x1275ab400>,
 'Processing': <gensim.models.keyedvectors.Vocab at 0x1275ab3c8>,
 'is': <gensim.models.keyedvectors.Vocab at 0x1275ab390>,
 'fun': <gensim.models.keyedvectors.Vocab at 0x1275ab358>,
 'learn': <gensim.models.keyedvectors.Vocab at 0x1275ab2e8>,
 'There': <gensim.models.keyedvectors.Vocab at 0x1275ab208>,
 'are': <gensim.models.keyedvectors.Vocab at 0x1275ab240>,
 'numerous': <gensim.models.keyedvectors.Vocab at 0x1275ab1d0>,
 'use': <gensim.models.keyedvectors.Vocab at 0x127591a20>,
 'cases': <gensim.models.keyedvectors.Vocab at 0x1275919e8
```

Word2vec models are generally stored as pickle files that serialize the model; the `save()` method can be used for this.

Limitations of Word2vec

Word2vec is a great tool for capturing semantic information from text, and we have seen how well it captures information. However, the Word2vec model has some limitations. Let's take the following two sentences:

```
I am eating an apple.
I am using an apple desktop.
```

`apple` in the first sentence signifies the fruit and, in the second sentence, it signifies the company. However, the word vector generated for `apple` would be the same for both the company and the fruit. In other words, since a static embedding is created for each word after the training, generating an embedding on the fly based on the context for a word's specific usage is a limitation of the Word2vec model.

Word2vec can also capture stereotypical or biased relationships depending on the text corpus it was trained on. These biases can be related to gender, ethnicity, religion, and so on. For example, some patterns that can be observed are as follows:

```
man:doctor what woman:nurse
man:computer programmer what woman:homemaker
```

This is another limitation of the Word2vec model, but this is highly dependent on the text provided and, as is always said, *the model is as good as the data it was trained on.*

Applications of the Word2vec model

Word2vec has a large-scale application. It can be used in search engines, building classification, and clustering models where sentences can be represented by using embeddings of the words in them. Another very important scenario where Word2vec is used is in capturing document similarity or how related two or more documents are to each other. These are only some of its use cases, and the internet is filled with other examples of where Word2vec finds its place and is highly relevant.

Word mover's distance

In the previous section, we discussed how measuring document similarity is one of the major use cases of Word2vec. Think of a problem statement, such as one where we are building an engine that can rank resumes based on their relevance to a job description. Here, we ideally need to figure out the distance between the job description and the set of resumes. The smaller the distance between the resume and the job description, the higher the relevance of the resume to the job description.

One measure we discussed in `Chapter 4`, *Transforming Text into Data Structures*, was to use cosine similarity to find how close or far text documents are to one another or how far removed they are from one another. In this section, we will discuss another measure, **Word Mover's Distance (WMD)**, which is more relevant than cosine similarity, especially when we base the distance measure for documents on word embeddings.

Kusner et al. devised the WMD algorithm. They define the dissimilarity between two text documents as the minimum amount of distance that the embedded words of one document need to *travel* to reach the embedded words of another document.

Let's look at an example that the authors use in their research paper:

```
Sentence 1: Obama speaks to the media in Illinois.
Sentence 2: President greets the press in Chicago.
```

Based on the Word2vec model, the embedding for `Obama` would be very close to `President`. Similarly, `speaks` would be pretty close to `greets`, `media` would be pretty close to `press`, and `Illinois` would map pretty closely to `Chicago`.

Let's take a look at a third sentence—`Apple is my favorite company`. Now, this is likely to be more distant to sentence 1 than sentence 2 is. This is because there is not much of a semantic relationship between the words in the first and third sentences.

WMD computes the pairwise Euclidean distance between words across the sentences and it defines the distance between two documents as the minimum cumulative cost in terms of the Euclidean distance required to move all the words from the first sentence to the second sentence.

Let's see how we implement this using `gensim`:

1. We will import the libraries using the following two lines of code:

```
import gensim
from gensim.models import KeyedVectors
```

2. Now, we will load our pretrained model:

```
model=KeyedVectors.load_word2vec_format('/Users/amankedia/Desktop/S
unday/nlp-book/Chapter 5/Code/GoogleNews-vectors-negative300.bin',
binary=True)
```

3. Now that we have loaded our model, let's define our data:

```
sentence_1 = "Obama speaks to the media in Illinois"
sentence_2 = "President greets the press in Chicago"
sentence_3 = "Apple is my favorite company"
```

We will get into the real action next!

4. We will now compute the WMD between the sentences from the data we just defined. Let's begin by calculating the WMD between `sentence_1` and `sentence_2` first:

```
word_mover_distance = model.wmdistance(sentence_1, sentence_2)
word_mover_distance
```

This is the WMD between `sentence_1` and `sentence_2`:

```
1.1642040735998236
```

5. Now, we will compute the distance between `sentence_1` and `sentence_3`:

```
word_mover_distance = model.wmdistance(sentence_1, sentence_3)
word_mover_distance
```

The distance between `sentence_1` and `sentence_3` is given in the following output block:

```
1.365806580758697
```

6. Let's normalize our word embeddings using the following line of code to get the best measure of distance:

```
model.init_sims(replace = True)
```

7. Let's now recompute the WMD between the sentences based on the normalized embeddings we created in the previous step. We will again start by calculating the WMD between `sentence_1` and `sentence_2`, this time with normalized embeddings:

```
word_mover_distance = model.wmdistance(sentence_1, sentence_2)
word_mover_distance
```

Here's the distance between `sentence_1` and `sentence_2` using normalized embeddings:

```
0.4277553083600646
```

8. Let's repeat this for `sentence_1` and `sentence_2`:

```
word_mover_distance = model.wmdistance(sentence_1, sentence_3)
word_mover_distance
```

The WMD between `sentence_1` and `sentence_3` based on normalized embeddings is as follows:

```
0.47793400675650705
```

As we can see, the distance between sentence 1 and sentence 2 is much smaller than the distance between sentence 1 and sentence 3. This indicates that sentence 2 is much more similar to sentence 1 compared to sentence 3. With this understanding of how WMD works, we are now better equipped to apply it to cases where we need to compute distances between documents based on their Word2vec representations. A simple use case would be to apply this to document clustering, where documents with small WMDs between them are clustered together and documents with larger WMDs are kept further apart.

Summary

In this chapter, we expanded on the ideas introduced in Chapter 4, *Transforming Text into Data Structures*. Instead of using the syntactical aspects of a document, we focused on capturing the semantics of words in a sentence. Properties such as the co-occurrence of words help in understanding the context of a word, and we tried to leverage this to build vector representations of text using the Word2vec algorithm. We explored the pretrained Word2vec model developed by Google and looked at a few relationships that it can capture. We followed this up by learning about the architecture of a Word2vec model. After that, we trained a few Word2vec models from scratch. Limitations and bias around the Word2Vec model were then discussed, followed by a discussion on some applications of the Word2vec model. Finally, we looked at how the WMD algorithm uses word vectors to capture document distances.

In the next chapter, we will take this idea further to build vectors for documents, sentences, and characters.

6
Exploring Sentence-, Document-, and Character-Level Embeddings

In Chapter 5, *Word Embeddings and Distance Measurements for Text*, we looked at how information related to the ordering of words, along with their semantics, can be taken into account when building embeddings to represent words. The idea of building embeddings will be extended in this chapter. We will explore techniques that will help us build embeddings for documents and sentences, as well as words based on their characters. We will start by looking into an algorithm called **Doc2Vec**, which, as the name suggests, provides document- or paragraph-level contextual embeddings. A sentence can essentially be treated as a paragraph, and embeddings for individual sentences can also be obtained using Doc2Vec. We will briefly discuss techniques such as **Sent2Vec**, which are focused on obtaining embeddings for sentences based on *n*-grams. Before Sent2Vec, we will discuss **fastText** extensively, which is a technique for building word representations using *n*-grams. An introduction to the **Universal Sentence Encoder** (USE) will be provided toward the end of this chapter.

The following topics will be covered in this chapter:

- Venturing into Doc2Vec
- Exploring fastText
- Understanding Sent2Vec and the Universal Sentence Encoder

Technical requirements

The code files for this chapter can be found at the following GitHub link: https://github.com/PacktPublishing/Hands-On-Python-Natural-Language-Processing/tree/master/Chapter06.

Venturing into Doc2Vec

As we saw in `Chapter 5`, *Word Embeddings and Distance Measurements for Text*, Word2Vec helped in fetching semantic embeddings for word-level representations. However, most of the NLP tasks we deal with are a combination of words or are essentially what we call a paragraph:

```
How do we fetch paragraph-level embeddings?
```

One simple mechanism would be to take the word embeddings for the words occurring in the paragraph and average them out to have representations of paragraphs:

```
Can we do better than averaging word embeddings?
```

Le and Mikolov extended the idea of Word2Vec to develop paragraph-level embeddings so that paragraphs of differing lengths can be represented by fixed-length vectors. In doing so, they presented the paper *Distributed Representations of Sentences and Documents* (`https://arxiv.org/abs/1405.4053`), which aimed at building paragraph-level embeddings. Similar to Word2Vec, the idea here is to predict certain words as well. However, in addition to using word representations for predicting words, as we did in the Word2Vec model, here, document representations are used as well.

These documents are represented using dense vectors, similar to how we represent words. The vectors are called document or paragraph vectors and are trained to predict words in the document. Documents vectors are updated similarly to how word vectors are. The paragraph vectors are concatenated with multiple word vectors to predict the next word in the context. Similar to Word2Vec, Doc2Vec also falls under the class of unsupervised algorithms since the data that's used here is unlabeled.

The paper described two ways of building paragraph vectors, as follows:

- **Distributed Memory Model of Paragraph Vectors (PV-DM)**: This is similar to the continuous bag-of-words approach we discussed regarding Word2Vec. Paragraph vectors are concatenated with the word vectors to predict the target word. Another approach is to use the average of the word and paragraph vectors to predict the target word. How are embeddings built for unseen documents after training? The model uses the built word matrix to develop embeddings for unseen documents, and these are added to the paragraph vector or document matrix. The following diagram shows how the PV-DM model is trained. In **Learn Natural Language Processing** (**NLP**), along with the word vectors of *Learn*, *Natural*, and *Language*, the *Document* vector is used to predict the next word, *Processing*. The model is tuned based on how it did in terms of predicting the word *Processing* and how it learned throughout:

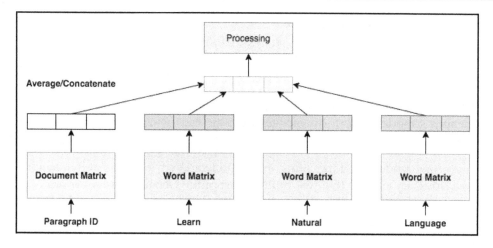

- **Distributed Bag-of-Words Model of Paragraph Vectors (PV-DBOW):** In this approach, word vectors aren't taken into account. Instead, the paragraph vector is used to predict randomly sampled words from the paragraph. In the process of using gradient descent and backpropagation, the paragraph vectors get adjusted and learning happens based on how good or bad they are doing in terms of making predictions. This approach is analogous to the Skip-gram approach used in Word2Vec.

The following diagram shows the architecture of a PV-DBOW model wherein the paragraph vector gets trained by predicting words in the paragraph itself:

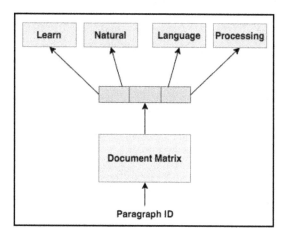

The PV-DBOW model is simpler and more memory-efficient as word vectors don't need to be stored in this approach. The learned representations that are obtained from both the distributed memory model and the distributed bag-of-words model can be combined to form the paragraph vector. Each of the learned representations can individually be treated as paragraph vectors, which are also used to represent the document. These learned representations serve as vector representations of documents and can be fed as input to any machine learning model to perform various tasks such as the classification/clustering of the documents and so on.

Now that we have understood the intuition behind Doc2Vec, let's look at it in action. We will use the Doc2Vec module that was built as part of the Gensim library for our experimentation. Here, we will look at some basic examples to understand the theory we described here. We will use these in conjunction with machine learning algorithms to solve actual problems in Chapter 7, *Identifying Patterns in Text Using Machine Learning*.

Building a Doc2Vec model

Next, we will look into the step-wise details of building a Doc2Vec model. Let's begin!

1. We will begin by importing `common_texts` from `genism`. This is a small document corpus. Along with this, we will import the `Doc2Vec` and `TaggedDocument` modules since `Doc2Vec` expects sentences in `TaggedDocument` format:

```
from gensim.test.utils import common_texts
from gensim.models.doc2vec import Doc2Vec, TaggedDocument
```

2. Now, let's check the training corpus:

```
common_texts
```

Here's our training corpus:

```
[['human', 'interface', 'computer'],
 ['survey', 'user', 'computer', 'system', 'response', 'time'],
 ['eps', 'user', 'interface', 'system'],
 ['system', 'human', 'system', 'eps'],
 ['user', 'response', 'time'],
 ['trees'],
 ['graph', 'trees'],
 ['graph', 'minors', 'trees'],
 ['graph', 'minors', 'survey']]
```

3. We will now convert the tokenized documents into `TaggedDocument` format and validate this:

```
documents = [TaggedDocument(doc, [i]) for i, doc in \
                            enumerate(common_texts)]
documents
```

Here is our corpus in the `TaggedDocument` form:

```
[TaggedDocument(words=['human', 'interface', 'computer'],
tags=[0]),
 TaggedDocument(words=['survey', 'user', 'computer', 'system',
'response', 'time'], tags=[1]),
 TaggedDocument(words=['eps', 'user', 'interface', 'system'],
tags=[2]),
 TaggedDocument(words=['system', 'human', 'system', 'eps'],
tags=[3]),
 TaggedDocument(words=['user', 'response', 'time'], tags=[4]),
 TaggedDocument(words=['trees'], tags=[5]),
 TaggedDocument(words=['graph', 'trees'], tags=[6]),
 TaggedDocument(words=['graph', 'minors', 'trees'], tags=[7]),
 TaggedDocument(words=['graph', 'minors', 'survey'], tags=[8])]
```

Here, we have used a simple iterator to act as a tag for the documents. This can be extended to a list of topics and so on. Also, note that Doc2Vec expects a list of tokens as input for each document.

4. Next, let's build and train a basic `Doc2Vec` model using the following code:

```
model = Doc2Vec(documents, vector_size=5, min_count=1, workers=4,
epochs = 40)
model.train(documents, total_examples=model.corpus_count,
epochs=model.epochs)
```

Here, `vector size` of 5 denotes that each document will be represented by a vector of five floating-point values. The `min_count` parameter sets a threshold so that only terms that occur at least `min_count` number of times will be considered in the vocabulary.

The `workers` parameter denotes the number of threads to be used while training to speed up the process. Finally, the `epochs` parameter represents the number of iterations that will be made over the corpus.

5. Now, we will validate the vector size for the document embeddings:

```
model.vector_size
```

Our vectors are of the following size:

```
5
```

6. Let's check whether the number of document vectors being built is equal to the number of documents being used in the training process:

```
len(model.docvecs)
```

There are 9 documents in total, as can be seen in the following output block. This is in line with our expectations:

```
9
```

7. Now, we need to check the vocabulary and the vocabulary size of the model we've developed. Let's begin by checking the length of our vocabulary:

```
len(model.wv.vocab)
```

Here's our vocabulary size:

```
12
```

Now, let's take a look at our vocabulary:

```
model.wv.vocab
```

Here's our vocabulary:

```
{'human': <gensim.models.keyedvectors.Vocab at 0x1275bfa58>,
 'interface': <gensim.models.keyedvectors.Vocab at 0x1275bfa90>,
 'computer': <gensim.models.keyedvectors.Vocab at 0x1275bfac8>,
 'survey': <gensim.models.keyedvectors.Vocab at 0x1275bfb00>,
 'user': <gensim.models.keyedvectors.Vocab at 0x1275bfb38>,
 'system': <gensim.models.keyedvectors.Vocab at 0x1275bfb70>,
 'response': <gensim.models.keyedvectors.Vocab at 0x1275bfba8>,
 'time': <gensim.models.keyedvectors.Vocab at 0x1275bfbe0>,
 'eps': <gensim.models.keyedvectors.Vocab at 0x1275bfc18>,
 'trees': <gensim.models.keyedvectors.Vocab at 0x1275bfc50>,
 'graph': <gensim.models.keyedvectors.Vocab at 0x1275bfc88>,
 'minors': <gensim.models.keyedvectors.Vocab at 0x1275bfcc0>}
```

8. Now that we have trained a very basic Doc2Vec model, let's build a document vector for a new sentence:

```
vector = model.infer_vector(['user', 'interface', 'for',
'computer'])
 print(vector)
```

Here's our vector for the document specified in the previous code block:

```
[-0.00837848  0.02508169 -0.07431821 -0.0596405  -0.0423368 ]
```

Now, let's experiment with the other important parameters. This can be useful for building paragraph vectors.

Changing vector size and min_count

We will begin by building a Doc2Vec model, but this time with vectors of size 50 and the min_count parameter set to 3. We will take a look at these in detail in the upcoming code and output blocks:

1. First, let's build our Doc2Vec model using the following code block:

```
model = Doc2Vec(documents, vector_size=50, min_count=3, epochs=40)
model.train(documents, total_examples=model.corpus_count,
epochs=model.epochs)
```

2. Now that we have built our models, let's do some basic checks in terms of the vocabulary and its size. Let's check the vocabulary size using the following code:

```
len(model.wv.vocab)
```

Here's our vocabulary size:

```
4
```

3. Now, let's check the vocabulary:

```
model.wv.vocab
```

Here's our vocabulary:

```
{'user': <gensim.models.keyedvectors.Vocab at 0x1275e5278>,
 'system': <gensim.models.keyedvectors.Vocab at 0x1275e52b0>,
 'trees': <gensim.models.keyedvectors.Vocab at 0x1275e52e8>,
 'graph': <gensim.models.keyedvectors.Vocab at 0x1275e5320>}
```

4. Let's build a new paragraph vector using the Doc2Vec model:

```
vector = model.infer_vector(['user', 'interface', 'for',
'computer'])
print(vector)
```

Here's our paragraph vector:

```
[-0.0007554    0.00245294 -0.00753151 -0.00607859 -0.00448105   0.00735318
 -0.00594467  0.00859313   0.00224831   0.00329965 -0.00813412 -0.00946166
 -0.00889105 -0.00073677   0.00183127   0.00870271   0.00402407 -0.00895064
 -0.00469407 -0.00866868   0.00176067 -0.00080887 -0.00720792   0.0097493
  0.00787539  0.00132159   0.00142888   0.00662106   0.00739355 -0.0035373
 -0.004258     0.00317122 -0.00414719   0.0087981    0.00254999   0.0062838
  0.00276298 -0.00396981   0.00029113   0.0015878    0.0088333    0.00634579
 -0.00670296  0.00886645 -0.00246914 -0.00679858 -0.0062902     0.00156767
  0.00728981  0.00063676]
```

As we can see, the vector size is now 50 and only 4 terms are in the vocabulary. This is because `min_count` was modified to 3 and, consequently, terms that were equal to or greater than 3 terms are present in the vocabulary now.

Earlier, we discussed that there are two approaches we can use to build paragraph vectors: the **PV-DM** and **PV-DBOW** approaches. Next, we'll check how we can change between them.

The dm parameter for switching between modeling approaches

The value of dm, when set to 1, indicates that the model should be based on the distributed memory approach.

The following code builds a PV-DM model:

```
model = Doc2Vec(documents, vector_size=50, min_count=2, epochs=40, dm=1)
  model.train(documents, total_examples=model.corpus_count,
epochs=model.epochs)
```

dm equal to 0 builds the Doc2Vec model based on the distributed bag-of-words approach, as shown in the following code block:

```
model = Doc2Vec(documents, vector_size=50, min_count=2, epochs=40, dm=0)
  model.train(documents, total_examples=model.corpus_count,
epochs=model.epochs)
```

The distributed memory model takes word vectors into account and comes with two additional parameters, dm_concat and dm_mean. We'll discuss them next.

The dm_concat parameter

The `dm_concat` parameter is used in the PV-DM approach. Its value, when set to `1`, indicates to the algorithm that the context vectors should be concatenated while trying to predict the target word. This, of course, leads to building a larger model since multiple word embeddings get concatenated.

Let's see how it can be built in the following code snippet:

```
model = Doc2Vec(documents, vector_size=50, min_count=2, epochs=40,
window=2, dm=1, alpha=0.3, min_alpha=0.05, dm_concat=1)
model.train(documents, total_examples=model.corpus_count,
epochs=model.epochs)
```

What to do if I don't wish to concatenate and use a lighter model?

The `dm_concat` parameter can be set to `0` for that:

```
However, how do I take into account information related to the context
vectors?
```

Next, we'll look at this in terms of the `dm_mean` parameter.

The dm_mean parameter

In the previous section, *The dm_concat parameter*, we saw that context vectors can be concatenated. Here, we will look at other options that can be used instead of concatenating the context vectors. Two alternative approaches are to sum or average the context vectors instead of concatenating them. Whether the context vectors should be summed up or averaged can be controlled by the `dm_mean` parameter.

When the `dm_mean` parameter is set to `1`, the mean of the context word vectors is taken. The sum of the context word vectors is taken into account when `dm_mean` is set to `0`. Let's see the two in action.

Using the code in the following code block, the mean of the context vectors can be taken:

```
model = Doc2Vec(documents, vector_size=50, min_count=2, epochs=40,
window=2, dm=1, dm_concat=0, dm_mean=1, alpha=0.3, min_alpha=0.05)
model.train(documents, total_examples=model.corpus_count,
epochs=model.epochs)
```

The following piece of code can be executed to take the sum of the context vectors:

```
model = Doc2Vec(documents, vector_size=50, min_count=2, epochs=40,
window=2, dm=1, dm_concat=0, dm_mean=0, alpha=0.3, min_alpha=0.05)
model.train(documents, total_examples=model.corpus_count,
epochs=model.epochs)
```

Now, we will see the effect the window size has.

Window size

The window size parameter controls the distance between the word under concentration and the word to be predicted, similar to the Word2Vec approach. The following code block illustrates the same:

```
model = Doc2Vec(documents, vector_size=50, min_count=2, epochs=40,
window=2, dm=0)
model.train(documents, total_examples=model.corpus_count,
epochs=model.epochs)
```

Now, let's explore what the learning rate is and how it can be leveraged.

Learning rate

Most machine learning models come with a learning rate, which we will look at in detail in Chapter 8, *From Human Neurons to Artificial Neurons for Understanding Text*. For Doc2Vec, the initial learning rate can be specified using the `alpha` parameter. With the `min_alpha` parameter, we can specify what value the learning rate should drop to over the course of training. These details have been specified in the following code block:

```
model = Doc2Vec(documents, vector_size=50, min_count=2, epochs=40,
window=2, dm=1, alpha=0.3, min_alpha=0.05)
model.train(documents, total_examples=model.corpus_count,
epochs=model.epochs)
```

Apart from these, there are other parameters, including `negative` for enabling negative sampling similar to Word2Vec, `max_vocab_size` to limit the vocabulary, and more.

Before we proceed and briefly discuss other algorithms that have been built for developing sentence-level representations, let's discuss a character-based n-gram approach known as fastText, which is used to build word-level embeddings that outperform Word2Vec in most use cases. We will build on the fastText approach later to see how sentence-level embeddings can be built in a similar manner.

Exploring fastText

We discussed and built models based on the Word2Vec approach in `Chapter 5`, *Word Embeddings and Distance Measurements for Text,* wherein each word in the vocabulary had a vector representation. Word2Vec relies heavily on the vocabulary it has been trained to represent. Words that occur during inference times, if not present in the vocabulary, will be mapped to a possibly unknown token representation. There can be a lot of unseen words here:

```
Can we do better than this?
```

In certain languages, sub-words or internal word representations and structures carry important morphological information:

```
Can we capture this information?
```

To answer the preceding code block, *yes, we can,* and we will use fastText to capture the information contained in the sub-words:

```
What is fastText and how does it work?
```

Bojanowski et al., researchers from Facebook, built on top of the Word2Vec Skip-gram model developed by Mikolov et al., which we discussed in `Chapter 5`, *Word Embeddings and Distance Measurements for Text,* by encapsulating each word as a combination of character *n*-grams. Each of these *n*-grams has a vector representation. Word representations are actually a result of the summation of their character *n*-grams:

```
What are the character n-grams?
```

Let's see the two- and three-character *n*-grams for the word `language`:

```
la, lan, an, ang, ng, ngu, gu, gua, ua, uag, ag, age, ge
```

fastText leads to parameter sharing among various words that have any overlapping *n*-grams. We capture their morphological information from sub-words to build an embedding for the word itself. Also, when certain words are missing from the training vocabulary or rarely occur, we can still have a representation for them if their *n*-grams are present as part of other words.

The authors kept most of the settings similar to the Word2Vec model. They initially trained fastText using a Wikipedia corpus based on 9 different languages. As of March 18, 2020, the fastText GitHub documentation states that fastText models have been built for 157 languages.

Facebook released the `fastText` library as a standalone implementation that can be directly imported and worked on in Python. Gensim offers its own `fastText` implementation and has also built a wrapper around Facebook's `fastText` library. Since we have focused on Gensim for most of our tasks, we will use Gensim's `fastText` implementation next to build word representations.

We will discuss parameters that are new to fastText as most of them are common to the Word2Vec and Doc2Vec models. We have taken the same `common_texts` data to explore fastText.

Building a fastText model

In this section, we will look at how to build a fastText model:

1. We will begin by importing the necessary libraries and dataset using the following code block:

```
from gensim.models import FastText
from gensim.test.utils import common_texts
```

2. Let's instantiate and train a basic `FastText` model using the following code:

```
model = FastText(size=5, window=3, min_count=1)

model.build_vocab(sentences=common_texts)
model.train(sentences=common_texts,
total_examples=len(common_texts), epochs=10)
```

3. Now, let's validate our vocabulary:

```
model.wv.vocab
```

Here's our vocabulary:

```
{'human': <gensim.models.keyedvectors.Vocab at 0x1103db780>,
 'interface': <gensim.models.keyedvectors.Vocab at 0x1103db7f0>,
 'computer': <gensim.models.keyedvectors.Vocab at 0x1274b84a8>,
 'survey': <gensim.models.keyedvectors.Vocab at 0x1274b8710>,
 'user': <gensim.models.keyedvectors.Vocab at 0x1274b8748>,
 'system': <gensim.models.keyedvectors.Vocab at 0x1274b8780>,
```

```
'response': <gensim.models.keyedvectors.Vocab at 0x1274b87b8>,
'time': <gensim.models.keyedvectors.Vocab at 0x1274b87f0>,
'eps': <gensim.models.keyedvectors.Vocab at 0x1274b8828>,
'trees': <gensim.models.keyedvectors.Vocab at 0x1274b8860>,
'graph': <gensim.models.keyedvectors.Vocab at 0x1274b8898>,
'minors': <gensim.models.keyedvectors.Vocab at 0x1274b88d0>}
```

Let's visualize the vector of the word human:

```
model.wv['human']
```

Here's the vector of the word human:

```
array([ 0.03953331, -0.02951075,  0.02039873,  0.00304991,
-0.00968183],
       dtype=float32)
```

The size of the vector is 6—it's size + 1 as we specified size = 5 in our fastText model.

4. Now, let's explore the most similar method to this, as we did with Word2Vec in Chapter 5, *Word Embeddings and Distance Measurements for Text*. We will see what the closest vector is to the following vector expression:

$$vec(computer) + vec(interface) - vec(human)$$

```
model.wv.most_similar(positive=['computer', 'interface'],
negative=['human'])
```

Here's the output:

```
[('system', 0.908109724521637),
 ('eps', 0.886881947517395),
 ('response', 0.6286922097206116),
 ('user', 0.38861846923828125),
 ('minors', 0.24753454327583313),
 ('time', 0.06086184084415436),
 ('survey', -0.0791618824005127),
 ('trees', -0.40337082743644714),
 ('graph', -0.46148836612701416)]
```

5. Let's understand the very important min_n and max_n parameters.

Since word representations in `FastText` are built using the `n-grams`, `min_n`, and `max_n` characters, this helps us by setting the minimum and maximum lengths of the character *n*-grams so that we can build representations. In the following code block, we have used a range of 1-gram to 5-grams to build our fastText model:

```
model = FastText(size=5, window=3, min_count=1, min_n=1, max_n=5)

model.build_vocab(sentences=common_texts)
model.train(sentences=common_texts,
total_examples=len(common_texts), epochs=10)
```

6. Now, we will try and build a representation of a word that does not occur in our vocabulary. Let's try and fetch the vector for the word `rubber`:

```
model.wv['rubber']
```

Here's the vector for `rubber`:

```
array([-0.01671136, -0.01868909, -0.03945312, -0.01389101,
-0.0250267 ],
        dtype=float32)
```

7. Now, let's use an out-of-vocabulary term in the `most_similar` function to validate whether it works:

```
model.wv.most_similar(positive=['computer', 'human'],
negative=['rubber'])
```

Here's the output:

```
[('time', 0.5615436434745789),
 ('system', 0.4772699475288391),
 ('minors', 0.3850055932998657),
 ('eps', 0.15983597934246063),
 ('user', -0.2565014064311981),
 ('graph', -0.411243200302124),
 ('response', -0.4405473470687866),
 ('trees', -0.6079868078231812),
 ('interface', -0.6381739377975464),
 ('survey', -0.8393087387084961)]
```

8. Now, we will try and extend our model so that it incorporates new sentences and vocabulary. This can be done using the following code snippet:

```
sentences_to_be_added = [["I", "am", "learning", "Natural",
"Language", "Processing"],
 ["Natural", "Language", "Processing", "is", "cool"]]
```

```
model.build_vocab(sentences_to_be_added, update=True)
 model.train(sentences=common_texts,
total_examples=len(sentences_to_be_added), epochs=10)
```

 Note: The `update` parameter is set to `True`.

Here's the output:

```
{'human': <gensim.models.keyedvectors.Vocab at 0x1103db908>,
 'interface': <gensim.models.keyedvectors.Vocab at 0x1274cbcf8>,
 'computer': <gensim.models.keyedvectors.Vocab at 0x1274cb9e8>,
 'survey': <gensim.models.keyedvectors.Vocab at 0x1274cba20>,
 'user': <gensim.models.keyedvectors.Vocab at 0x1274cba58>,
 'system': <gensim.models.keyedvectors.Vocab at 0x1274cba90>,
 'response': <gensim.models.keyedvectors.Vocab at 0x1274cbac8>,
 'time': <gensim.models.keyedvectors.Vocab at 0x1274cbdd8>,
 'eps': <gensim.models.keyedvectors.Vocab at 0x1274cbcc0>,
 'trees': <gensim.models.keyedvectors.Vocab at 0x1274cbe10>,
 'graph': <gensim.models.keyedvectors.Vocab at 0x1274cbb38>,
 'minors': <gensim.models.keyedvectors.Vocab at 0x1274cbef0>,
 'I': <gensim.models.keyedvectors.Vocab at 0x1274cb320>,
 'am': <gensim.models.keyedvectors.Vocab at 0x1274cb240>,
 'learning': <gensim.models.keyedvectors.Vocab at 0x1274cb2b0>,
 'Natural': <gensim.models.keyedvectors.Vocab at 0x1274cbf28>,
 'Language': <gensim.models.keyedvectors.Vocab at 0x1274cbbe0>,
 'Processing': <gensim.models.keyedvectors.Vocab at 0x1274cb5c0>,
 'is': <gensim.models.keyedvectors.Vocab at 0x1274cb550>,
 'cool': <gensim.models.keyedvectors.Vocab at 0x1274cbc88>}
```

As we can see, the model was updated to incorporate the new vocabulary terms.

The original fastText research paper extended on the Skip-gram approach for Word2Vec, but today, both the Skip-gram and continuous bag-of-words approach can be used. Pre-trained fastText models across multiple languages are available online and can be directly used or fine-tuned so that we can understand a specific dataset better.

fastText can be applied to solve a plethora of problems such as spelling correction, auto suggestions, and so on since it is based on sub-word representation. Datasets such as user search query, chatbots or conversations, reviews, and ratings can be used to build fastText models. We can apply them to enhance the customer experience in the future by providing information such as better suggestions, displaying better products, autocorrecting user input, and so on. In the next section, we'll take a look at the spelling corrector/auto-suggestion use case and build a fastText model for it.

Building a spelling corrector/word suggestion module using fastText

Let's try and build a fastText model based on some comments data that can be obtained from Kaggle's toxic comment classification challenge. This data can be sourced from https://www.kaggle.com/c/jigsaw-toxic-comment-classification-challenge. We will take the comments column from the dataset and build a fastText model on top of it. We will also provide some incorrect spellings to the built model and see how well the model does in terms of correcting them. The same code can be extended to the problem statements mentioned in the previous section. We will use the Gensim implementation of fastText for this exercise. Let's begin!

1. We will start by importing the necessary libraries:

```
import nltk
import re
nltk.download('stopwords')
nltk.download('wordnet')
from nltk.corpus import stopwords
from nltk.stem.porter import PorterStemmer
from nltk.stem.snowball import SnowballStemmer
from nltk.stem.wordnet import WordNetLemmatizer
from gensim.models import FastText
import io
import collections
```

2. Let's read the data into basic data structures using the following code snippet:

```
words = []
data = []
with io.open('comment_text.txt', 'r') as file:
    for entry in file:
        entry = entry.strip()
        data.append(entry)
        words.extend(entry.split())
```

3. Let's fetch some basic information about the data in terms of the most common words in the corpus using the following code snippet:

```
unique_words = []
unique_words = collections.Counter(words)
unique_words.most_common(10)
```

Here are our most common terms:

```
[('the', 445892),
 ('to', 288753),
 ('of', 219279),
 ('and', 207335),
 ('a', 201765),
 ('I', 182618),
 ('is', 164602),
 ('you', 157025),
 ('that', 140495),
 ('in', 130244)]
```

As we can see, the data is dominated by stopwords. We can apply necessary preprocessing in terms of keeping only alphanumeric data, case-folding, and removing stopwords. We won't lemmatize or stem because we want the model to understand incorrect spellings as well.

4. Let's `preprocess` the data using the preprocessing pipeline we built in Chapter 3, *Building Your NLP Vocabulary*:

```
data = preprocess(data)
```

You can learn about the `preprocess` method in more detail by reading Chapter 3, *Building Your NLP Vocabulary*, or by viewing the code files.

5. fastText expects data to be in a certain format, so let's modify our data so that it comprehends our requirements. The following code block does that for us:

```
preprocessed_data = []
for line in data:
    if line != "":
        preprocessed_data.append(line.split())
```

6. Now, we will initialize our fastText model:

```
model = FastText(size=300, window=3, min_count=1, min_n=1, max_n=5)
```

7. Now, let's build our vocabulary and check the size of the built vocabulary. Here, we're building the vocabulary:

```
model.build_vocab(sentences=preprocessed_data)
```

Now, let's check the size of our vocabulary:

```
len(model.wv.vocab)
```

Here's our vocabulary size:

```
182228
```

The size would have been smaller if we had applied stemming or lemmatization.

8. Let's train our model now:

```
model.train(sentences=preprocessed_data,
total_examples=len(preprocessed_data), epochs=10)
```

9. Now, we will check whether our model can actually predict the correct spelling for the incorrect words as part of the top 5 similar suggestions.

Let's see what autocorrect suggestion our model provides for the word `eplain`:

```
model.wv.most_similar('eplain', topn=5)
```

Here's the output:

```
[('xplain', 0.8792348504066467),
 ('eexplain', 0.8370275497436523),
 ('explain', 0.8350315093994141),
 ('plain', 0.8258184194564819),
 ('reexplain', 0.8141466379165649)]
```

`explain` and `plain` occur in the top 5 most similar words to `eplain`, which is very positive for us.

Now, let's see the outputs for the term `reminder`:

```
model.wv.most_similar('reminder', topn=5)
```

Here's the output:

```
[('remainder', 0.9140011668205261),
 ('rejoinder', 0.9139667749404907),
 ('reminde', 0.9069227576255798),
 ('minderbinder', 0.9042780995368958),
 ('reindeer', 0.9034557342529297)]
```

Even though `reminder` is a correct word in itself, the model suggests `remainder` as a potential correct spelling:

```
How does our model do for the incorrectly spelled term relevnt?
```

Now, let's check out how the model does for `relevnt`:

```
model.wv.most_similar('relevnt', topn=5)
```

Here are the top 5 suggestions for `relevnt`:

```
[('relevant', 0.7919449806213379),
 ('relev', 0.7878341674804688),
 ('relevanmt', 0.7624361515045166),
 ('releant', 0.7576485276222229),
 ('releve', 0.7547794580459595)]
```

`relevant` appears right at the top of the suggestions for `relevnt`, which is what we wanted:

What suggestions does my model provide for the possibly correctly spelled word, `purse`?

Next, let's look at how the model does for `purse`:

```
model.wv.most_similar('purse', topn=5)
```

Here are the top 5 suggestions for `purse`:

```
[('purpse', 0.9245591163635254),
 ('cpurse', 0.910297691822052),
 ('pursue', 0.8908491134643555),
 ('pure', 0.8890833258628845),
 ('pulse', 0.8745534420013428)]
```

Again, `purse` is a correctly spelled word; however, `pursue` and `pulse` are valid suggestions provided by the model.

Our fastText model does a good job in terms of suggesting corrections and potential alternatives for input text. This model can further be improved by providing better data where incorrect and correct spellings have been used in the same context across different sentences. An ideal example of such data would be conversations, wherein a lot of short forms and incorrect spellings are typed in by users. Next, we'll learn how document distances can be computed using fastText.

fastText and document distances

Let's use the model we built for spelling correction to check for document distances using the **Word Mover's Distance** (**WMD**) algorithm. We will use the same example that we used in the Word2Vec section in Chapter 5, *Word Embeddings and Distance Measurements for Text*.

Let's get started:

1. We will start by initializing the sentences that we wish to compute the distances between:

   ```
   sentence_1 = "Obama speaks to the media in Illinois"
   sentence_2 = "President greets the press in Chicago"
   sentence_3 = "Apple is my favorite company"
   ```

2. Let's compute the distance between the document pairs using WMD, which we discussed extensively in Chapter 5, *Word Embeddings and Distance Measurements for Text*.

   Let's compute the WMD between sentence_1 and sentence_2 using fastText-based vectors:

   ```
   word_mover_distance = model.wmdistance(sentence_1, sentence_2)
   word_mover_distance
   ```

   Here's the distance between sentence_1 and sentence_2:

   ```
   16.179816809121103
   ```

   Now, we can compute the distance between sentence_2 and sentence_3:

   ```
   word_mover_distance = model.wmdistance(sentence_2, sentence_3)
   word_mover_distance
   ```

   Here's the corresponding distance:

   ```
   21.01126373005312
   ```

   As expected, sentences 1 and 2 have a smaller distance compared to the distance between sentences 2 and 3.

The results that we obtained in the spelling correction and distance calculations would be potentially better if pre-trained fastText models were used since those are mostly built on Wikipedia text corpora and are more generalized to understand different data points.

fastText is a very convenient technique for building word representations using character-level features. It outperformed Word2Vec since it incorporated internal word structure information and associated it with morphological features, which are very important in certain languages. It also allows us to represent words not present in the original vocabulary. Now, we will extend our understanding of *n*-grams and briefly discuss how this can be extended to build embeddings for documents and sentences by using an approach called Sent2Vec. We will also briefly touch upon the Universal Sentence Encoder, which is one of the most recent algorithms that's used to build sentence-level embeddings.

Understanding Sent2Vec and the Universal Sentence Encoder

In the previous sections, we discussed Doc2Vec and fastText extensively. We will build on the concepts we learned about there and try to understand the basic underlying concepts of another algorithm, called Sent2Vec. We will briefly touch on the **Universal Sentence Encoder** (**USE**) in the second part of this section.

Sent2Vec

Sent2Vec combines the continuous bag-of-words approach we discussed regarding Word2Vec, along with the fastText thought process of using constituent *n*-gram, to build sentence embeddings.

Matteo et al. devised the Sent2Vec approach, wherein contextual word embeddings and target word embeddings were learned by trying to predict the target words based on the context of the words, similar to the C-BOW approach. However, they extended the C-BOW methodology to define sentence embeddings as the average of the context word embeddings present in the sentence, wherein context word embeddings are not restricted to unigrams but extended to *n*-grams in each sentence, similar to the fastText approach. The sentence embedding would then be represented as the average of these *n*-gram embeddings. Research has shown that Sent2Vec outperforms Doc2Vec in the majority of the tasks it undertakes and that it is a better representation method for sentences or documents. The Sent2Vec library is an open sourced implementation of the model that's built on top of fastText and can be used similar to the Doc2Vec and fastText models, which we have discussed extensively so far.

Before we close this chapter, we will briefly look at the Universal Sentence Encoders, which is a very recent technique that has been open sourced by Google to build sentence or document-level embeddings.

The Universal Sentence Encoder

The **Universal Sentence Encoder** (USE) is a model for fetching embeddings at the sentence level. These models are trained using Wikipedia, web news, web question-answer pages, and discussion forums. The pre-trained generalized model can be used for transfer learning directly or can be fine-tuned to a specific task or dataset. The basic building block of USE is an encoder (we will learn about this in Chapter 9, *Applying Convolutions to Text*). The USE model can be built using the transformers methodology, which will be discussed in Chapter 10, *Capturing Temporal Relationships in Text*, or it can be built by combining unigram and bigram representations and feeding them to a neural network to output sentence embeddings through a technique known as deep averaging networks. Several models that have been built using USE-based transfer learning have outperformed state-of-the-art results in the recent past. USE can be used similar to TF-IDF, Word2Vec, Doc2Vec, fastText, and so on for fetching sentence-level embeddings.

Summary

In this chapter, we began by extending our discussion on Word2Vec, applied a similar thought process to building document-level embedding, and discussed the Doc2Vec algorithm extensively. We followed that up by building word representations using character *n*-grams from the words themselves, a technique referred to as fastText. The fastText model helped us capture morphological information from sub-word representations. fastText is also flexible as it can provide embeddings for out-of-vocabulary words since embeddings are a result of sub-word representations. After that, we briefly discussed Sent2Vec, which combines the C-BOW and fastText approaches to building sentence-level representations. Finally, we introduced the Universal Sentence Encoder, which can also be used for fetching sentence-level embeddings and is based on complex deep learning architectures, all of which we will read about in the upcoming chapters.

In the next chapter, we will use whatever we have discussed so far in terms of text cleaning, preprocessing, and word and document representations to build models that can solve real-life machine learning tasks.

Section 3: NLP and Learning 3

This section deep dives into the application of machine learning and deep learning algorithms in NLP. Each algorithm will be explained in detail and a real-world application will be discussed to provide you with a hands-on understanding.

This section comprises the following chapters:

- Chapter 7, *Identifying Patterns in Text Using Machine Learning*
- Chapter 8, *From Human Neurons to Artificial Neurons for Understanding Text*
- Chapter 9, *Applying Convolutions to Text*
- Chapter 10, *Capturing the Temporal Relationship in Text*
- Chapter 11, *State of the Art in NLP*

7

Identifying Patterns in Text Using Machine Learning

In the previous chapter, we learned about advanced vector representation methodologies such as Doc2Vec and Sent2Vec, which significantly improve text processing accuracy. In this chapter, we will explore the applications of **Machine Learning (ML)** algorithms in **Natural Language Processing (NLP)**. We will start with a gentle introduction to ML and learn about some additional preprocessing steps required for ML model training. We will then gain a thorough understanding of Naive Bayes and **Support Vector Machine (SVM)** algorithms and build a sentiment analyzer using them. By the end of this chapter, you will have gained a sound understanding of the application of ML algorithms for text processing and will be able to build a production-ready ML-based sentiment analyzer.

The following topics will be covered in this chapter:

- Introduction to ML
- Data preprocessing
- The Naive Bayes algorithm
- The SVM algorithm
- Productionizing a trained sentiment analyzer

Let's get started!

Technical requirements

The code files for this chapter can be found at the following GitHub link: `https://github.com/PacktPublishing/Hands-On-Python-Natural-Language-Processing/tree/master/Chapter07`.

Introduction to ML

ML is a subfield of artificial intelligence and aims at building systems that are capable of performing tasks without being explicitly programmed to do so. ML algorithms employ mathematical models that learn from existing data to perform tasks such as prediction, classification, decision-making, and so on. The *learning* bit of the model is also called training, where the model analyzes large volumes of data to identify patterns. This process is computationally intensive as the model needs to perform numerous calculations for the given data. However, with the continual advancement in computational power at our disposal, training, and the deployment of ML models, this has become fairly easy and quite popular. Since NLP also requires that we analyze large volumes of data, ML algorithms are widely applied in terms of text processing.

ML algorithms can be divided into three categories, as shown in the following diagram:

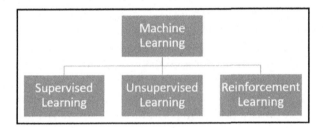

Let's look at these in more depth:

- **Supervised learning**: Supervised learning algorithms involve training the model using labeled data. The training dataset contains values of independent variables (also called a feature set) and the corresponding values of dependent variables. The algorithm analyzes these values and tries to learn a function that maps the independent variables to the dependent variables. Some widely used supervised learning algorithms include linear regression, k-nearest neighbor, decision tree, random forest, SVMs, Naive Bayes, and so on.
- **Unsupervised learning**: Unsupervised learning algorithms involve training the model using unlabeled data. The training process involves studying the dataset to understand the underlying structure of the data. Unsupervised learning is mostly used to cluster data and to perform anomaly detection by analyzing a data point with respect to other data points in the training set. Popular unsupervised algorithms include k-means, k-medoids, BIRCH, DBSCAN, and so on.

- **Reinforcement learning**: Reinforcement learning algorithms involve training the model based on simulations wherein the model learns based on the rewards that it receives for performing certain actions. Examples of popular reinforcement learning algorithms include Q-learning, SARSA, and so on.

While all three categories of ML algorithms have found applications in the field of text processing, NLP tools based on supervised learning algorithms are the most popular among the three categories. Supervised learning-based tools have a sizable adoption in the industry and they enjoy an established track record. Given their importance, we will delve into the nitty-gritty of two popularly used supervised learning algorithms. We will then combine our understanding of these algorithms with the tools we have learned so far to create and deploy a reasonably accurate NLP tool (sentiment analyzer).

Data preprocessing

Before we delve into these models and gain familiarity with some of these algorithms, we must learn about preprocessing the training data. We covered some of the preprocessing steps when working with text data such as tokenization, stop word removal, lemmatization, stemming, and so on in Chapter 3, *Building Your NLP Vocabulary*. However, there are some additional data preprocessing steps that are extremely crucial in ML as the training data needs to adhere to certain rules to be of any value to the model. Poorly processed data is guaranteed to train low accuracy models. It should be noted that data preprocessing is a vast field and that you may be required to perform various preprocessing steps based on the data you are working with. For example, you may be required to handle unstructured data; perform outlier analysis, invalid data analysis, and duplicate data analysis; identify correlated features; and more. However, we will focus on some of the most widely used preprocessing steps that are almost always required.

We will be performing preprocessing on the Tips dataset, which comes with the seaborn Python package. First, let's import the dataset and print out the first five lines to gain a basic understanding of the dataset:

```
import seaborn as sns

tips_df = sns.load_dataset('tips')
tips_df.head()
```

Here's the output:

```
   total_bill tip sex smoker day time size
0 16.99 1.01 Female No Sun Dinner 2
1 10.34 1.66 Male No Sun Dinner 3
```

```
2 21.01 3.50 Male No Sun Dinner 3
3 23.68 3.31 Male No Sun Dinner 2
4 24.59 3.61 Female No Sun Dinner 4
```

This dataset contains information about tips that have been paid in a particular restaurant by its patrons. Other than the tip amount, the dataset contains information regarding the total bill amount, the gender of the person paying the bill, the number of people in the group, the day and time of the visit, and whether there were any smokers in the group. Per the output, we can figure out that the `sex`, `smoker`, `day`, and `time` features are categorical features, whereas the others are numeric.

From the outset, we can see that there are some clear challenges with the data. Let's address them one by one.

NaN values

Data needs to be checked for NaN values after it's been imported. This is important because undetected NaN values can be very problematic for training and may even cause the training process to fail. Detecting NaN values is easy and can be done in various ways. The following is an example of how the pandas `isnull()` function can be used to figure out if there are any NaN values in the dataset:

```
tips_df.isnull().values.any()
```

The preceding command scans the entire dataset and returns `True` if there is even a single NaN in the dataset. The following is the output:

```
False
```

For this dataset, we do not have any NaN values. However, had the output been true, you would then be interested to determine which column or which row contains the NaN values. This can be done by running the following command:

```
tips_df.isnull().any()
```

This will output the result of the NaN search, which provides the results for each column, as follows:

```
total_bill False
tip False
sex False
smoker False
day False
time False
```

```
size False
dtype: bool
```

To identify the rows with NaN values, we need to pass the value 1 for the axis parameter of the `any()` function, which will scan the data for NaN values along the rows. The updated command is as follows:

```
tips_df.isnull().any(axis=1)
```

The following is the partial output of the preceding command, which shows the results of the search along the rows:

```
0 False
1 False
2 False
3 False
4 False
5 False
6 False
7 False
```

Once the NaN values have been identified, you need to decide what to do with them. Among the many methods for addressing NaN values, some of the popular methods are as follows:

- Dropping the row/column with NaN value(s). The `dropna()` function can be used to drop rows/columns containing NaN value(s).
- Replacing the NaN value with another value. The value could be the previous value, the next value, zero, the mean of the row or column, and so on. This can be done using the `fillna()` function.

There is no boilerplate solution to addressing NaN values, and how to deal with NaN values is a question that needs to be answered by the user.

Label encoding and one-hot encoding

In the `Tips` dataset, we can see that there are four categorical variables, namely `sex`, `smoker`, `day`, and `time`. The values of these variables are non-numeric, which is problematic because the mathematical models underpinning our ML system only understand numeric inputs. Therefore, we need to convert these non-numeric values into numeric values, which can be done by label encoding. As the name suggests, we use label encoding to map non-numeric values to numeric values.

To perform label encoding, we import the `LabelEncoder` class from sklearn's preprocessing module and apply the `fit_transform()` function to the non-numeric categorical variables of the DataFrame, as follows:

```
from sklearn.preprocessing import LabelEncoder
label_encoding = LabelEncoder()
tips_df.iloc[:,[2,3,4,5]] =
tips_df.iloc[:,[2,3,4,5]].apply(label_encoding.fit_transform)
```

This transforms the `tips_df` DataFrame containing all the non-numeric categorical variables so that they're encoded as numeric variables, as shown in the following partial output of `tips_df`:

```
   total_bill  tip sex smoker day time size
0       16.99 1.01   0      0   2    0    2
1       10.34 1.66   1      0   2    0    3
2       21.01 3.50   1      0   2    0    3
3       23.68 3.31   1      0   2    0    2
4       24.59 3.61   0      0   2    0    4
```

To map non-numeric values to the encoded value, you can use the `fit` function on the relevant column and then print out the unique values for that column, as well as the corresponding encoding (using the `transform()` method), as follows:

```
label_encoding = LabelEncoder()
col_fit = label_encoding.fit(tips_df["day"])
dict(zip(col_fit.classes_, col_fit.transform(col_fit.classes_)))
```

The following is the output of the preceding code, along with the encoded values for the `day` column of the DataFrame:

```
{0: 0, 1: 1, 2: 2, 3: 3}
```

By using label encoding, we have addressed the issue of non-numeric data values in the dataset. However, encoding categorical variables that are nominal (where the values of the variable can't be ordered; for example, gender, days in a week, color, and so on) and not ordinal (the values of the variable can be ordered; for example, rank, size, and so on) creates another complication. For example, in the preceding case, we encoded `Friday` as 0 and `Saturday` as 1. When we feed these values to a mathematical model, it will consider these values as numbers and therefore will consider 1 to be greater than 0, which is not a correct treatment of these values.

To address this issue, we can use one-hot encoding, which splits a column with categorical variables into multiple columns, with each new column corresponding to a unique value of the categorical variable. In the preceding example, using one-hot encoding on the day column will result in four columns (Fri, Sat, Sun, Thur), with each column containing only 0 or 1, depending on whether the unique value occurred in a given row. We introduced one-hot encoding in the *One-hot vectorization* section in Chapter 4, *Transforming Text into Data Structures*, where we built a one-hot matrix for a corpus. We will now learn how to use sklearn's OneHotEncoder method to do the same. Please note that we will be applying one-hot encoding only after performing label encoding.

To perform one-hot encoding, we need to import the ColumnTransformer class from sklearn's compose module and the OneHotEncoder class from sklearn's preprocessing module. Since we are essentially transforming the columns of the DataFrame by splitting categorical features, we need to use this class. The OneHotEncoder class goes as an argument to the ColumnTransformer object which tells our program what kind of transformation we seek. We also need to pass the list of columns on which we seek to perform the transformation and use the remainder=passthrough argument to ignore other columns. Finally, just like label encoding, we'll apply the fit_transform() function to the DataFrame and store the output as an array called tips_df_ohe, as follows:

```
from sklearn.preprocessing import OneHotEncoder
from sklearn.compose import ColumnTransformer
oh_encoding = ColumnTransformer([('OneHotEncoding', OneHotEncoder(), \
                                 [2,3,4,5])],remainder='passthrough')
tips_df_ohe = oh_encoding.fit_transform(tips_df)
tips_df_ohe
```

This splits all the labeled categorical variables in the tips_df DataFrame into columns for each unique value, as shown in the following output of tips_df_ohe:

```
array([[ 1. , 0. , 1. , ..., 16.99, 1.01, 2. ],
       [ 0. , 1. , 1. , ..., 10.34, 1.66, 3. ],
       [ 0. , 1. , 1. , ..., 21.01, 3.5 , 3. ],
       ...,
       [ 0. , 1. , 0. , ..., 22.67, 2. , 2. ],
       [ 0. , 1. , 1. , ..., 17.82, 1.75, 2. ],
       [ 1. , 0. , 1. , ..., 18.78, 3. , 2. ]])
```

There is still an outstanding issue that we need to resolve and that is the issue of the dummy variable trap. Say we use one-hot encoding on the `day` variable, which has four unique values. Splitting this variable into four columns will cause collinearity in our data (high correlation between variables) because we can always predict the outcome of the fourth column with the three other columns (if the day is not Friday, Saturday, or Sunday, then it will have to be Thursday). To address this issue, we will need to drop one dummy variable from the split columns of each categorical variable. This could be done by simply passing the argument `drop='first'` when defining the `OneHotEncoder` class.

Data standardization

Standardization is a data preprocessing step that attempts to equalize the range of values for all the columns. This is important because most ML algorithms require data to be in the same range, and non-uniform value ranges can impair the model's ability to learn from the data. For example, if all the columns in a dataset are in the range of `[0, 10]`, whereas values in one column range from `[-1000, 1000]`, then there is a high likelihood that this column will have a disproportionate influence over the model and that the trained model will be pretty much a one-to-one mapping between this column and the dependent variable. Therefore, you should always try to standardize the data before feeding it into the model for training. There are various standardization techniques we can use, but the two most popular techniques are min-max standardization and z-score standardization.

Min-max standardization

Each value in a column is transformed using the following formula:

$$X_{STD} = \frac{X - min(X)}{max(X) - min(X)}$$

Here, X is the vector representing the column. Each value in the column is subtracted by the minimum value of the column and divided by the column range. Post transformation, the range of the column becomes `[0, 1]`.

Min-max standardization is quite simple to implement using the pandas `min()` and `max()` functions. However, since we have been discussing sklearn, here is how we can import the `MinMaxScaler` class from sklearn's `preprocessing` module to implement min-max standardization:

```
from sklearn.preprocessing import MinMaxScaler
minmax = MinMaxScaler()
tips_df_std = minmax.fit_transform(tips_df_ohe)
tips_df_std
```

The following is the output of the `tips_df_std` DataFrame. We can see that the one-hot encoded vectors remain the same, whereas other vectors are transformed so that they fit in the range `[0, 1]`:

```
array([[1. , 0. , 1. , ..., 0.29157939, 0.00111111, 0.2 ],
       [0. , 1. , 1. , ..., 0.1522832 , 0.07333333, 0.4 ],
       [0. , 1. , 1. , ..., 0.3757855 , 0.27777778, 0.4 ],
       ...,
       [0. , 1. , 0. , ..., 0.41055718, 0.11111111, 0.2 ],
       [0. , 1. , 1. , ..., 0.30896523, 0.08333333, 0.2 ],
       [1. , 0. , 1. , ..., 0.32907415, 0.22222222, 0.2 ]])
```

Z-score standardization

Z-score standardization transforms the column by calculating the z-score for each value, as per the following formula:

$$X_{STD} = \frac{X - mean(X)}{std.\,dev(X)}$$

Here, X is the vector representing the column. The z-score is the numerical measurement of how many standard deviations away a value from the mean of the group is. Post transformation, most values are expected to fall in the range of `[-3, 3]`.

We can use the `StandardScaler()` class of sklearn's `preprocessing` module to implement z-score standardization, as shown here:

```
from sklearn.preprocessing import StandardScaler
zs = StandardScaler()
tips_df_std = zs.fit_transform(tips_df_ohe)
tips_df_std
```

The following is the output of the `tips_df_std` DataFrame. We can see that z-score standardization transforms each vector, depending on the mean and standard deviation:

```
array([[-0.06415003, -0.06415003, -0.09090909, ..., -0.42278122,
        -0.14463921, -0.12909944],
       [-0.06415003, -0.06415003, -0.09090909, ..., -0.42278122,
        -0.14463921, -0.12909944],
       [-0.06415003, -0.06415003, -0.09090909, ..., -0.42278122,
        -0.14463921, -0.12909944],
       ...,
       [-0.06415003, -0.06415003, -0.09090909, ..., -0.42278122,
        -0.14463921, -0.12909944],
       [-0.06415003, -0.06415003, -0.09090909, ..., -0.42278122,
        -0.14463921, -0.12909944],
       [-0.06415003, -0.06415003, -0.09090909, ..., -0.42278122,
        -0.14463921, -0.12909944]]])
```

Now that we have covered various preprocessing techniques, we will explore some ML algorithms we can use to build NLP applications.

The Naive Bayes algorithm

In this section, we will delve into the Naive Bayes algorithm and build a sentiment analyzer. Naive Bayes is a popular ML algorithm based on the Bayes' theorem. The Bayes' theorem can be represented as follows:

$$P(A|B) = \frac{P(B|A) \cdot P(A)}{P(B)}$$

Here, A, B are events:

- $P(A|B)$ is the probability of A given B, while $P(B|A)$ is the probability of B given A.
- $P(A)$ is the independent probability of A, while $P(B)$ is the independent probability of B.

Let's say we have the following fictitious dataset containing information about applications to Ivy League schools. The independent variables in the dataset are the applicant's SAT score, applicant's GPA, and information regarding whether the applicant's parents are alumni to an Ivy League school. The dependent variable is the outcome of the application. Based on this data, we are interested in calculating the likelihood of an applicant getting admission to an Ivy League school given that their SAT score is greater than 1,500, their GPA is greater than 3.2, and their parents are not alumni:

SAT Score	GPA	Alumni Parents	Ivy League Admission?
1,580	4.0	0	1
1,450	3.1	1	1
1,480	3.6	0	0
1,410	3.33	0	0
1,280	3.0	1	1
1,440	3.7	0	0
1,560	3.9	1	1
>1,500	>3.2	0	?

The likelihood of an applicant being admitted to an Ivy League school can be represented as a probability expression, as follows:

$$P(Ivy\ League\,|\,(SAT>1500,\ GPA>3.2,\ AP=0))$$

Using Bayes' theorem, the preceding probabilistic expression can be represented as follows:

$$\frac{P((SAT > 1500, GPA > 3.2, AP = 0)|IvyLeague) * P(IvyLeague)}{P(SAT > 1500, GPA > 3.2, AP = 0)}$$

We can solve the given equation by calculating the respective joint probabilities given in the previous table. However, for bigger datasets, calculating joint probability can get a bit challenging. To get around this problem, we use Naive Bayes, which assumes that all the features are independent of each other, so the joint probability is simply the product of independent probabilities. This assumption is naive because it is almost always wrong. Even in our example, an applicant having a high SAT score is more likely to have a high GPA, so these two events are not independent. However, the Naive Bayes assumption has been proved to work well for classification problems.

Using the Naive Bayes assumption we provided in the previous example, the Bayes' theorem expression can be written as follows:

$$\frac{P(SAT > 1500 | IvyLeague) * P(GPA > 3.2 | IvyLeague) * P(AP = 0 | IvyLeague) * P(IvyLeague)}{P(SAT > 1500) * P(GPA > 3.2) * P(AP = 0)}$$

This equation can easily be solved by calculating the respective probabilities. The numerator can be calculated as follows:

$$(2/4) * (2/4) * (1/4) * (4/7)$$

The denominator can be calculated as follows:

$$(2/7) * (5/7) * (4/7)$$

By calculating the ratio of the products, the final answer as *0.306*, which can be rounded to *0*. So, based on the data, Naive Bayes calculation predicts that an applicant with a *SAT score > 1,500, GPA > 3.2*, and parents not being alumni is not likely to be admitted to Ivy League. This is an unfair world!

Building a sentiment analyzer using the Naive Bayes algorithm

Sentiment analysis, sometimes called opinion mining or polarity detection, refers to the set of algorithms and techniques that are used to extract the polarity of a given document; that is, it determines whether the sentiment of a document is positive, negative, or neutral. Sentiment analysis is gaining popularity in the industry as it allows organizations to mine opinions of a large group of users or potential customers in a cost-efficient way. Sentiment analysis is now used extensively in advertisement campaigns, political campaigns, stock analysis, and more.

Now that we understand the mathematics behind the Naive Bayes algorithm, we will build a sentiment analyzer by training our Naive Bayes model on a labeled product review dataset gathered from Amazon. This dataset was created for the paper, *From Group to Individual Labels using Deep Features, Kotzias et. al., KDD 2015*, and can be accessed at `http:/ /archive.ics.uci.edu/ml/datasets/Sentiment+Labelled+Sentences`.

Dua, D. and Graff, C. (2019). UCI Machine Learning Repository [http://
archive.ics.uci.edu/ml]. Irvine, CA: University of California, School of
Information and Computer Science.

The data is stored in a text file. The following is a partial snapshot of the text file:

```
So there is no way for me to plug it in here in the US unless I go by a converter.        0
Good case, Excellent value.        1
Great for the jawbone.  1
Tied to charger for conversations lasting more than 45 minutes.MAJOR PROBLEMS!! 0
The mic is great.        1
I have to jiggle the plug to get it to line up right to get decent volume.        0
If you have several dozen or several hundred contacts, then imagine the fun of sending each of them one by one. 0
If you are Razr owner...you must have this!    1
Needless to say, I wasted my money.      0
What a waste of money and time!.      0
```

As we can see, the document contains a list of customer reviews and each review is
assigned a sentiment score, with 0 representing negative sentiment and 1 representing
positive sentiment.

First, we will import the raw data into a DataFrame called data, as follows:

```
import pandas as pd
data = pd.read_csv("amazon_cells_labelled.txt", sep='\t', header=None)
data.head()
```

Here are the first five lines of the DataFrame:

```
0 So there is no way for me to plug it in here i... 0
1 Good case, Excellent value. 1
2 Great for the jawbone. 1
3 Tied to charger for conversations lasting more... 0
4 The mic is great. 1
```

Next, we will separate the columns that contain text reviews and the column containing
sentiment labels:

```
X = data.iloc[:,0] # extract column with reviews
y = data.iloc[:,-1] # extract column with sentiments
```

We're doing this because the text data needs to be preprocessed for the ML model. Following this, we will import the CountVectorizer class, which performs key preprocessing steps on the text data such as tokenization, stop word removal, one-hot encoding, and so on. The following code snippet shows how CountVectorization is used to preprocess the text data:

```
from sklearn.feature_extraction.text import CountVectorizer
vectorizer = CountVectorizer(stop_words='english')
X_vec = vectorizer.fit_transform(X)
X_vec.todense() # convert sparse matrix into dense matrix
```

The following is the matrix, with each row representing a review and each column representing a unique word in the corpus. Each row vector represents the word count in that row for each unique word:

```
matrix([[0, 0, 0, ..., 0, 0, 0],
        [0, 0, 0, ..., 0, 0, 0],
        [0, 0, 0, ..., 0, 0, 0],
        ...,
        [0, 0, 0, ..., 0, 0, 0],
        [0, 0, 0, ..., 0, 0, 0],
        [0, 0, 0, ..., 0, 0, 0]], dtype=int64)
```

Next, we import the TfidfTransformer class to transform word counts into their respective tf-idf values (refer to Chapter 4, *Transforming Text into Data Structures*, for more details). Here is how we can transform the word count matrix into a matrix with corresponding tf-idf values:

```
from sklearn.feature_extraction.text import TfidfTransformer
tfidf = TfidfTransformer()
X_tfidf = tfidf.fit_transform(X_vec)
X_tfidf = X_tfidf.todense()
```

The following is the tf-idf matrix. Please note that because each review in the corpus is quite brief, the majority of the values in each row of the matrix are set to 0:

```
matrix([[0, 0, 0, ..., 0, 0, 0],
        [0, 0, 0, ..., 0, 0, 0],
        [0, 0, 0, ..., 0, 0, 0],
        ...,
        [0, 0, 0, ..., 0, 0, 0],
        [0, 0, 0, ..., 0, 0, 0],
        [0, 0, 0, ..., 0, 0, 0]], dtype=int64)
```

With this, we've completed the preprocessing part and are now ready to train the model using the processed data. However, before we do that, we need to split the data into training and testing sets so that we can evaluate the performance of our trained model. This is called **cross-validation** and is an important part of ML model training. We can easily split the data manually but for the sake of consistency, let's use the `train_test_split` class of sklearn's `model_selection` module to do this. For this, we pass our processed reviews data (`X_tfidf`) and the sentiment data to the `train_test_split` object and pass another argument regarding the desired ratio of the split, as follows:

```
from sklearn.model_selection import train_test_split
X_train, X_test, y_train, y_test = train_test_split(X_tfidf, y, test_size =
0.25, random_state = 0)
```

The preceding code splits both independent variables (the `tfidf` matrix) and the dependent variable (sentiment) into training and testing data.

We now have everything we need to train our model. For this, we need to import the `MultinomialNaive Bayes` class from sklearn's `naive_bayes` module and fit the training data to the model, as follows:

```
from sklearn.naive_bayes import MultinomialNaive Bayes
clf = MultinomialNaive Bayes()
clf.fit(X_train, y_train)
```

Fitting the training data essentially means that our Naive Bayes classifier has now learned the training data and is now in a position to calculate relevant probabilities. Therefore, if an out-of-sample review (such as *I was very disappointed with this product*) is now passed to the classifier, it will try to calculate the probability of the sentiment being positive or negative given that the words *this, disappointed,* and *product* exist in the review. Here is how we obtain the predicted sentiment values from the classifier for the test reviews that are stored in the `y_pred` array:

```
y_pred = clf.predict(X_test)
```

To determine the performance of our model, we will create a confusion matrix that calculates the number of correct predictions, broken down for each classification:

```
from sklearn.metrics import confusion_matrix
confusion_matrix(y_test, y_pred)
```

The following is the output of the confusion matrix. The vertical axis of sklearn's confusion matrix should be interpreted as the actual values, while the horizontal axis should be interpreted as the predicted values. Therefore, our model predicted `107` `(87 + 20)` values as having a sentiment score of `0`, out which `87` were correctly predicted and `20` were incorrectly predicted. Likewise, the model predicted `143` `(33+110)` values as having a sentiment score of `1`, out of which `110` were correctly predicted and `33` were incorrectly predicted:

```
array([[ 87,  33],
       [ 20, 110]], dtype=int64)
```

Therefore, the total number of correct predictions is obtained by summing the left diagonal (in this case, `87 + 110`). The accuracy is the ratio of the total correct predictions divided by the total count of the test set (obtained by summing all the numbers in the confusion matrix). Therefore, the accuracy, in this case, is *197/250 = 78.8%*. This is a decent accuracy score given the simple model and limited training data we had (only 750 abridged reviews). Tuning model parameters and performing further preprocessing steps such as lemmatization, stemming, and so on can improve the accuracy further.

The SVM algorithm

SVM is a supervised ML algorithm that attempts to classify data within a dataset by finding the optimal hyperplane that best segregates the classes. Each data point in the dataset can be considered a vector in an *N*-dimensional plane, with each dimension representing a feature of the data. SVM identifies the frontier data points (or points closest to the opposing class), also known as support vectors, and then attempts to find the boundary (also known as the hyperplane in the *N*-dimensional space) that is the farthest from the support vector of each class.

Say we have a fruit basket with two types of fruits in it and we want to create an algorithm that segregates them. We only have information about two features of the fruits; that is, their weight and radius. Therefore, we can abstract this problem as a linear algebra problem, with each fruit representing a vector in a two-dimensional space, as shown in the following diagram. In order to segregate the two types of fruit, we will have to identify a hyperplane (in two dimensions, the hyperplane would be a line) whose equation can be represented as follows:

$$w1 * radius + w2 * weight - c = 0$$

Here, *w1* and *w2* are coefficients and *c* is a constant. The equation of the hyperplane in the *n* dimension can be generalized as follows:

$$W^T * X - c = 0$$

Here, *W* is a vector of coefficients and *X* represents each dimension of the space.

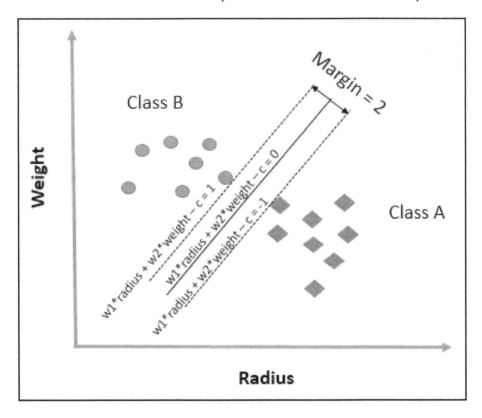

From the preceding diagram, it is obvious that there are many hyperplanes that can segregate the two classes in this case. However, the SVM algorithm tries to find the optimum *W* (coefficients) and *c* (constant) so that the hyperplane is at the maximum distance from both support vectors. To perform this optimization, the algorithm starts with a hyperplane with random parameters and then calculates the distance of each point from the hyperplane using the following equation:

$$\frac{W^T * X_0 - c}{\|W\|}$$

Knowing the distance of the hyperplane from each point, the algorithm can easily figure out the frontier points and calculate the distance from each support vector. The algorithm creates a number of hyperplanes and repeats this calculation to identify the hyperplane that's the most equidistant from both support vectors. This algorithm is also called linear SVM as the points are linearly separable. It should be noted that the SVM algorithm can also be applied to non-linearly separable data points, albeit after applying various transformations to the data.

Building a sentiment analyzer using SVM

In this section, we will build a sentiment analyzer using a linear SVM. We will be using the same dataset that we used to build the Naive Bayes-based sentiment analyzer for the sake of comparison. The feature matrix that was created while training the Naive Bayes sentiment analyzer had 1,642 columns, so the objective, in this case, is to identify a hyperplane that segregates vectors in a 1,642-dimensional space into positive sentiment classes and negative sentiment classes. This hyperplane will then be used to predict the sentiment of the newly vectorized and tf-idf transformed documents.

All the data preprocessing steps will be identical to those in the Naive Bayes sentiment analyzer section, as follows:

```
import pandas as pd
data = pd.read_csv("amazon_cells_labelled.txt", sep='\t', header=None)

X = data.iloc[:,0] # extract column with review
y = data.iloc[:,-1] # extract column with sentiment

# tokenize the news text and convert data in matrix format
from sklearn.feature_extraction.text import CountVectorizer
vectorizer = CountVectorizer(stop_words='english')
X_vec = vectorizer.fit_transform(X)
X_vec = X_vec.todense() # convert sparse matrix into dense matrix

# Transform data by applying term frequency inverse document frequency (TF-
IDF)
from sklearn.feature_extraction.text import TfidfTransformer
tfidf = TfidfTransformer()
X_tfidf = tfidf.fit_transform(X_vec)
X_tfidf = X_tfidf.todense()
```

Again, we will split the processed input data into training data and testing data, as follows:

```
from sklearn.model_selection import train_test_split
X_train, X_test, y_train, y_test = train_test_split(X_tfidf, y, test_size =
0.25, random_state = 0)
```

The previous code splits both the independent variables (the tfidf matrix) and the dependent variable (sentiment) into training and testing data. Now, we import the **Support Vector Classification (SVC)** class from sklearn's svm module and fit the training data to the model, as follows:

```
from sklearn.svm import SVC
classifier = SVC(kernel='linear')
classifier.fit(X_train, y_train)
```

Fitting the training data means that the classifier has identified the optimum hyperplane after identifying the frontier points and calculating the relevant distances based on the training data. To assess the accuracy of the hyperplane, we will fit the vectorized test reviews (stored in the y_pred array) to the hyperplane equation. Based on the sign of the value of the equation, the model will predict the sentiment analysis score. The following command shows how the predicted values are calculated using the predict() function:

```
y_pred = classifier.predict(X_test)
```

Once again, we will be using a confusion matrix to measure the performance of our model, as follows:

```
from sklearn.metrics import confusion_matrix
confusion_matrix(y_test, y_pred)
```

Here is the output of the confusion matrix. Our model predicted 135 (102 + 33) values as having a sentiment score of 0, out which 102 were correctly predicted and 33 were incorrectly predicted. Likewise, the model predicted 115 (18+97) values as having a sentiment score of 1, out of which 97 were correctly predicted and 18 were incorrectly predicted:

```
array([[102, 18],
       [ 33, 97]], dtype=int64)
```

Therefore, the total number of correct predictions is obtained by summing the left diagonal (in this case, `102 + 97`). The accuracy is the ratio of the total correct predictions divided by the total count of the test set (obtained by summing all the numbers in the confusion matrix). Therefore, the accuracy, in this case, *199/250 = 79.6%*, which is marginally better than the Naive Bayes model's accuracy. The model's performance can be further improved by improving input data preprocessing (via lemmatization, stemming, and so on) and optimizing various SVM hyperparameters.

Productionizing a trained sentiment analyzer

Now that we have trained our sentiment analyzer, we need a way to reuse this model to predict the sentiment of new product reviews. Python provides a very convenient way for us to do this through the `pickle` module. **Pickling** in Python refers to serializing and deserializing Python object structures. In other words, by using the `pickle` module, we can save the Python objects that are created as part of model training for reuse. The following code snippet shows how easily the trained classifier model and the feature matrix, which are created as part of the training process, can be saved in your local machine:

```
import pickle
pickle.dump(vectorizer, open("vectorizer_sa", 'wb')) # Save vectorizer for reuse
pickle.dump(classifier, open("nb_sa", 'wb')) # Save classifier for reuse
```

Running the previous lines of code will save the Python object's vectorizer and classifier, which were created as part of the model training exercise we discussed in the *Building a sentiment analyzer* sections. These objects are saved as the `vectorizer_sa` and `nb_sa` files in your working directory. We can now import these pickled objects as we wish. We will use the same trained classifier and feature matrix as the ones we created during the training exercise.

Now, we will create a function that predicts the sentiment of any new product review. We will pass the trained classifier, feature matrix, and the new product review as parameters to this function and the function will return the predicted sentiment. The function simply vectorizes the new product review (passed as a string) based on the feature matrix that we have passed. The feature matrix is the matrix that contains all the words we learned from our training sample.

When we use the `transform()` function of the feature matrix on the new document, it simply creates a vector with the same number of elements as the number of columns (words) in the feature matrix and updates each element with the frequency of the corresponding word in the new document. The frequency vector is then transformed into a `tf-idf` vector before it's passed to the classifier. The function returns a positive or negative sentiment based on the classifier's output. Here is the implementation of the function:

```
def sentiment_pred(classifier, training_matrix, doc):
    """function to predict the sentiment of a product review
       classifier : pre trained model
       training_matrix : matrix of features associated with the trained
       model
       doc = product review whose sentiment needs to be identified"""
    X_new = training_matrix.transform(pd.Series(doc))
    #don't use fit_transform here because the model is already fitted
    X_new = X_new.todense() #convert sparse matrix to dense

    from sklearn.feature_extraction.text import TfidfTransformer
    tfidf = TfidfTransformer()
    X_tfidf_new = tfidf.fit_transform(X_new)
    X_tfidf_new = X_tfidf_new.todense()

    y_new = classifier.predict(X_tfidf_new)
    if y_new[0] == 0:
        return "negative sentiment"
    elif y_new[0] == 1:
        return "positive sentiment"
```

Now that the function is ready, all we need to do is unpickle and import the classifier and feature matrix and pass them to the function, along with the new product review. The following code snippet shows how we can unpickle objects by using the `load()` function:

```
nb_clf = pickle.load(open("nb_sa", 'rb'))
vectorizer = pickle.load(open("vectorizer_sa", 'rb'))
new_doc = "The gadget works like a charm. Very satisfied with the product"
sentiment_pred(nb_clf, vectorizer, new_doc)
```

After this, we pass a fictitious product review to the function. The following is the output:

```
'positive sentiment'
```

Let's try passing another fictitious product review to our function:

```
new_doc = "Not even close to the quality one would expect"
sentiment_pred(nb_clf, vectorizer, new_doc)
```

Here is the output:

```
'negative sentiment'
```

As we can see, our ML-based sentiment analyzer is live and performing decently.

However, the following are some important things to consider while creating and deploying the sentiment analyzer:

- The training data should be consistent with the objective of the sentiment analyzer. Don't train the model using movie reviews if the objective is to predict the sentiment of financial news articles.
- Accurately labeling the training data is critical for the model to perform well. We have used pre-labeled data in this chapter. However, if you are creating a real-world application, you will have to spend time labeling the training documents. Typically, labeling should be done by someone with a good understanding of industry jargon.
- Sourcing training data is a difficult task. You can use tools such as web scraping or social media scraping, subject to permissions. Effort should be spent on sourcing data from multiple platforms and you shouldn't rely too much on a particular source.
- Evaluate the performance of your model regularly and retrain the model if required.

With that, we have come to the end of this chapter!

Summary

In this chapter, we built on our understanding of text vectorization, data preprocessing, and so on to gain an end-to-end understanding of applying ML algorithms to develop NLP applications. We learned about the additional pre-processing steps required for ML training and gained a thorough understanding of the Naive Bayes and SVM algorithms. We applied our understanding of text data processing and ML algorithms to build a sentiment analyzer and deployed the model to perform sentiment analysis in real-time. We also learned how to measure the performance of ML models and discussed some important dos and don'ts about building ML-based applications.

In the next chapter, we will learn how to apply deep learning to text processing and cover how neural networks can help us improve the accuracy of our applications.

8
From Human Neurons to Artificial Neurons for Understanding Text

There has been an unprecedented rise in the use of neural network-based applications and architectures in the first two decades of the twenty-first century. This has been largely catered to by the extensive research that has been carried out over the past few decades. The evolution of high-end processors in the form of **graphical processing units (GPUs)** and **tensor processing units (TPUs)** has supplemented the rise of neural network-based applications by making it possible to perform heavy calculations that are very commonly encountered in any neural network. Self-driving cars, language translation services, chatbots, document summarization, and image captioning are some common modern-day use cases that are powered by neural networks.

In this chapter, we will begin by looking at how the idea of an **artificial neural network (ANN)** came into being thanks to neurons in the human brain. We will learn about the various components that make up an ANN and learn how the network as a whole works and how it learns. We will briefly talk about Keras, which is a popular framework for building deep learning models. Based on the knowledge we will gain about ANNs, we will apply it to solve the real-life NLP task of classifying questions. By the end of the chapter, based on the theoretical discussions and hands-on exercises, we will be comfortable in using neural networks for solving tasks related to text processing.

In this chapter, the following topics will be covered:

- Exploring the biology behind neural networks
- How does a neural network learn?
- Understanding regularization
- Let's talk Keras
- Building a question classifier using neural networks

Technical requirements

The code files for this chapter can be found at the following GitHub link: `https://github.com/PacktPublishing/Hands-On-Python-Natural-Language-Processing/tree/master/Chapter08`.

Exploring the biology behind neural networks

Neural networks were based on the functioning of neurons in the brain. Dendrites in the brain receive input signals from the neighboring neurons. Each dendrite has a weight associated with it and the signal coming in from a specific dendrite gets multiplied by its corresponding weight. These incoming signals are then summed up in the cell body. As this summed-up value reaches a particular threshold, the summed-up signal is then sent across through the neuron's axon and is further propagated forward. The weights associated with a dendrite dictate the importance of the signal coming in through a particular dendrite. These values get changed dynamically. ANNs build upon the same context. Let's look at the structure of a basic ANN in the next section.

Neurons

An ANN is an interconnected network of neurons. Each neuron, as shown in the diagram at the end of this section, receives n input signals that are nothing but a set of features, represented by X in the following equation:

$$X = [x_1, x_2, ..., x_n]$$

These input features are multiplied by a set of weights, W, depending on the edge they are coming in from:

$$W = [w_1, w_2, ..., w_n]$$

These are then summed up. In reality, it boils down to the following equation:

$$z = x_1w_1 + x_2w_2 + x_3w_3 + b \quad \text{(Equation. 1)}$$

But there are two questions that arise from this:

1. What is b?
2. Isn't it a simple linear equation?

Let's answer question 1 first.

b is referred to as the bias, and it is analogous to the intercept term in linear equations. It can be seen as the property of the neuron and is trained like the other parameters in the network. It allows the model to fit the data better:

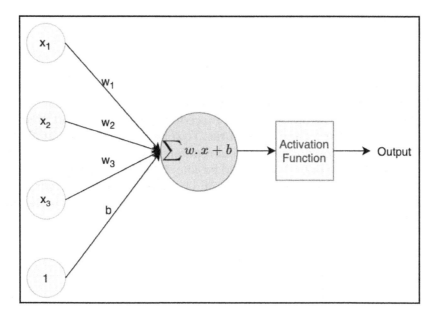

To answer the second question, yes: until now, everything has been a multivariate linear equation; however, these multivariate linear equations coupled with activation functions offer a powerful way to theoretically classify any decision boundary in any dimensional space. Let's illustrate this through an example. Let's assume that we have been provided with two types of objects and the objects are defined by two features, **X1** and **X2**, as shown in the following diagram:

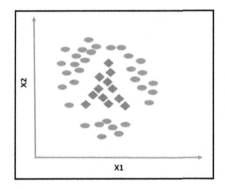

These two input features could be the radius and weight for fruits, age and salary for employees, annual returns and volatility for stocks, and so on. Now, let's say that we are asked to build a classifier that learns from the preceding training data and predicts the type of new objects based on their X1 and X2 features. To solve this problem, our classifier will have to figure out the decision boundaries that separate one class of object from others. Any new object falling within the boundary would be categorized as one type of object, and any object falling outside the decision boundary would be categorized as another type of object (assuming binary classification). The decision boundary for this problem is shown in the following diagram:

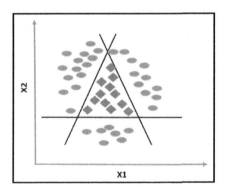

Recall high school coordinate geometry and how we define the equation of a line in a two-dimensional plane. The equation of a line is as follows:

$$ax + by + c = 0$$

Here, x and y are the axes (the same as X1 and X2 in our example) and a, b, and c are the coefficients. The slope ($-a/b$) and the intercept ($-c/b$) of the line can be calculated using the coefficients.

Therefore, all that our classifier needs to do is to calculate the value of the coefficients (a, b, and c) for the three lines that constitute our decision boundary. Now let's revisit the neuron architecture and appreciate how linear equations coupled with activation functions help us replicate the same decision boundary. In the following neuron architecture diagram, the three weighted sums of the input **X1** and **X2** (and bias) coupled with a simple activation function will mimic the three lines that constitute our decision boundary:

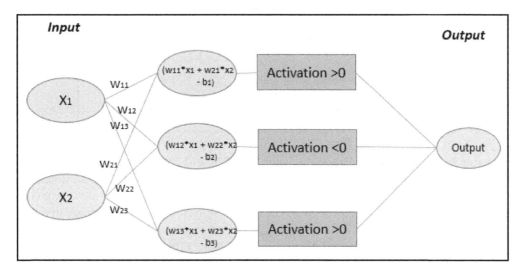

The following diagram shows how the linear system of equations coupled with the activation functions in the preceding neuron architecture is the same as the equations of the decision boundary:

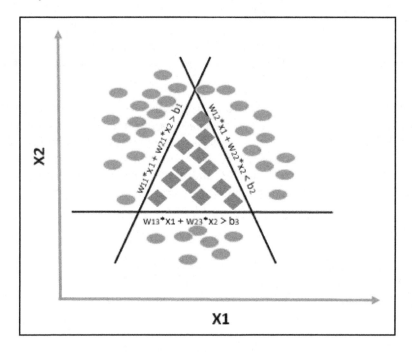

If we are able to find the optimum value of the weights and the biases of the neuron architecture, then we have solved the problem of creating the classifier. Please note that the same concept applies to higher dimensional spaces (more than two input features) as well, and therefore neural networks can help us create decision boundaries in any dimensional space. In theory, we can use neural networks to create a decision boundary of any shape by increasing or decreasing the number of intermediate nodes (also called hidden nodes), as illustrated in the following diagram:

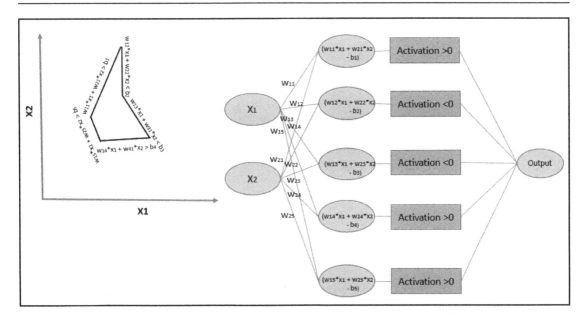

Based on the neuron architecture described in the preceding diagram, it can be deduced that activation functions play a key role in transforming the system of linear equations to a nonlinear construct (complex nonlinear decision boundaries). Choosing an appropriate activation function for a neural network is key to its performance. Let's now delve into the various types of activation functions.

Activation functions

Activation functions introduce nonlinearity in the network. Without nonlinearity, the network would be performing linear mappings between the input, which would be nothing but a multivariate linear equation. Activation functions control the threshold that decides what the neuron would provide as output, analogous to what was mentioned when we discussed biological neurons. In *Equation 2*, $f()$ is the activation function. The input to the activation function is z, which we computed in *Equation. 1*. The final output, y, is released from the neuron at the particular instance:

$$y = f(z) \quad \text{(Equation. 2)}$$

There are various types of activation functions. We will look into three of them in this chapter, as others would be beyond the scope of this book. More can be read about different types of activation functions at `https://en.wikipedia.org/wiki/Activation_function`.

Sigmoid

The sigmoid activation function constrains the output in a range between 0 and 1. It is defined using the following mathematical equation:

$$Sigmoid(x) = \frac{1}{1 + e^{-x}}$$

The curve of the sigmoid function is as follows:

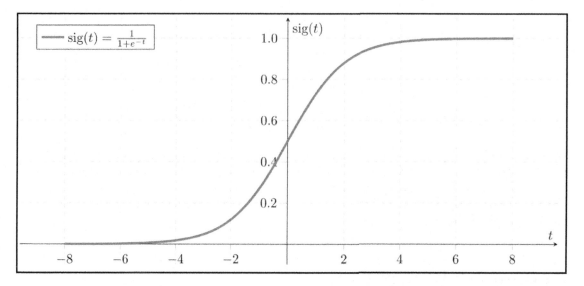

The sigmoid function will pull down very large values to 1 and very small values to 0. It is very commonly used for tasks involving binary outputs; however, due to issues such as values not being zero-centered and gradients getting killed because of the saturation of the sigmoid function for the majority of the values, its usage has dropped significantly.

Tanh activation

The tanh activation function is pretty similar to the sigmoid function; however, it's a zero-centered function, unlike sigmoid, and overcomes this drawback associated with sigmoid functions. It converts the input values within the range of -1 to 1. The equation governing tanh is as follows:

$$tanh(x) = \frac{e^x - e^{-x}}{e^x + e^{-x}}$$

You can see the curve of the tanh function in the following diagram:

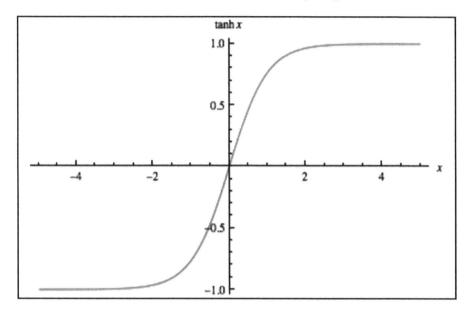

The tanh function is used primarily in place of sigmoid in most of the networks today since it overcomes the zero-centered problem associated with the sigmoid function. However, similar to the sigmoid function, the tanh function also saturates quickly and, as a result, the gradients get killed.

Rectified linear unit

Rectified linear unit (ReLU) is probably the most commonly used activation function today. It is defined by the following formula:

$$ReLu(x) = max(0, x)$$

ReLU's charm is its very simple formula, which does not require complex computations and, at the same time, overcomes the problems associated with the sigmoid and tanh nonlinearity functions. However, if you look at the graph of ReLU in the following diagram, you may note that for negative values, the neuron with ReLU as the activation function would never get triggered and would die. This problem can be solved by using similar activation functions, such as leaky ReLU; however, details of these are beyond the scope of this book:

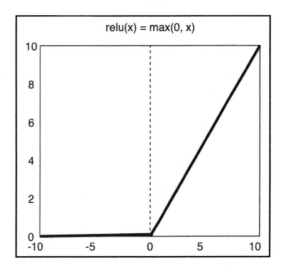

Now that we have understood neurons and activation functions, let's see how these all come together to form a neural network.

Neurons form an interconnected network that we call an ANN. An ANN consists of three layers, with each layer consisting of a particular number of neurons or nodes. Let's look at the various ANN layers next.

Layers in an ANN

An ANN consists of three types of layers:

- **Input layer**: This is the first layer in a neural network, and the number of nodes or neurons in this layer is equal to the number of features that would be fed to the network.
- **Hidden layer**: An ANN can have one or more hidden layers. These are the intermediate layers in a network. The relationships and patterns in data are derived in these layers. The number of hidden layers is a hyperparameter that needs to be tuned. The number of nodes in each hidden layer is a hyperparameter. For fairly simple datasets, an ANN with only one hidden layer will suffice. However, depending on the complexity of the data and the features that need to be extracted, the number of hidden layers can be varied, along with the number of nodes in each hidden layer.
- **Output layer**: This is the final layer in an ANN that provides the output for a particular input. It receives the results from the hidden layers and puts it across. The number of nodes in the output layer depends on the type of problem being solved. The output layer has only one node if it is a binary classification problem since this node itself can emit *0* or *1* depending on which class the data point is categorized into. For multiclass classification problems, the number of nodes in the output layer is equal to the number of classes so that each node portrays the probability of the data point belonging to a particular class.

The nodes in an ANN are connected across the layers and there is no connection between the nodes in the same layer.

The following diagram shows a neural network with an input layer comprising four nodes catering to four input features. The input layer is followed by a hidden layer consisting of three neurons. As expected, the final layer is an output layer that has one node. The ANN structure shown can work for both binary classification and regression problems. The summation sign in the diagram shows the operations taking place in a neuron followed by the application of the activation function:

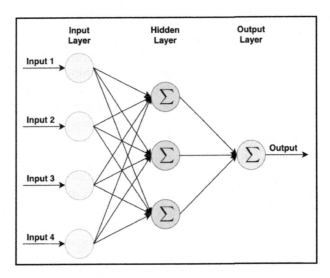

Okay. I have understood the structure of a neural network, but how does it learn?

We will answer this question in the following section.

How does a neural network learn?

The following steps represent step-by-step description of how information goes forward in a neural network. This process is referred to as forward propagation:

1. The input values arrive at the input layer and are processed in the neurons.
2. The outputs are then forwarded to the hidden layers wherein the randomly initialized weights are multiplied by the values and the bias is added.
3. These values are then passed through the activation function.
4. Finally, the values reach the output layer and the neurons perform the processing and emit an output value, y'.
5. This y' is the predicted value for the input that came in.

Everything that we have discussed hitherto falls under the category of forward propagation.

As we saw, a value y' was predicted by the network. No learning has happened yet.

Now we need to judge the performance of our network, in terms of how far away or close it was to predicting the correct value. We do this by measuring something called the loss function. There are multiple kinds of loss function that can be used. Loss functions provide an indication of how well the network performed in terms of predicting the output for a particular data point. The objective of the network is to minimize the loss function by improving its prediction ability.

 There are techniques for initializing weight matrices, such as Xavier initialization, that result in better results than randomly initialized weight matrices.

How does the network get better at making predictions?

Depending on the value of the loss function, the weight matrices and bias vector are updated to figure out their optimal values so that the neural network as a whole improves in making predictions. This is referred to as **gradient descent**, and in using it, we try to go down the slope of the weights versus loss function curve so that we can reach a minimum loss function value. This is performed by calculating the partial derivatives of the loss function with respect to the individual weights and biases. The details of this process are beyond the scope of this book. However, in a nutshell, by calculating the partial derivatives, each weight and bias tries to understand how responsible it was for the prediction and updates itself accordingly. This process is illustrated by the following formula:

$$W_{new} = W_{old} - alpha \times \frac{\partial J}{\partial W_{old}}$$

Let's look at each of the components:

- W_{old} and W_{new} represent the present and modified weights, respectively.
- J represents the loss function.

$$\frac{\partial J}{\partial W_{old}}$$ is the partial derivative of the loss function with respect to the weight W_{old}.

- *alpha* represents the learning rate.

In the aforementioned formula, we have essentially discussed everything except alpha. The learning rate, alpha, controls how big or small a step to take when updating values. We would ideally want to modify the learning rate during training so that larger steps are taken when we are far away from the optimum value of the loss function, and smaller steps are taken as we progress towards the optimal value of the loss function.

Essentially, this process is referred to as backpropagation, wherein the signal flows backward to the network in terms of how good or bad the network performed in predicting values. Accordingly, the various parameters in the network get updated so that the optimal value of the loss function can be achieved and the network can learn in the process.

Before we proceed and solve an NLP problem using an ANN, let's learn about the concept of regularization, which is a very critical concept to know before training any machine learning or deep learning model. We will also discuss dropout, which is a regularization technique for neural networks.

Understanding regularization

During model training, two problems come up quite often: *underfitting* and *overfitting*. Let's learn about them next:

- **Underfitting**: When our model performs poorly on both training and test data, it is said to be underfitting. This basically means that the model was not able to capture patterns or underlying trends in our data, and so it could not generalize well when working with unseen data. For such models, we can try out the tuning of various hyperparameters so that it can fit data well. In the case of neural networks, we can add more layers and create a bigger network so that the model can capture complex patterns in data.
- **Overfitting**: Overfitting is another problem that can happen during model training. When the model performs very well on training data, but does not generalize well and performs poorly on test data, it is said to be overfitting. Basically, the model is trying to memorize data here rather than learn patterns. It can, at times, model noise and inaccurate data points as well. In order to solve the problem of overfitting, regularization is a very useful technique that can be used.

We do not want a model that performs very well on training data. Rather, we want a model that generalizes well and performs decently on both training data that it has already seen and test data that is unseen. Regularization helps us with that. It prevents the model from overfitting by penalizing it when it performs too well on training data. A penalty term is added to the loss function that will take care of preventing overfitting by incorporating regularization. Details of this are beyond the scope of this book. The popular forms of regularization include L1 or Lasso, L2 or Ridge, and Elastic Net.

Dropout is another very commonly used and effective form of regularization that helps prevent overfitting in neural networks. Let's look at dropout in the next section to understand how exactly it achieves this.

Dropout

We discussed how regularization can help us prevent overfitting. Dropout is an extremely efficient regularization technique for preventing overfitting in neural networks. As part of dropout, every neuron in a network is only active with a probability, p. Essentially, a particular percentage of signals going to the subsequent layers are turned off. This helps the model to prevent overfitting as the model would not concentrate on the specifics of data but generalize better, since in every pass, a different variation of weights would be used corresponding to the active neurons.

In addition to L1, L2, Elastic Net, and dropout, another technique that helps in preventing dropout is early stopping. As part of early stopping, the model is asked to look at a parameter or function during the training phase. As soon as the value for the parameter is met, the training stops. One of the commonly used parameters is validation accuracy, wherein during training, the model's performance is evaluated on an unseen dataset, called the validation set. When the performance of the model degrades on the validation dataset, training is stopped. At this point, the model can be seen as generalizing well to the data.

We now have a decent theoretical understanding of neural networks. In order to get practical exposure, we need to understand how we can code neural networks. For this, we will next discuss Keras, which is a very convenient framework for building deep learning models.

Let's talk Keras

Keras is a high-level framework that can be used to build neural networks. It is written in Python and provides numerous APIs and modules for defining, building, and training neural networks with ease. It can use multiple platforms, such as TensorFlow, in its backend.

TensorFlow is an open source library developed by Google for machine learning model building and deployment. It provides several low-level controls as well.

Keras provides a wrapper around frameworks such as TensorFlow and hides low-lying implementations that let developers concentrate on solving problems using deep learning by taking care of all internal implementations and interfacing with backend frameworks, such as TensorFlow.

A neural network can be envisioned as a computational graph in which layers are stacked. Keras provides an interface to build these stacks of layers. The simplest among these is the sequential model, which is nothing but a linear stack of layers. It can be imported and instantiated in Keras using the following code snippet:

```
from keras.models import Sequential
model = Sequential()
```

We have already looked into the concept of fully connected layers and dropout. These layers can be added to the sequential stack by using the following piece of code:

```
from keras.layers import Dense, Dropout
model.add(Dense(units=64, activation='relu'))
model.add(Dropout(0.3))
```

The dense layer is synonymous with the fully connected layer, and here it has 64 neurons. The ReLU activation function is used. The dropout layer is added when the value 0.3 indicates that 30% of the neurons would be dropped randomly. Similarly, we can add or move layers, such as convolutions, and pooling, which we will see in the next sections and subsequent chapters. Now, once we define our network architecture, we need to build it. The compile method in Keras helps us to build the architecture, and here we can specify the loss function, optimizer, and other features that we will be using in our model. We can build our model using the following code snippet:

```
model.compile(loss='binary_crossentropy',
              optimizer= 'adam',
              metrics=['accuracy'])
```

Here, we would want to use binary cross-entropy for loss computation and Adam as our optimization technique.

Now that everything is defined and built, Keras provides the `fit()` method to actually train our model, as can be seen in the following code snippet:

```
model.fit(x_train, y_train, epochs=5, batch_size=32)
```

We provide the training data, predictor variable, the number of epochs that the training will happen for, and the batch size or the number of samples to be used during one input pass, before updating the weights for the parameters, respectively.

Finally, the `evaluate()` API in Keras provides us with a mechanism for evaluating the performance of our model on test data and the `predict()` API helps make predictions for new data.

> We talked about early stopping when discussing regularization. Keras provides a method called `EarlyStopping` in its `callback` module. You should check it out.

Now that we have a fair understanding of neural networks and how can we use Keras to leverage it, let's apply what we have learned to solve an NLP problem of classifying questions.

Building a question classifier using neural networks

We have used a **question classification** dataset that is open sourced by the University of Illinois, Urbana Champaign. We will try and classify questions based on their text into one of the following six classes:

- ABBREVIATION
- ENTITY
- DESCRIPTION
- HUMAN
- LOCATION
- NUMERIC

More about the dataset can be found at `https://cogcomp.seas.upenn.edu/Data/QA/QC/`.

Go through the following steps to classify the questions based on their text:

1. Import the basic libraries:

```
import nltk
nltk.download('stopwords')
nltk.download('wordnet')
from nltk.corpus import stopwords
from nltk.stem.porter import PorterStemmer
from nltk.stem.snowball import SnowballStemmer
from nltk.stem.wordnet import WordNetLemmatizer
import pandas as pd
import re
import numpy as np
from sklearn.feature_extraction.text import TfidfVectorizer
from sklearn.preprocessing import LabelEncoder
```

2. Now, we will read the dataset using the following code snippet:

```
train_data = open('Dataset/training_data.txt', 'r+')
test_data = open('Dataset/test_dataset.txt', 'r+')
train = pd.DataFrame(train_data.readlines(), columns =
['Question'])
test = pd.DataFrame(test_data.readlines(), columns = ['Question'])
```

3. Let's look at some data points next:

```
train.head()
```

Here's what our data looks like in raw form:

	Question
0	DESC:manner How did serfdom develop in and the...
1	ENTY:cremat What films featured the character ...
2	DESC:manner How can I find a list of celebriti...
3	ENTY:animal What fowl grabs the spotlight afte...
4	ABBR:exp What is the full form of .com ?\n

Our dataset offers a unique challenge in terms of segregating it into **Questions** and **Question Types**, which are attached together. Furthermore, as the **Question Type** consists of both coarse and fine classes, we will need to perform separation for these as well. Our focus should be on the questions and determining which coarse classes they fall into as part of this exercise. Let's do that next.

4. Split the data points to obtain question strings and coarse and fine question categories:

```
train['QType'] = train.Question.apply(lambda x: x.split(' ', 1)[0])
train['Question'] = train.Question.apply(lambda x: x.split(' ',
1)[1])
train['QType-Coarse'] = train.QType.apply(lambda x:
x.split(':')[0])
train['QType-Fine'] = train.QType.apply(lambda x: x.split(':')[1])
test['QType'] = test.Question.apply(lambda x: x.split(' ', 1)[0])
test['Question'] = test.Question.apply(lambda x: x.split(' ',
1)[1])
test['QType-Coarse'] = test.QType.apply(lambda x: x.split(':')[0])
test['QType-Fine'] = test.QType.apply(lambda x: x.split(':')[1])
```

5. Now let's look at our grained dataset:

```
train.head()
```

Here's our segregated dataset:

	Question	QType	QType-Coarse	QType-Fine
0	How did serfdom develop in and then leave Russ...	DESC:manner	DESC	manner
1	What films featured the character Popeye Doyle...	ENTY:cremat	ENTY	cremat
2	How can I find a list of celebrities' real na...	DESC:manner	DESC	manner
3	What fowl grabs the spotlight after the Chines...	ENTY:animal	ENTY	animal
4	What is the full form of .com ?	ABBR:exp	ABBR	exp

6. Next, we will use the following code snippet to pop out the `QType` and `QType-Fine` variables, as our focus is on predicting the coarse classes for a question:

```
train.pop('QType')
train.pop('QType-Fine')
test.pop('QType')
test.pop('QType-Fine')
```

7. Let's look at the classes in our dataset:

```
classes = np.unique(np.array(train['QType-Coarse']))
classes
```

Here's our array of classes:

```
array(['ABBR', 'DESC', 'ENTY', 'HUM', 'LOC', 'NUM'], dtype=object)
```

8. In Chapter 7, *Identifying Patterns in Text Using Machine Learning*, we looked at label encoding. Next, we will use this to convert our classes into integral identifiers:

```
le = LabelEncoder()
le.fit(pd.Series(train['QType-Coarse'].tolist() + test['QType-Coarse'].tolist()).values)
train['QType-Coarse'] = le.transform(train['QType-Coarse'].values)
test['QType-Coarse'] = le.transform(test['QType-Coarse'].values)
```

9. We will preprocess our dataset using the preprocessing pipeline that we developed in Chapter 3, *Building Your NLP Vocabulary*:

```
all_corpus = pd.Series(train.Question.tolist() +
test.Question.tolist()).astype(str)
all_corpus = preprocess(all_corpus, remove_stopwords = True)
```

 The preprocess method can be viewed in Chapter 3, *Building Your NLP Vocabulary*, or the code files.

10. Now, we will split our data back into a training and test corpus, which we had combined for preprocessing:

```
train_corpus = all_corpus[0:train.shape[0]]
test_corpus = all_corpus[train.shape[0]:]
```

Hey, I converted my classes into integral identifiers. But how do I convert my text into numbers?

Let's make use of TF–IDF for building embeddings that we discussed in Chapter 4, *Transforming Text into Data Structures*.

11. We will vectorize our text data using TF–IDF, making use of the following code block:

```
vectorizer = TfidfVectorizer()
tf_idf_matrix_train = vectorizer.fit_transform(train_corpus)
tf_idf_matrix_test = vectorizer.transform(test_corpus)
```

Our embeddings are ready now. Next, let's make use of Keras to build our network architecture.

12. Import the Keras library and various modules:

```
import keras
from keras.models import Sequential, Model
from keras import layers
from keras.layers import Dense, Dropout, Input
from keras.utils import np_utils
```

13. We discussed one-hot encoding in Chapter 7, *Identifying Patterns in Text Using Machine Learning*, as well. Since we have multiple possibilities in our problem statement, we need to one-hot encode the class labels that are expected by the network:

```
y_train = np_utils.to_categorical(train['QType-Coarse'],
train['QType-Coarse'].nunique())
y_test = np_utils.to_categorical(test['QType-Coarse'],
train['QType-Coarse'].nunique())
```

14. Next, let's define our network architecture by using the following code block:

```
model = Sequential()
model.add(Dense(128, activation='relu',
input_dim=tf_idf_matrix_train.shape[1]))
model.add(Dropout(0.3))
model.add(Dense(6, activation='softmax'))
model.compile(optimizer='adam', loss='categorical_crossentropy',
metrics=['categorical_accuracy'])
model.summary()
```

Here is the summary of the model we just defined.

```
Model: "sequential_1"
```

Layer (type)	Output Shape		Param #
dense_1 (Dense)	(None, 128)		1027968
dropout_1 (Dropout)	(None, 128)		0
dense_2 (Dense)	(None, 6)	Eq.	774

```
Total params: 1,028,742
Trainable params: 1,028,742
Non-trainable params: 0
```

We have added a fully connected layer that will accept the inputs. It will apply the ReLU activation function to the processed values before emitting the output from each neuron.

Next, we apply dropout. Since we have provided a value of 0.3, it will randomly delete 30% of the neurons during each training epoch so as to prevent overfitting.

The dropout layer is followed by the output layer comprising six neurons, where each neuron caters to one class in our dataset.

We have used the Adam optimizer and categorical cross-entropy function for loss computation, the details of which are beyond the scope of this chapter. More about the Adam optimizer can be read at https://arxiv.org/pdf/1412.6980.pdf, and you can check out the link at https://arxiv.org/pdf/1702.05659.pdf for reading about loss functions for deep neural networks in classification.

Softmax is used in our network for computing the normalized probabilities for each of the six classes. We have discussed softmax extensively in Chapter 5, *Word Embeddings and Distance Measurements for Text*.

15. Let's train our model next:

```
training_history = model.fit(tf_idf_matrix_train, y_train,
epochs=10, batch_size=100)
```

16. Let's evaluate the model that we built using accuracy as the metric:

```
loss, accuracy = model.evaluate(tf_idf_matrix_test, y_test,
verbose=False)
print("Testing Accuracy:  {:.4f}".format(accuracy))

Testing Accuracy:  0.8580
```

Our model achieves a performance of 85.8% on test data.

17. Let's save the model architecture and weights using the following code block:

```
import h5py
model_structure = model.to_json()
with open("Output Files/question_classification_model.json", "w")
as json_file:
    json_file.write(model_structure)
model.save_weights("Output
Files/question_classification_weights.h5")
```

Alongside our method, you can try fine-tuning the various hyperparameters, including the following:

- Number of hidden layers
- Number of neurons in each layer
- Different activation functions
- Learning rate
- Different optimizers
- Batch size
- The number of epochs, among other things

Let's summarize what we have learned from this chapter.

Summary

We made attempts to understand neural networks by looking into the working of a biological neuron and how a similar setup is imitated to build artificial neurons. We looked at the various components of neural networks, including neurons, layers, activation functions, and dropout, among other components. We attempted to answer how a signal flows through a neural network and how it learns. We discussed Keras, which conveniently helps us build our neural networks by providing high-level APIs. Finally, we applied our understanding to solve an NLP problem of classifying questions using an ANN so that the input to the network could comprise embeddings that were built using the TF–IDF vectorization technique.

Now that we have understood the architecture of ANNs and have seen the NLP applications that are based on it, let's take this forward and discuss the interaction of convolutional neural networks with text data in the next chapter.

Applying Convolutions to Text

9

The relationships between words can be derived by looking at their relative placement with respect to each other. These relationships can be viewed as a time series wherein words that are spoken can be thought of as constituting a time series database. On the other hand, we can view their relative positions and derive relationships out of these. These approaches are used by more complex and modern forms of **Artificial Neural Networks (ANNs)**, known as **Convolutional Neural Networks (CNNs)** and **Recurrent Neural Networks (RNNs)**. Here, we will deep dive into CNNs and understand how they help us solve problems for the textual domain.

We will begin by understanding what a CNN is and view the various components in the CNN architecture. We will try and form an understanding of convolutions as an operation, followed by exploring the various layers that comprise a CNN. Based on the knowledge we gain, we will make use of Keras to solve a very challenging NLP problem of detecting sarcasm in text.

The following topics will be covered in this chapter:

- What is a CNN?
- Detecting sarcasm in text using CNNs

Let's get started!

Technical requirements

The code files for this chapter can be found at the following GitHub link: `https://github.com/PacktPublishing/Hands-On-Python-Natural-Language-Processing/tree/master/Chapter11`.

What is a CNN?

CNNs try to capture the spatial relationships in data. These are ideally suited for capturing patterns in images since images have spatial relationships in those pixels that are in the same vicinity contribute to making sense of the object. The nature of convolutions, as we will see in the upcoming sections, is more suited for pictures, so we will try and see how they can be used to make sense of the text and capture spatial relationships in text data as well. First, let's try and understand convolutions and the other components that come with them. After doing this, we will extend our learning to text.

Understanding convolutions

Images are described using pixels. These pixels can have varying values, depending on whether the image is black and white, grayscale, or color. The values in the pixels are reflective of the patterns they might be carrying. As part of convolution, we try and slide (perform a dot product) what we call filters across the image so as to capture patterns from the pixels. Let's look at an example of an image and filter it to understand this better:

Let's say that the preceding image can be represented by the following *4 x 4* pixel matrix, where each value indicates the intensity of that pixel in the image:

6	1	4	3
8	6	7	9
4	3	2	7
1	3	5	4

We can apply the following filter to the image:

1	0	-1
1	0	-1
1	0	-1

Now, using this filter, we want to find the pattern specified in the filter across the image. What we can do here is perform an element-wise multiplication, which is nothing but a dot product across the image. The element-wise multiplication results are summed up for each pass the filter took over the image. By doing this, we get the resultant matrix, which shows the intensity of the pattern or filter at various points in the image. The following matrix is obtained after applying the filter to the image:

5	-9
-1	-8

Let's pick up 5 from the output matrix and understand how we got that.

We performed element-wise multiplication between the entries from *(1, 1)* to *(3, 3)* in the input matrix. This filter looks as follows:

$$(6*1) + (1*0) + (4*-1) + (8*1) + (6*0) + (7*-1) + (4*1) + (3*0) + (2*-1) = 5$$

Similarly, we obtain other values. Here, we assumed that the matrix was indexed starting from *1*.

These values are then passed through activation functions, which can be thought of as being present inside the filter, along with the weights.

The process we described here is primarily what happens in the convolutional layer. Each convolutional layer can have multiple filters, also known as kernels. The values in these filters are weights that the network updates in order to fit those patterns to the data. We used a filter of size *3 x 3* in the example we discussed. These filters can take different dimensions as well.

There is a simple formula governing what we discussed here.

If we have an image of $n \times n$ and a filter of size $f \times f$, then the output would be a matrix of dimensions, as follows:

$$(n-f+1)*(n-f+1)$$

Let's see what we have got in the preceding image:

- A *4 x 4* image
- A *3 x 3* filter

The expected output is as follows:

$$(4-3+1)*(4-3+1)$$

This is exactly what we got – a 2 x 2 output matrix.

As you may have noticed, our filter started with a sidewise movement at *1 x 1*, moved to *1 x 2*, followed by *2 x 1* and *2 x 2*. However, it never went to *1 x 3* or *1 x 4* since we would have overshot our boundaries since the image is *4 x 4*. In simple terms, the leftmost column in our filter was never applied to the rightmost column in our image. In certain situations, the filter pattern in the leftmost column might be present in the rightmost column of our image. Somewhere, it is being provided a fewer number of times to the network as input compared to the rows or columns toward the beginning or internal in the input matrix.

Now, let's learn how to enable our network so that it captures this information.

Let's pad our data

What we essentially do is use a technique called padding, which is like applying pseudo entries containing 0s as the values to the end. This is referred to as zero-padding and as a result of this, the values toward the edges can also be perceived as being internal in the matrix. No value is under-sampled compared to others. It also enables the filter to find patterns at all the places in the image, irrespective of their position.

Here's how the equation changes after applying padding:

- A *4 x 4* image
- Padding of size *1* around the image
- A *3 x 3* filter size

Here's how things change when padding of size *1* is applied all around the image. The image, along with the padding, is now of size *n + 2p* since padding of size *p* is applied to all the outer edges.

The output matrix will now use the following equation:

$$(n+2p-f+1)*(n+2p-f+1)$$

Let's try and understand what the size of the padding we need to apply is. The size will depend on the size of the filters we wish to apply. This generally follows the following equation:

$$p = floor(\frac{f-1}{2})$$

Understanding strides in a CNN

One more thing we should discuss here is that we moved sideways *1* pixel at a time. This value is a configurable parameter referred to as the stride. It helps to determine how an overlap or transition from one pixel to another should be captured.

Here's how we can generalize the equation to accommodate different strides by using strides as a parameter.

Let's say we apply a stride of *s* when performing convolutions. Here, our output matrix will use the following equation:

$$(\frac{n+2p-f}{s}+1) * (\frac{n+2p-f}{s}+1)$$

Along with convolutions, we are using a pooling and a fully connected layer. Next, we'll figure out how these layers work and what happens after filters are applied to the input data.

What is pooling?

In the convolution operation, what we tried to capture were features or patterns in data using some filters. The objective is to keep computation as minimal as possible while capturing as much information as possible. Hence, at all times, we should try and keep only required information that can describe the feature that's been captured. This is performed using pooling layers. The pooling operation helps in downsampling the data so that only relevant information is preserved. We let go of most of the unwanted information so that minimal computation is required. As a result, this helps prevent overfitting. Another thing you may have realized is that even if the data shifts somewhat, pooling allows us to capture the information we need, irrespective of where the feature is located in the data. This property is referred to as **spatial invariance**.

Now, let's try and understand some commonly used pooling techniques. There are various types of pooling that can be performed. Let's take a matrix and see how the various pooling strategies can be applied to it. We will take a stride of 2:

6	1	4	3
8	6	7	9
4	3	2	7
1	3	5	4

Let's take a look at the various types of pooling:

- **Max pooling**: This is the most common pooling technique that can be applied. In max pooling, the maximum value across a filter window is taken up. The max that's pooled out for our matrix with a stride of 2 would be as follows:

8	9
4	7

  We have basically taken the maximum over every 2 x 2 block in the matrix.

- **Average pooling**: This technique, as the name suggests, takes the average across the 2 x 2 blocks. Let's see what the results of average pooling on the matrix would be:

5	6
3	5

  Here, we have rounded our averages to the nearest integer. In most use cases, max pooling outperforms and proves to be more efficient compared to average pooling.

- **Sum pooling**: The next technique we will discuss is sum pooling, where we just take the sum of the values across the filter. The following matrix shows the result that's obtained by using sum pooling. Sum pooling is the least used pooling method among the ones we'll discuss:

21	23
11	18

- **Global max pooling**: This pooling technique comes into effect for temporal data primarily. A global outlook for the data is taken and the maximum value across the input is the output. For an image of *height x width* dimensions, the output of global max pooling would be tensor of size k, where k is the number of filters. Basically, after the dot product is performed between the input and each filter, the maximum value among the resultants is added to the output. The global max pooling operation can replace the flatten option in neural networks.

There are other forms of pooling as well, such as min pooling and L2 pooling, but these are rarely used.

Now that we have made sense of pooling and how it helps us, let's put that last piece of the puzzle into place and look at the fully connected layer.

The fully connected layer

The convolutional and pooling layers help us extract and refine features from the inputs the network receives. We need something in place that can actually classify or do things with these features. The results after performing convolutions and pooling are flattened into a vector that is fed to a **feedforward neural network**, as we discussed in the previous chapter. After sending the feature vector through a neural network containing possibly multiple layers and activation functions, we get our final classification results.

The learning process in a CNN happens similarly to how it does in ANNs, where the weights get updated based on the losses encountered and the corresponding gradient calculation. The details of these are beyond the scope of this book.

So far, we have understood how a CNN captures features from images, but how does all this make sense with text data?

We'll try and answer this question in the next section.

Detecting sarcasm in text using CNNs

The convolutions that we have seen so far capture spatial relations in data as specific images. However, text has more of a sequential relationship, where words in the vicinity of a given account for more information for that particular word rather than any word appearing in a line right above them. Hence, for text data, we look at one-dimensional spatial relationships and leverage the Conv1D layer for this purpose. This is similar to going through n-grams, wherein there would be overlaps in consecutive n-gram windows. The value of n would be specified by the kernel size parameter you provide as input to the Conv1D layer.

The following diagram will help us understand how CNNs can be used to find patterns in text data:

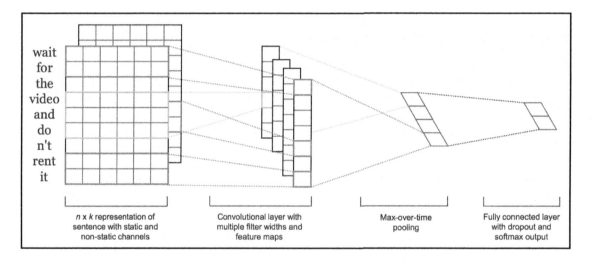

This image has been sourced from the paper, *Convolutional Neural Networks for Sentence Classification* by *Yoon Kim*, which was released in 2014

The preceding diagram shows how word embeddings are sent across as inputs to the convolutional layer, which contains multiple filters. This is followed by max pooling and, finally, the fully connected layer and dropout are applied with the appropriate activation function. We will use a similar architecture in our sarcasm detection study.

Now that we have understood convolutions and how they capture features, we are now well equipped to use them to perform text analysis.

Sarcasm detection is a big NLP challenge in today's world, from print media to commentaries and so on. Let's try and use CNNs to detect sarcasm in text. We will use the word embeddings we discussed in `Chapter 5`, *Word Embeddings and Distance Measurements for Text*, to understand the interaction between CNNs and text. The word embeddings will be sent as input to the CNN-based architecture.

Loading the libraries and the dataset

Perform the following steps to load the required libraries and dataset:

1. First, we need to import the various libraries that we'll be using during the course of this exercise, as follows:

```
import pandas as pd
import numpy as np
import re
import json
import gensim
import math
import nltk
nltk.download('stopwords')
nltk.download('wordnet')
from nltk.corpus import stopwords
from nltk.stem.porter import PorterStemmer
from nltk.stem.snowball import SnowballStemmer
from nltk.stem.wordnet import WordNetLemmatizer
from gensim.models import KeyedVectors
import keras
from keras.models import Sequential, Model
from keras import layers
from keras.layers import Dense, Dropout, Conv1D, GlobalMaxPooling1D
import h5py
```

2. Let's add the following code block to read our data:

```
def parse_data(file):
    for l in open(file,'r'):
        yield json.loads(l)

data = 
list(parse_data('Dataset/Sarcasm_Headlines_Dataset_v2.json'))
df = pd.DataFrame(data)
```

The data that we will be using for this exercise has been taken from `https://www.kaggle.com/rmisra/news-headlines-dataset-for-sarcasm-detection`. This is primarily data from news headlines sourced from The Onion and the Huffington Post.

Performing basic data analysis and preprocessing our data

Next, let's perform some basic data analysis:

1. First, let's understand our data better:

   ```
   df.head(5)
   ```

   Here's what the first five rows in our data will look like:

	is_sarcastic	headline	article_link
0	1	thirtysomething scientists unveil doomsday clo...	https://www.theonion.com/thirtysomething-scien...
1	0	dem rep. totally nails why congress is falling...	https://www.huffingtonpost.com/entry/donna-edw...
2	0	eat your veggies: 9 deliciously different recipes	https://www.huffingtonpost.com/entry/eat-your-...
3	1	inclement weather prevents liar from getting t...	https://local.theonion.com/inclement-weather-p...
4	1	mother comes pretty close to using word 'strea...	https://www.theonion.com/mother-comes-pretty-c...

   The preceding output shows five rows from the data. Our data consists of three columns:

   - `headline` that contains sarcastic and non-sarcastic text.
   - `is_sarcastic`, which is the class variable. This tells us if a headline is sarcastic or not.
   - `article_link`, which contains the link to the original article for the headline.

   Since `article_link` is not of much use in our analysis, we can eliminate the column using the following command:

   ```
   df.pop('article_link')
   ```

   What's the size of our data? Let's take a look:

   ```
   len(df)
   ```

The size of our data can be seen in the following output:

```
28619
```

2. Let's clean and preprocess our data using the same pipeline that we've used throughout this book. Details can be found in `Chapter 3`, *Building Your NLP Vocabulary*. Here, we do the following:

   - Remove special characters.
   - Keep only alphanumeric data.
   - Remove stopwords
   - Lemmatize our data
   - Perform case-folding on the data:

   ```
   headlines = preprocess(df['headline'], lemmatization = True,
   remove_stopwords = True)
   ```

Loading the Word2Vec model and vectorizing our data

Next, let's load the Word2Vec model:

1. First, we will convert the text into numbers using an embedding technique we have already discussed.

   We use Word2Vec to fetch embeddings of our data. For this, we would use the pre-trained Word2Vec model, as we discussed in `Chapter 5`, *Word Embeddings and Distance Measurements for Text*:

   ```
   model = KeyedVectors.load_word2vec_format('GoogleNews-vectors-
   negative300.bin', binary=True)
   ```

2. In the upcoming steps, we will be sending the word vectors, each of size 300, to our CNN model. However, for that, our data dimensions should be standardized. Since our data is from headlines, we will standardize them so that they have a length of 10. If any of the headlines contain more than 10 characters, they will be subsampled to keep the word embeddings for the first 10 characters. If any of the headlines contain less than 10 characters, we will pad them so that they have vectors with values of 0.

We define this using the following parameters:

```
MAX_LENGTH = 10
VECTOR_SIZE = 300
```

Now, let's define a code snippet that will convert the preprocessed headlines into their respective vectors and also pad or subsample the data based on whether the size of the data is greater or less than the maximum length we have defined:

```
def vectorize_data(data):

    vectors = []

    padding_vector = [0.0] * VECTOR_SIZE

    for i, data_point in enumerate(data):
        data_point_vectors = []
        count = 0

        tokens = data_point.split()

        for token in tokens:
            if count >= MAX_LENGTH:
                break
            if token in model.wv.vocab:
                data_point_vectors.append(model.wv[token])
            count = count + 1

    if len(data_point_vectors) < MAX_LENGTH:
        to_fill = MAX_LENGTH - len(data_point_vectors)
        for _ in range(to_fill):
            data_point_vectors.append(padding_vector)

    vectors.append(data_point_vectors)

return vectors
```

Now, let's call our `vectorize_data()` method:

```
vectorized_headlines = vectorize_data(headlines)
```

The `vectorized_headlines` parameter contains our headlines after they've been converted into vectors using Word2Vec.

3. Let's add a small validation to ensure that the 10 vectors are present for each headline, as defined in the MAX_LENGTH parameter:

```
for i, vec in enumerate(vectorized_headlines):
    if len(vec) != MAX_LENGTH:
    print(i)
```

The output of the previous code snippet is null, as expected, indicating that all the headlines have been defined using 10 word vectors.

Splitting our dataset into train and test sets

Follow these steps:

1. We need to split our data into train and test sets. We'll use the following code snippet to do so. We can also verify the size of each component using a simple print statement:

```
X_train = vectorized_headlines[:train_div]
y_train = df['is_sarcastic'][:train_div]
X_test = vectorized_headlines[train_div:]
y_test = df['is_sarcastic'][train_div:]
print('The size of X_train is:', len(X_train),
      '\nThe size of y_train is:', len(y_train),
      '\nThe size of X_test is:', len(X_test),
      '\nThe size of y_test is:', len(y_test))
```

Here's the output of the print statement:

```
The size of X_train is: 20033
The size of y_train is: 20033
The size of X_test is: 8586
The size of y_test is: 8586
```

2. We need to reshape our data in order to convert it into the form expected by our CNN model. The following code snippet helps us with that:

```
X_train = np.reshape(X_train, (len(X_train), MAX_LENGTH,
VECTOR_SIZE))
X_test = np.reshape(X_test, (len(X_test), MAX_LENGTH, VECTOR_SIZE))
y_train = np.array(y_train)
y_test = np.array(y_test)
```

Building the model

Follow these steps:

1. Now that we are ready with our vectorized data, let's get into the CNN part. We begin by defining the hyperparameters of our network:

```
FILTERS=8
KERNEL_SIZE=3
HIDDEN_LAYER_1_NODES=10
HIDDEN_LAYER_2_NODES=5
DROPOUT_PROB=0.35
NUM_EPOCHS=10
BATCH_SIZE=50
```

We have specified the following hyperparameters:

- The number of filters.
- The kernel size, which indicates the number of tokens in the text we will look at.
- The number of nodes to be used in each of the hidden layers.
- The dropout, indicating the percentage of nodes to be dropped at random.
- The number of epochs or number of times we'll see the entire data.
- The batch size, which specifies the number of vectorized headlines to input to the model in each batch.

2. Now, let's define our convolutional layer using the following code snippet:

```
model = Sequential()model.add(Conv1D(FILTERS, KERNEL_SIZE,
padding='same',                                  strides=1,
activation='relu', input_shape =
(MAX_LENGTH, VECTOR_SIZE)))
```

Here, we have defined a stride of 1 and ReLU as the activation function.

We have used one-dimensional convolutions due to the signal dimensionality associated with text data. We'll define our pooling layer next. We will use global max pooling for this:

```
model.add(GlobalMaxPooling1D())
```

3. Next, we will define our feedforward neural network, along with the dropout layers:

```
model.add(Dense(HIDDEN_LAYER_1_NODES, activation='relu'))
model.add(Dropout(DROPOUT_PROB))
model.add(Dense(HIDDEN_LAYER_2_NODES, activation='relu'))
model.add(Dropout(DROPOUT_PROB))
model.add(Dense(1, activation='sigmoid'))
```

We have only defined one node in our output layer since sarcasm detection boils down to a binary classification problem. In the earlier layers, we used ReLU as the activation function and sigmoid in the last layer since we are trying to solve a binary classification problem.

4. Let's take a look at the summary of our model:

```
print(model.summary())
```

Here's our model summary:

```
Model: "sequential_1"
```

Layer (type)	Output Shape	Param #
conv1d_1 (Conv1D)	(None, 10, 8)	7208
global_max_pooling1d_1 (Glob	(None, 8)	0
dense_1 (Dense)	(None, 10)	90
dropout_1 (Dropout)	(None, 10)	0
dense_2 (Dense)	(None, 5)	55
dropout_2 (Dropout)	(None, 5)	0
dense_3 (Dense)	(None, 1)	6

```
Total params: 7,359
Trainable params: 7,359
Non-trainable params: 0
```

We have 7,359 trainable parameters in our model. You can add more layers so as to have more parameters in the model.

5. Now, let's build our model using the `compile` command:

```
model.compile(loss='binary_crossentropy', optimizer='adam',
metrics=['accuracy'])
```

Our loss can be calculated using binary cross-entropy. We have used the Adam optimizer here.

6. We are now ready to train our model. Use the following code block to do so:

```
training_history = model.fit(X_train, y_train, epochs=NUM_EPOCHS,
batch_size=BATCH_SIZE)
```

Here are some snippets from our model training process over time:

```
Epoch 1/10
20033/20033 [==============================] - 2s 88us/step - loss:
0.6523 - acc: 0.6119
Epoch 2/10
20033/20033 [==============================] - 1s 73us/step - loss:
0.5698 - acc: 0.7280
Epoch 3/10
20033/20033 [==============================] - 1s 69us/step - loss:
0.5224 - acc: 0.7642
Epoch 4/10
20033/20033 [==============================] - 1s 73us/step - loss:
0.4946 - acc: 0.7842
Epoch 5/10
20033/20033 [==============================] - 1s 74us/step - loss:
0.4703 - acc: 0.8002
Epoch 6/10
20033/20033 [==============================] - 2s 79us/step - loss:
0.4460 - acc: 0.8124
Epoch 7/10
20033/20033 [==============================] - 2s 75us/step - loss:
0.4302 - acc: 0.8251
Epoch 8/10
20033/20033 [==============================] - 1s 70us/step - loss:
0.4128 - acc: 0.8326
Epoch 9/10
20033/20033 [==============================] - 1s 71us/step - loss:
0.3986 - acc: 0.8410
Epoch 10/10
20033/20033 [==============================] - 1s 71us/step - loss:
0.3850 - acc: 0.8488
```

Evaluating and saving our model

Perform the following steps to evaluate and save the model:

1. Now, we need to evaluate our model on the test data we have, as follows:

```
loss, accuracy = model.evaluate(X_test, y_test, verbose=False)
print("Testing Accuracy:  {:.4f}".format(accuracy))
```

Here's the model's accuracy on the test data:

```
Testing Accuracy:  0.7616
```

You can fine-tune various parameters and add/delete layers to obtain other results.

2. Finally, we need to save our model. The following code snippet will help us with that:

```
model_structure = model.to_json()
with open("Output Files/sarcasm_detection_model_cnn.json", "w") as
json_file:
    json_file.write(model_structure)
model.save_weights("Output Files/sarcasm_detection_model_cnn.h5")
```

With that, we have successfully built a model for sarcasm detection using Word2Vec and CNNs. CNNs can be extended to various flavors. Research into the CNN architecture has led to the rise of standard CNN-based architectures such as VGGNet, **ResNet (Residual Networks)**, Inception networks, and so on, all of which build on the ideas on CNN and experiment with various filter sizes, combine the results from such filters, and so on. You are encouraged to further read about these architectures and try them out.

Summary

In this chapter, we understood a specialized form of neural network, that is, CNNs, which help us capture spatial relationships and patterns in data. We looked at the various components involved in a CNN for encompassing convolutions, pooling, fully connected layers, and their functionality. We understood the way spatial relationships can exist in text and how can we extract them using CNNs. Finally, we applied all our understanding to solve a fairly complex problem regarding detecting sarcasm from text data using CNNs and pre-trained word embeddings from the Word2Vec algorithm.

In the next chapter, we will expand on the knowledge we gained in this chapter and look at another specialized form of neural network known as RNNs. We will look at the improvements we can make to the RNN architecture, which are suited for natural language data as they tend to capture temporal relationships in data.

10
Capturing Temporal Relationships in Text

In the previous chapters, we saw how we could leverage **Artificial Neural Networks (ANNs)** and **Convolutional Neural Networks (CNNs)** to mine patterns in text and apply them to various tasks such as classifying questions and sarcasm detection in news headlines. With ANNs, we primarily saw that inputs are independent of one another. With CNNs, we went one step further and tried to capture spatial relationships in the inputs by trying to extract patterns across a set of tokens together. However, our scope was limited to only a few tokens in the vicinity.

Sentences are essentially sequences of words, and the contextual meaning of a particular word in a sentence may not be derived solely from the immediately surrounding words. It might actually be a result of some words far away in the sentence as well. Also, the sense behind the usage of the word might be a result of a word or words in the past or in the future. In this chapter, we will look at **Recurrent Neural Networks (RNNs)** and improvements built on them to help us capture context and temporal relationships in sequences. In addition to discussing basic RNNs, we will also discuss their various use case-based forms and variants.

We will see how the **Long Short-Term Memory (LSTM)** cell, a memory-based variant of the RNN, helps us solve some issues pertaining to RNNs. An LSTM-based architecture will be used to generate text for a practical use case of generating descriptions. In this exercise, we will try to generate descriptions of hotels for the city of Mumbai, but the same concept can be extended to other similar problems such as music generation and lyrics generation, among other things. Finally, we will look at other variants of the memory-based RNN and discuss **Gated Recurrent Units (GRUs)** and stacked LSTM cells in brief.

The following topics will be covered in this chapter:

- Baby steps toward understanding RNNs
- Vanishing and exploding gradients
- Architectural forms of RNNs
- Giving memory to our networks—LSTMs
- Building a text generator using LSTMs
- Exploring memory-based variants of the RNN architecture

Now that the plot is set up, let's begin!

Technical requirements

The code files for this chapter can be found at the following GitHub link: `https://github.com/PacktPublishing/Hands-On-Python-Natural-Language-Processing/tree/master/Chapter10`.

Baby steps toward understanding RNNs

Sentences can be thought of as combinations of words, such that words are spoken over time in a sequential manner. It is essential to capture this temporal relationship in natural language data. The presence of a word in a lot of scenarios might be influenced by words not necessarily in the immediate neighborhood. Think of the following sentences:

She went on a walk along with her dog.

He went on a walk with his dog.

The sentences are exactly similar except in the usage of words for the identification of gender. The usage of the term *her* or *his* is directly dependent on the term *She* or *He* used toward the beginning of the sentence. With CNNs, we only looked at the immediate proximity of a word. Text data, as we saw in the examples, offers a unique challenge wherein we need to preserve context and have some notion of memory, which can help in making judgments at various points in time. RNNs are the go-to thing in such scenarios as they keep a notion of what happened in the past. Let's dig in and understand their structure in depth.

Every recurrent neuron takes in two inputs—one is the current or external input at that state and the other is called a hidden state, which is basically an output from the previous state. You may have noticed, this is in contrast to **Feedforward Neural Networks (FNNs)**, wherein only the current input is taken into account when predicting anything. These inputs are independent of one another.

In an RNN, the output from a time step t depends on the input at time step t and the hidden state from the time step t-1. The following figure shows the structure of an RNN. It shows the input x_t going into the network at time step t and producing an output y_t for the corresponding time step. The interesting part is the feedback loop, which shows how the hidden state from the previous time step is also provided as input to the recurrent neuron in addition to the input x_t, as can be seen in the following figure:

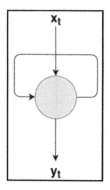

In simple terms, the circle in the middle is basically an FNN, such that at each time step it outputs something based on the input to the network at that time step, along with the hidden state received from the previous time step. Let's look at the unrolled version of this so that things get clearer.

The following figure shows an unrolled version of an RNN wherein each rectangular block containing the circles is the neural network. Two outputs are emitted at every time step, one being the external output and the other being the hidden state, which is fed as input to the subsequent step. A many-to-many RNN is what's shown in the figure. It can be used for tasks such as music and lyrics generation, among other things. There can be multiple variations of RNNs, as we will see later. One thing to be careful about is that we should not think of these as n different neural networks. Instead, each of them is a snapshot of the same FNN with parameters shared across the time steps.

This can be illustrated as shown in the following figure:

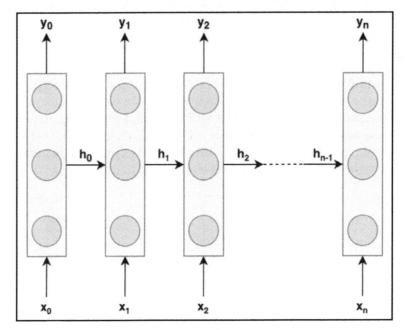

While discussing CNNs, we took a window size, such that the network tried to find patterns among the word vectors for the tokens in each window by sliding over them at once. In contrast with RNNs, we would send across one token as input to the network at each time step. Let's take in the sentence *She went on a walk along with her dog* to understand this better.

The input to the RNN at time step 0 is the embedding for the word *She*. At time step 1, the input is the embedding of the word *went* along with the hidden state output from time step 0. As a result, the contextual information from the word *She* is captured in the hidden state, and it can be used when working with the word *her* at a later time step. This is illustrated in the following figure:

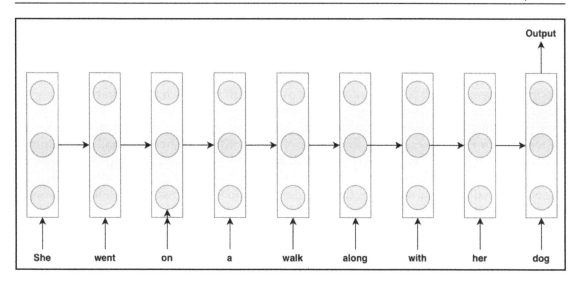

The following figure shows how the sentence would be processed by the RNN over time. In figure 2, we showed a many-to-many RNN, whereas, in figure 3, we have portrayed a many-to-one RNN, which takes in multiple inputs in the form of a sequence of words and provides one output at the last time step. An ideal use case for such an RNN would be a text classification problem where multiple tokens are used to predict the class label for a document.

Forward propagation in an RNN

Forward propagation is pretty straightforward in an RNN, whereby an input vector along with a hidden state vector is taken as input at each time step to produce an output that is further used as the hidden state for the next time step. There can be variations in terms of the output layer where the RNN can produce an output at each time step, as we saw in figure 2, or just the last time step, as we witnessed in figure 3.

Now that we have understood the basic structure of an RNN, let's next understand how it actually learns by backpropagating results through time in the next section.

Backpropagation through time in an RNN

One of the key concepts to understand in RNNs is the process of **backpropagation through time (BPTT)**. We discussed backpropagation in detail in Chapter 8, *From Human Neurons to Artificial Neurons for Text Understanding*, where we saw that for each input, there is an output label based on which the algorithm computes the loss or error in a prediction. The error propagates back to the network and the parameters understand how much they were responsible for the error, and they tune themselves accordingly. There, we had one output for one input. However, as we have discussed, for RNNs each token is an input, and figure 3 shows that we need not have one output per token but a single output for a group of tokens, and, while forward propagating, we use snapshots of the network itself at various time steps. As a result, parameters are shared across the time steps.

How do we backpropagate in this scenario?

As we discussed, since the parameters are shared across the time steps, the gradient calculated at each of the time steps would not only be dependent on the computations of the present time step but also on the previous time steps. Essentially, this can be thought of as the same neurons firing differently across various points in time. At each time step, these neurons can be thought of as unrolling themselves one by one, and, finally, we reach the end state and get our output. The error calculated at the final step can be sent back the same way the network forward-propagated results at the various time steps. We can now see which neuron fired what at each time step, and this can be propagated back to the network in the same way as it's done for normal ANNs. One difference here would be that, as with normal ANNs, we go to the previous layer while backpropagating using the chain rule, but here, we go to the layer in the past time step since we are thinking of each unrolled version of the network we discussed previously as a different network altogether. While going back in time, we make use of the chain rule to do the math. At each step, the gradient with respect to the more recent time step is calculated. All these gradients and changes across each time step are aggregated. Since the weights are shared across time steps, we cannot apply the changes to the weights at each time step since the same weights may have produced different outputs for the changing inputs across time. Here, we try to backpropagate from the final time step to the initial time step, keeping track of the weight corrections at each time step, and, in the end, applying these aggregated changes all at once to the shared weights in our network, as illustrated in the following figure:

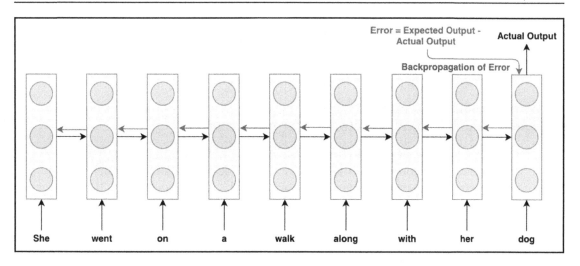

Why did we sum up the weight corrections at each time step and apply them all at once instead of making the corrections at each time step?

This is because, during the forward pass at each time step for an input, the weight was the same. If we computed the gradient at time step *t* and applied the changes to the weights there and then, the weights at time step *t-1* would be different and the error calculation would be wrong since, during the forward pass, we had the same weights at every time step. If we had updated the weights at each time step, we would have simply penalized the weights while computing the gradient for something it did not do at all.

> Sequences need not always be at the word level. Characters can be used as input sequences as well.

We saw how RNNs can help us perform a better analysis of sequential data and capture relationships over time, a case ideally suited to temporal dependencies such as usage of words in a sentence or time-series data, and so on. However, everything comes at a price, and, for RNNs, the problem is related to either vanishing or exploding gradients. Let's understand these in the next section.

> Keras provides a SimpleRNN wrapper **application programming interface (API)** layer that helps us in building RNNs.

Vanishing and exploding gradients

Gradients help us to update weights in the right direction and at the right amount. What if these values become too high or too low?

The weights would not be updated correctly, the network would become unstable, and, consequently, our training of the network as a whole would fail.

The problem of vanishing and exploding gradients is seen predominantly in neural networks with a large number of hidden layers. When backpropagating in such neural networks, the error can become too large or too small whenever we compute the gradient, leading to instability in weight updates.

The exploding gradient problem occurs when large error gradients pile up and cause huge updates to the weights in our network. On the other hand, when the values of these gradients are too small, they effectively prevent the weights from getting updated in a network. This is called the **vanishing gradient problem**. Vanishing gradients can lead to the stopping of training altogether since the weights would not get updated.

We discussed that vanishing and exploding gradients can be troublesome when training neural networks with a lot of hidden layers. Now, imagine training an RNN wherein going back in each time step is like backpropagating the error to the previous layer in an ANN. Now, ANNs are generally a few layers deep. RNNs, on the other hand, can process sequences of sizes greater than 100 easily. As the error flows back in time, it can easily diminish or become huge. While going back in time, these gradients can take in vanishingly small or explodingly large values. The weight corrections for the time steps in the past can diminish when we encounter a vanishing gradient problem; this would feel as if the inputs in those time steps had no effect on the output at all. When encountering an exploding gradient problem, the gradients in the past time steps or for the initial inputs for the RNN can be very large and may subsequently lead to huge weight updates, causing instability in the model.

One technique for preventing the exploding gradient problem is called **gradient clipping**. As part of gradient clipping, the gradient is capped at a maximum value.

Vanishing and exploding gradients are very common problems in RNNs and there are ways to encounter these, as we will see when we discuss LSTMs.

Architectural forms of RNNs

In this section, we will begin by taking a look into what forms an RNN can take, depending on the application it is being built for. After that, we will dive into bidirectional RNNs, and, finally, we'll end this section by looking into how RNNs can be stacked to build deep RNNs.

Different flavors of RNN

RNNs can take multiple forms, depending on the type of use case it is applied to. Let's see the various forms an RNN can take, as follows:

- **One-to-one**: This is the simplest form of RNN and is very similar to a traditional neural network, wherein the RNN takes in a single input and provides a single output. An example of a one-to-one RNN is shown in the following figure:

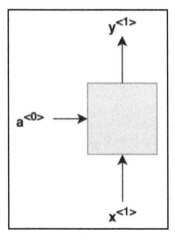

- **One-to-many**: In a one-to-many RNN, the network takes in only one input and produces multiple outputs. Such an RNN is used for solving problems such as music generation, wherein music is generated on the input of a single musical note. An example of a one-to-many RNN is shown in the following figure:

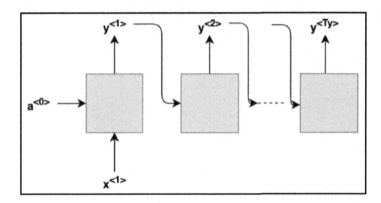

- **Many-to-one**: As the name suggests, this form of RNN takes in multiple inputs and produces one output. This can be used in applications such as sentiment analysis applications, wherein multiple words are fed into the network as input to produce an output depicting the sentiment from the input sentence. An example of a many-to-one RNN is shown in the following figure:

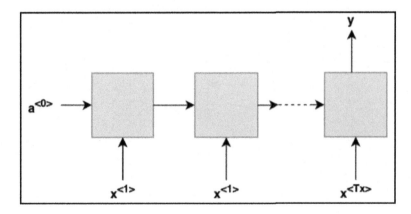

- **Many-to-many**: These RNNs take in multiple inputs and produce multiple outputs. These RNNs can take two forms, depending on whether the size of the input is equal or not to the size of the output. Let's discuss the two forms depending on the variation in the sizes of the input and output, as follows:
    - **Tx = Ty**: This is the many-to-many form in which the size of the input is equal to the size of the output. A common use case for this is named entity recognition, where we try to classify each input token into entity groups such as person names, locations, organizations, and so on. An example of such an RNN is shown in the following figure:

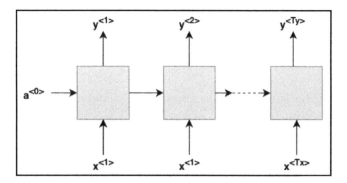

    - **Tx != Ty**: In this form, the size of the input is not equal to the size of the output. Machine translation problems encountered when we try to convert one language to another is an example of such an RNN. Think of the string *Goodbye* in English. We need to convert it into German so as to produce the output, *Auf Wiedersehen*. The input is of size 1, whereas the output is of size 2. Essentially, these RNNs can produce an output string greater than or less than the size of the input string. An example of such an RNN is shown in the following figure:

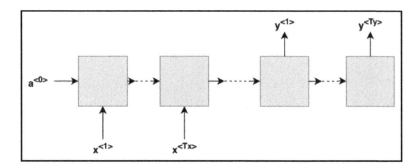

We have learned about the various flavors that an RNN can take based on the application. In the next section, let's see whether RNNs can use information from the beginning as well as the end of some input data.

Carrying relationships both ways using bidirectional RNNs

The RNNs we have discussed so far carry relationships from the beginning to the end using a hidden state.

Is that all we need?

Let's look at the following two sentences:

The boy named Harry became the greatest wizard.

The boy named Harry became a Duke: the Duke of Sussex.

The first sentence talks about the fictional character Harry Potter created by author J.K. Rowling, whereas the second sentence talks about Prince Harry from the United Kingdom. Until we arrive at the word *Harry*, both the sentences are exactly the same: *The boy named Harry*. Using a simple RNN, we cannot infer much about *Harry* from the words before its occurrence. Once we see the latter half of the sentence, we know who's being talked about: the wizard or the prince. It would be good if, using an RNN architecture, we could carry things from the end as well to infer things at a point in time. Bidirectional neural networks help us in this situation.

Bidirectional RNNs, as shown in the following figure, are essentially two independent RNNs such that one of them processes the inputs in the correct time order, whereas the other processes the inputs in the reverse time order. The outputs for these two networks are concatenated at every time step. This formation allows a network to have information from both directions at every time step. An example of such an RNN is shown in the following figure:

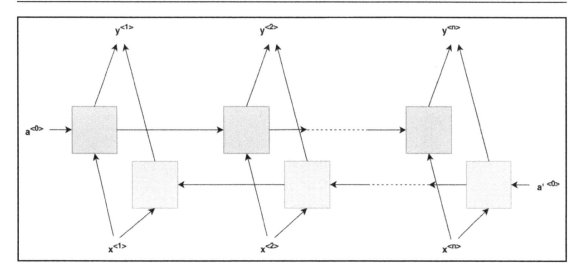

Bidirectional RNNs can be built by wrapping the SimpleRNN API from Keras into the bidirectional wrapper offered by Keras.

Before we begin discussing LSTMs, let's briefly talk about deep RNNs.

Going deep with RNNs

At times, it becomes essential to capture complex relationships in text that can be difficult to capture using a standard RNN. In such scenarios, we resort to stacking RNNs in order to capture the complex relationships. The following figure shows what a deep RNN looks like. The deep RNN shown has three hidden layers. The middle and outer layers do not receive input directly but, instead, they compute their activation outputs using the output at that time step from the previous hidden layer and the output of the previous time step in the same layer. Standard RNNs can be computationally expensive because of the notion of time steps. Deep RNNs take that one step further by stacking these RNNs on top of each other, and a deep RNN with three hidden layers can itself be highly expensive to compute. Also, instead of getting outputs ($y^{<1>}, y^{<2>},..., y^{<n>}$) directly from the RNN, these RNN cell outputs can be fed to FNNs or other neural networks to get outputs from those instead of RNN cells.

An example of a deep RNN is shown in the following figure:

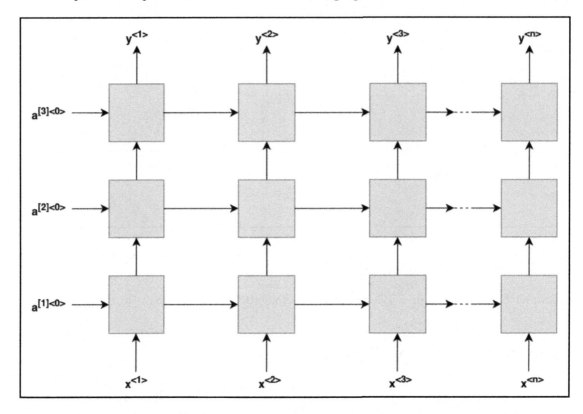

In this section, we looked at what an RNN is and how it uniquely helps capture sequential information and temporal relationships by combining previous outputs with present inputs. We looked at the various forms of RNN and also explored bidirectional RNNs, which help carry information from both directions. The major problem associated with RNNs is that they suffer in terms of capturing and making sense of long-term dependencies. Vanishing and exploding gradients can take a huge toll on the performance of such networks, as we discussed. In the next section, we will look into LSTM, which helps in overcoming the vanishing and exploding gradient problems by providing memory to our networks. Let's begin, then!

Giving memory to our networks – LSTMs

If the word in the eighth position in a sentence has a causal relationship with the word used in the first position, it becomes essential to remember this and apply it in the eighth position. However, RNNs are poor at capturing long-term dependencies because of the vanishing gradient problem, and for such use cases, it is important to remember these relationships. Along with remembering, we also need to understand what should be remembered from the past and what should be forgotten. An LSTM cell will help us with what we discussed here. LSTM cells help in remembering by using a structure called gates that help keep the necessary information in memory as long as it's required.

LSTM cells use the concept of state or memory to retain long-term dependencies. At every stage, it is decided as to what to keep in memory and what to discard. All this is done using gates. Let's look at the working of an LSTM cell in detail (this is shown in the following figure).

Understanding an LSTM cell

The input to an LSTM cell, as with RNNs, is a concatenation of the input for that time step and the output of the previous time step. These values are passed on to the gates in the LSTM cell, which are nothing but an FNN along with some form of activation function. These gates are referred to as the forget gate, input gate, and output gate. The neural networks in each of these gates get trained and allow the signal to flow through them into the memory in different amounts. They decide as to what information should be remembered, forgotten, or discarded at each step. An example of an LSTM cell is shown in the following figure:

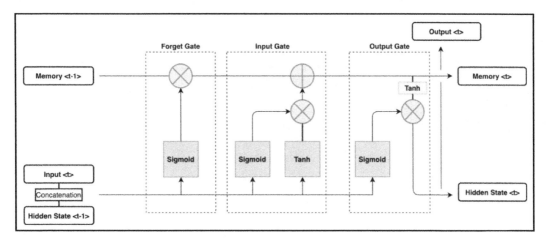

Let's look at the workings of each of these gates individually.

Forget gate

The first juncture in an LSTM cell is the forget gate. The concatenated vector from the present state's input along with the previous state's output goes to the forget gate first. The forget gate's job is to decide how much of the information should be removed from memory.

Hey, hold on a second!

We wanted to remember things using LSTMs, and we are suddenly discarding things from memory.

Yes! That is absolutely right. It is as important to understand what should be forgotten as it is to understand what should be remembered. Think of the following example:

> *Leonardo is a good actor. He won at the Oscars. Brad is a good actor too.*

Initially, our cell should remember that Leonardo is being talked about. However, as soon as we arrive in the third sentence, it should now remember that Brad is being talked about and it should discard information about Leonardo from its memory. Basically, our network should have the ability to forget long-term dependencies as soon as new dependencies worth remembering arrive in our data. Forget gates help us exactly with this by allowing space for new dependencies.

The forget gate is an FNN, as we mentioned, and the activation function applied here is `sigmoid`, which brings the output between 0 and 1, helping us figure out how much of the information must be forgotten. An output of 0 from this gate would indicate that we should forget everything from the past. On the contrary, an output of 1 indicates that the memory state should be retained.

The values from the forget gate are multiplied with the values in the memory cell in order to maintain only relevant information from the past.

We understood why forgetting is important and how the forget gate helps us with it. Now that we have understood how to forget, let's try to understand how to remember next.

Input gate

We should next understand what we need to remember and how much of it should be remembered. This is exactly what the input gate does for us.

Think of the following example:

Ronaldo is a good football player. Messi is another good player.

As soon as we arrive at the second sentence, the forget gate will help us forget about Ronaldo, but it is the job of the input gate to ensure that we now remember about Messi.

The input gate has two parts, which simultaneously help in figuring out what is to be remembered and how much of it needs to be remembered. Let's understand the functioning of the two parts next.

Part 1 in the input gate uses a `sigmoid` activation function, to pinpoint which part of the input values needs to be remembered by creating a sort of a mask with values between 0 and 1. A value of 0 would indicate that nothing is worth remembering from the inputs of this state, whereas a value of 1 would indicate everything from this input state must be remembered.

Part 2 uses a tanh activation function to help us figure out what is potentially the relevant information from the present state that the memory cell can get updated with. This part is also often referred to as the candidate vector since this vector holds the values that the memory cell might get updated with. The output ranges between –1 and 1 from this FNN.

An element-wise multiplication is performed between the outputs from part 1 and part 2. Essentially, what we did is we understood how relevant various components of part 2 are based on the values from part 1. The resultant output is added to the memory vector, thus updating the information in the memory cell.

Now that we have understood how to forget and remember, let's understand how to output next.

Output gate

The job of the output gate is to understand which bits of information in the current step should be sent across as output from the cell. With the forget gate and input gate, we always update our memory cell, but with the output gate, we will make use of our updated memory to see what information should be sent across as output from this LSTM cell.

There are two things that happen at this stage in the LSTM cell, as follows:

1. First, the output gate receives the input that was received by the LSTM cell initially, and these inputs are applied to the FNN in the output gate. Thereafter, the `sigmoid` activation function is applied to the computed values to bring the output in the range of 0 to 1.
2. Second, the memory at this juncture is already updated based on what should have been forgotten and what should have been remembered from the computations performed at the forget gate and input gate stages. This memory state is now passed through a tanh activation function at this stage to bring the values between -1 and 1.

Finally, the tanh-applied values from memory along with the sigmoid-applied values from the output gate are multiplied element-wise to get the final output from this LSTM cell in the network. This value can be taken as output and can also be sent across as the hidden state for the next LSTM time step.

Thus, we have sent across an output at this time step and also put forward the hidden state, which can be sent across to the next time step.

Backpropagation through time in LSTMs

The backpropagation in LSTMs works similarly to RNNs. However, unlike RNNs, we don't encounter the problem of vanishing or exploding gradients, wherein the gradients either become exceedingly small or large. It is primarily because of the memory component we introduced in LSTMs. The weights in the neural networks of each of the gates were used to update the memory cells. These weights get updated, using the various derivatives of the functions applied during the forward pass to update the memory cell. Consequently, the updates on these weights are only dependent on the state of the memory at the previous and present time steps.

We have had enough of theory. Now, let's try to solve an interesting problem of text generation using LSTMs.

Building a text generator using LSTMs

Text generation is a unique problem wherein, given some data, we should be able to predict the next occurring data. Good examples of where text generation is required include predicting the next word in our mobile phone keyboards, generating stories, music, and lyrics and so on. Let's try to build a model that can generate text related to describing hotels for the city of Mumbai, as follows:

1. We will begin by importing the various libraries we will be using during the course of solving this problem, as follows:

```
import nltk
from nltk.corpus import stopwords
import pandas as pd
import numpy as np
import re
from keras.preprocessing.sequence import pad_sequences
from keras.utils import np_utils
from keras.models import Sequential
from keras.layers import Dense, LSTM, Dropout, Embedding
```

2. Now that we have loaded our libraries, let's load our dataset. For this exercise, we will use the Hotels on MakeMyTrip dataset, obtained from https://data.world/promptcloud/hotels-on-makemytrip-com. Run the following code:

```
data = pd.read_csv('Dataset/hotel_data.csv')
```

3. Let's try to see how our data looks, using the `head()` command offered by the pandas library, as follows:

```
data.head(5)
```

Here are a few rows of our data:

	area	city	country	crawl_date	highlight_value	hotel_overview	hotel_star_rating
0	Hardasji Ki Magri	Udaipur	India	2016-06-21	{{facility}}	|Zion Home Stay is located in a city that sets...	1 star
1	Near Nai Gaon	Udaipur	India	2016-06-21	{{facility}}	| Araliayas Resorts is a 3 star hotel located ...	3 star
2	Near Bagore Ki Haveli	Udaipur	India	2016-06-21	{{facility}}	|A 2 star property is located at 24 km from Ma...	2 star
3	Dabok	Udaipur	India	2016-06-21	Airport Transfer|Car rental|Conference Hall|Cu...	|SNP House Airport Hotel And Restaurant is loa...	1 star
4	East Udaipur	Udaipur	India	2016-06-21	{{facility}}	| Hotel Pichola Haveli is situated in the beau...	2 star

4. Let's see information on how many hotels per city are available in our dataset, using the following command:

```
data.city.value_counts()
```

Here's the output:

```
NewDelhiAndNCR          1163
Goa                     1122
Mumbai                   543
Jaipur                   534
Bangalore                512
                        ...
Gajraula                   1
Chamba Uttaranchal         1
Krishnanagar               1
Nagarholae                 1
Bijapur                    1
Name: city, Length: 770, dtype: int64
```

A substantial amount of hotel data from the city of Mumbai in India is available in this dataset. Let's concentrate on generating descriptions for Mumbai hotels.

5. As discussed, let's focus on data for `Mumbai`, as follows:

```
array = ['Mumbai']
data = data.loc[data['city'].isin(array)]
```

You can add in more cities to your array in order to use data from them as well.

6. Let's see whether we were able to filter out data for `Mumbai`, as follows:

```
data.head(5)
```

Here's the output—we were able to filter out data for `Mumbai`, as illustrated in the following figure:

	area	city	country	crawl_date	highlight_value	hotel_overview	hotel_star_rating
294	Charai	Mumbai	India	2016-08-28	Doctor on Call|Front desk|Laundry Service|Park...	Nestled in Mumbai, a city with strong historic...	3
309	Andheri (East)	Mumbai	India	2016-08-28	Air Conditioned|Airport Transfer|Conference Ha...	3 km from Chhatrapati Shivaji International Ai...	2
321	Khar	Mumbai	India	2016-08-28	Airport/Rlwy Stn Transfer|Bar|Conference Hall|...	Location Hotel Royal Garden is situated on Juh...	3
334	Andheri (East)	Mumbai	India	2016-08-28	24 Hour Check in-Icon|24 hour reception|24 hou...	City Guest House is a beautiful property locat...	2
1238	Andheri (East)	Mumbai	NaN	2016-08-22	24 Hour Check in-Icon|24 hour reception|24 hou...	Sai Residency Hotel is situated in the City of...	2

7. Since we are interested in generating hotel descriptions, we will only keep the `hotel_overview` column, since others will not be required in our analysis. We will also follow that up by removing descriptions that are empty. The following code block helps us with this:

```
data = data.hotel_overview
data = data.dropna()
```

8. We now need to preprocess our data and, as part of preprocessing, we need to perform case-folding (converting to lowercase, stopword removal, and keeping only alphabetic data). Also, we will not keep single-character words. The following code block will help us do that:

```
stop = set(stopwords.words('english'))
def stopwords_removal(data_point):
    data = [x for x in data_point.split() if x not in stop]
    return data
```

9. Here's our method for overall data cleansing:

```
def clean_data(data):
    cleaned_data = []
    all_unique_words_in_each_description = []
    for entry in data:
        entry = re.sub(pattern='[^a-zA-Z]',repl=' ',string = entry)
        entry = re.sub(r'\b\w{0,1}\b', repl=' ',string = entry)
        entry = entry.lower()
        entry = stopwords_removal(entry)
        cleaned_data.append(entry)
        unique = list(set(entry))
        all_unique_words_in_each_description.extend(unique)
    return cleaned_data, all_unique_words_in_each_description
```

10. Let's figure out the unique words in our data. This will basically be our vocabulary. We can do this using the following code block:

```
def unique_words(data):
    unique_words = set(all_unique_words_in_each_description)
    return unique_words, len(unique_words)
```

11. Apply the cleansing and unique word-finding methods we described on our data, as follows:

```
cleaned_data, all_unique_words_in_each_description = \
    clean_data(data)
unique_words, length_of_unique_words = \
    unique_words(all_unique_words_in_each_description)
```

We now have the following outcome:

- The `cleaned_data` parameter contains our preprocessed data.
- The `unique_words` parameter contains our list of unique words.
- The `length_of_unique_words` parameter is the number of unique words in the data.

12. Let's look at one cleaned entry from our dataset and also figure out the number of unique words, as follows:

```
cleaned_data[0]
```

Here's a cleaned output block:

```
['nestled',
 'mumbai',
 'city',
 'strong',
 'historical',
 'links',
 'wonderful',
 'british',
 'architecture',
 'museums',
 'beaches',
 'places',...
```

13. Now, let's see the total number of unique words we have, as follows:

```
length_of_unique_words
```

Here is the number of unique words in our data:

```
3395
```

14. Next, we need to build a mapping of words to an index and a reverse mapping from an index to a word, which will help us give out the word given by an index and vice versa, as follows:

```
def build_indices(unique_words):
    word_to_idx = {}
    idx_to_word = {}
    for i, word in enumerate(unique_words):
        word_to_idx[word] = i
        idx_to_word[i] = word
    return word_to_idx, idx_to_word
```

15. Now, let's build our indices using the following code block, which calls the method defined in the previous code block:

```
word_to_idx, idx_to_word = build_indices(unique_words)
```

16. The next step is to prepare our training corpus. As part of this, let's see what we aim to do, given the following excerpt from a sentence:

```
nestled mumbai city
```

The sequences of training data we generate from this three-word sentence would be the following:

- `nestled, mumbai`
- `nestled, mumbai, city`

17. We essentially have generated continuous sequences of a size greater than 1 from the sentence. This is followed by converting the words into their index values, which we build in the last step, as follows:

```
def prepare_corpus(corpus, word_to_idx):
    sequences = []
    for line in corpus:
        tokens = line
        for i in range(1, len(tokens)):
            i_gram_sequence = tokens[:i+1]
            i_gram_sequence_ids = []
            for j, token in enumerate(i_gram_sequence):
                i_gram_sequence_ids.append(word_to_idx[token])
            sequences.append(i_gram_sequence_ids)
    return sequences
```

18. Let's call the defined `prepare_corpus` method next, as follows:

```
sequences = prepare_corpus(cleaned_data, word_to_idx)
max_sequence_len = max([len(x) for x in sequences])
```

Here, we have the following outcome:

- The `sequences` parameter contains all the sequences from our data.
- The `max_sequence_len` parameter conveys the length of the maximum sequence size that was built based on our data.

19. Let's validate what we built just now, as follows:

```
print(sequences[0])
print(sequences[1])
```

We get the following output:

```
[1647, 867]
[1647, 867, 1452]
```

20. Let's see which words are mapped to these indices, using the following code block:

```
print(idx_to_word[1647])
print(idx_to_word[867])
print(idx_to_word[1452])
```

Here's the output:

```
nestled
mumbai
city
```

So, we have correctly built our sequences.

21. Next, let's figure out some metadata about the sequences built, as follows:

```
len(sequences)
```

The total number of sequences we have is the following:

```
51836
```

Now, we will see the size of the longest sequence we have, as follows:

```
max_sequence_len
```

Here's the output:

```
308
```

Now that we have built our sequences, how do we use those to build a text generator?

Let's answer that in this step. What we will do is try and predict the last entry in our sequence, using the rest of the entries from the sequence.

The last entry in the sequences we generated becomes our class or dependent variable, and the entries prior to that become our independent variable. We will build a model that can predict one single value based on the input value of some length.

Let's see our example again.

The first sequence was this:

- `nestled, mumbai`

Here, we would have `nestled` as our *independent* variable and `mumbai` as our *dependent* variable.

Similarly, for the second sequence, we have the following:

- `nestled, mumbai, city`

`nestled, mumbai` forms our *independent* variable or X, and `city` is our *dependent* variable or Y.

Also, since our input size should be consistent for all training samples, we will pad our data to make this the same size. The size of each training sample after padding would be equal to the size of the longest sequence, which we captured in the `max_sequence_len` parameter in *step 18*. Here's the code for splitting our data into independent and dependent variables and also for padding the input samples:

1. Define `build_input_data`, as follows:

```
def build_input_data(sequences, max_sequence_len, \
                     length_of_unique_words):
    sequences = np.array(pad_sequences(sequences, \
                    maxlen = max_sequence_len, padding = 'pre'))
    X = sequences[:,:-1]
    y = sequences[:,-1]
    y = np_utils.to_categorical(y, length_of_unique_words)
    return X, y
```

2. Let's call our `build_input_data` method defined in the previous code block next, as follows:

```
X, y = build_input_data(sequences, max_sequence_len,
length_of_unique_words)
```

3. Now, we are ready with our data, so let's go ahead and define and build our model next, as follows:

```
def create_model(max_sequence_len, length_of_unique_words):
    model = Sequential()
    model.add(Embedding(length_of_unique_words, 10, \
                        input_length=max_sequence_len - 1))
    model.add(LSTM(128))
    model.add(Dropout(0.2))
    model.add(Dense(length_of_unique_words, activation='softmax'))
    model.compile(loss='categorical_crossentropy', \
                  optimizer='adam')
    return model
```

4. Let's bring our model into existence, using the following code block:

```
model = create_model(max_sequence_len, length_of_unique_words)
model.summary()
```

Here's the summary of our model:

```
Model: "sequential_1"
```

Layer (type)	Output Shape	Param #
embedding_1 (Embedding)	(None, 307, 10)	33950
lstm_1 (LSTM)	(None, 128)	71168
dropout_1 (Dropout)	(None, 128)	0
dense_1 (Dense)	(None, 3395)	437955

```
Total params: 543,073
Trainable params: 543,073
Non-trainable params: 0
```

Here are the components in our model:

- The `Embedding` layer, which provides us embeddings for each training sample in our data. The parameters are as follows:
  - `length_of_unique_words` tells the model the size of our vocabulary.
  - `10` indicates that we want a `Dense` embedding of size 10 as output from our model.

- `(input_length=max_sequence_len - 1)` indicates that each training sample to the layer would have a size of `max_sequence_len - 1`.
- The `Embedding` layer is followed by the `LSTM` layer, where we define `128` as the dimensionality of the inner cells in the `LSTM` layer.
- Next, we randomly drop off 20% of neurons from the network using the `Dropout` layer.
- Finally using the `Dense` layer from Keras, we define our `output` layer, where the number of neurons is equal to the size of our `length_of_unique_words` vocabulary. We have translated this problem into a multi-class classification problem, and so the `softmax` activation function is used.
- Finally, we have calculated our loss using the `categorical_crossentropy` technique and used `adam` for optimization.

All these values and techniques are hyperparameters that can be tuned to obtain other results. We can, in fact, try adding more LSTM layers, adding more units to each layer, among others methods.

5. Next, we will train our model, as follows:

```
model.fit(X, y, batch_size = 512, epochs=100)
```

We have used the following:

- A batch size of `512`
- A number of epochs of `100`

These are, again, hyperparameters that can be tuned, as follows:

```
Epoch 1/100
51836/51836 [==============================] - 157s 3ms/step -
loss: 6.9315
Epoch 2/100
51836/51836 [==============================] - 152s 3ms/step -
loss: 6.5816
Epoch 3/100
51836/51836 [==============================] - 156s 3ms/step -
loss: 6.5273
Epoch 4/100
51836/51836 [==============================] - 159s 3ms/step -
loss: 6.4325
Epoch 5/100
51836/51836 [==============================] - 157s 3ms/step -
```

```
loss: 6.2997
Epoch 6/100
51836/51836 [==============================] - 157s 3ms/step -
loss: 6.2009
```

This can be viewed in its entirety in the code files of this book.

Now that we have trained our model, let's put it to the test and see how it works.

The following code block helps us to generate the next_words number of words based on the input we provide to the method:

```
def generate_text(seed_text, next_words, model, max_seq_len):
    for _ in range(next_words):
        cleaned_data = clean_data([seed_text])
        sequences= prepare_corpus(cleaned_data[0], word_to_idx)
        sequences = pad_sequences([sequences[-1]], maxlen=max_seq_len-1, \
                                 padding='pre')
        predicted = model.predict_classes(sequences, verbose=0)
        output_word = ''
        output_word = idx_to_word[predicted[0]]
        seed_text = seed_text + " " + output_word
    return seed_text.title()
```

Let's try the method we defined to generate some text, as follows:

```
print(generate_text("in Mumbai there we need", 30, model,
max_sequence_len))
```

Here's our generated text:

```
In Mumbai There We Need Located Mumbai City Mumbai Charismatic Electrifying
Open Hearted Mumbai Bombay City Dreamers Stalwarts Common Man Guests Visit
Majestic Places Like Gateway India Chhatrapati Shivaji International
Airport Km Chhatrapati Shivaji International
```

Let's try for another input, as follows:

```
print(generate_text("The beauty of the city", 30, model, max_sequence_len))
```

Here's our generated text:

```
The Beauty Of The City World Pilgrimage Employment Opportunities Park Km
Chhatrapati Shivaji International Airport Km Chhatrapati Shivaji
International Airport Km Vile Parle Railway Station Km Kamgar Hospital Bus
Stand Prominent Tourist Spots Like Tikuji
```

We can see that the generated text captures a lot of meaningful information and is in line with the initial text we provided it as input. It does a decent job.

Hyperparameter tuning, along with building more complex and larger models, can help in generating better results.

Now that we have generated some beautiful text using LSTMs, let's go ahead and look at some other memory-based variants built on the foundation of RNNs.

Exploring memory-based variants of the RNN architecture

Before we close this chapter, we will briefly look at GRUs and stacked LSTMs.

GRUs

As we saw, LSTMs are huge networks and they have a lot of parameters. Consequently, we need to update a lot of parameters that are highly computationally expensive. Can we do better?

Yes! GRUs can help us with it.

GRUs use only two gates instead of three, as we used in LSTMs. They combine the forget gate and the candidate-choice part in the input gate into one gate, called the **update gate**. The other gate is the reset gate, which decides how the memory should get updated with the newly computed information. Based on the output of these two gates, it is decided what to send across as the output from this cell and how the hidden state is to be updated. This is done via using something called a **content state**, which holds the new information. As a result, the number of parameters in the network is drastically reduced.

You can read more about GRUs here: https://en.wikipedia.org/wiki/Gated_recurrent_unit.

Stacked LSTMs

Stacked LSTMs follow an architecture similar to deep RNNs, which we discussed earlier in this chapter. During the discussion on deep RNNs, we mentioned that stacking RNN layers one above the other helps the network capture highly complex patterns and relationships. The same idea is used when building stacked LSTMs, which can help us capture highly complex patterns from data. Each LSTM layer in a stacked LSTM model has its own gates and memory vector.

We saw that LSTMs can be highly computationally expensive because of the huge number of parameters involved. Stacked LSTMs take that forward as the number of parameters becomes even more dependent upon the number of LSTM layers involved. Hence, stacked LSTMs are very expensive in terms of computational requirements.

Summary

In this chapter, we began with understanding RNNs and how they enable us to capture sequential dependencies in data. We made an effort to understand the problem of the RNN in terms of it not being able to capture long-term dependencies because of vanishing and exploding gradient issues. We also looked at various forms an RNN can take, depending on the type of problem it is being used to solve. We followed that up with a brief discussion on some variants of RNNs by talking about bidirectional and deep RNNs. We went a step further next and looked at how the vanishing and exploding gradient problem can be solved by adding memory to the network and, as a result, we had an expansive discussion on LSTM, which is a variant of an RNN, using the concept of a memory state. We tried to solve the problem of text generation, where we used LSTMs to generate text for describing hotels in the city of Mumbai. Finally, we had a brief discussion on other memory variants of an RNN, including GRUs and stacked LSTMs.

We will take the knowledge from this chapter forward into the next chapter, where we look into sequence-to-sequence modeling using encoders and decoders. We will also discuss some of the state-of-the-art methodologies in **Natural Language Processing** (**NLP**) and talk about attention and transformers, among other topics.

State of the Art in NLP

11

Applications based on **Natural Language Processing** (**NLP**) have witnessed a tremendous rise in the last few years. New use cases are coming along every day and in order to keep pace with the ever-evolving demand, the need of the hour is to research, innovate, and build efficient solutions for solving the complex problems we face. Innovation in the field of NLP over the years has made it possible to solve some of the most challenging problems, such as language translation and building chatbots, among others.

In this chapter, we will take a look at some of the recent advancements in the field of NLP. We will begin by developing an understanding of **Sequence-to-Sequence** (**Seq2Seq**) models and discuss encoders and decoders in the process. We will use this new knowledge to build a French-to-English translator using Seq2Seq modeling. After that, we will have a look at the attention mechanism, one of the key recent developments. The attention mechanism has not only improved the inferencing abilities of existing architectures but has also paved the way for the development of other amazingly efficient architectures such as Transformers and **Bidirectional Encoder Representations from Transformers** (**BERT**), which we will look at toward the end of this chapter.

The following topics will be covered in this chapter:

- Seq2Seq modeling
- Translating between languages using Seq2Seq modeling
- Let's pay some attention
- Transformers
- BERT

Technical requirements

The code files for this chapter can be found at the following GitHub link: `https://github.com/PacktPublishing/Hands-On-Python-Natural-Language-Processing/tree/master/Chapter11`.

Seq2Seq modeling

Before we begin with Seq2Seq modeling, I would like to share an anecdote that I witnessed at Bengaluru Airport in India. A traveler from China was trying to order a meal at one of the airport restaurants and the butler was unable to comprehend Mandarin. An onlooker stepped in and used Google Translate to convert the English being spoken by the store owner into Mandarin and vice versa. Seq2Seq modeling has helped build applications such as Google Translate, which made the conversation between these folks possible.

When we try to build chatbots or language translating systems, we essentially try to convert a sequence of text of some arbitrary length into another sequence of text of some unknown length. For example, the same chatbot might respond with one word or multiple words depending on the conversational prompts coming from the other party involved in the conversation. We do not always respond with text of the same length. We saw this as one of the *many-to-many* variants of the RNN architecture in `Chapter 10`, *Capturing Temporal Relationships in Text*. This architecture is referred to as Seq2Seq modeling, where we try to convert one sequence into another.

Let's consider the example of language translation.

The English sentence *how are you doing?* is written as *como estas?* in Spanish. These two sentences are of different lengths. Let's think of another example: *can we do this?* in English is represented as *podemos hacer esto?* in Spanish. Even though both English sentences have four words in them, their Spanish counterparts are of differing lengths. When building such systems, we try to map an input sequence to an output sequence that can be of varying lengths.

Okay. Now that we understand what Seq2Seq modeling is, how do we do it? We use two building blocks, called **Encoders** and **Decoders** and shown in the following diagram, to build our Seq2Seq modeling systems:

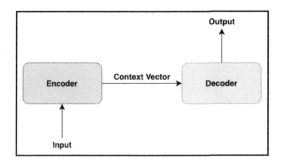

These encoders and decoders can be built using **Long Short Term Memory (LSTM)** networks, **Gated Recurrent Units (GRU)**, and so on. Let's take a deep dive and understand how these encoders and decoders enable us to build these systems.

Encoders

The encoder is the first component in the encoder-decoder architecture. The input data is fed to the encoder and it builds a representation of the input data. This low-dimensional representation of the input data is referred to as the **context** vector. Some literature also refers to it as the **thought** vector. The context vector tries to capture the meaning in the input data. Essentially, it tries to build an embedding for the input data.

The encoder can be built using RNNs, LSTMs, GRUs, or bidirectional RNNs, among others. We saw that RNN-based architectures hold the context of the inputs that they saw in the hidden state. Hence, the last hidden state will hold the context of the entire sentence. The hidden state from the last timestep is what we want. It is our context vector since it has seen all the input and has maintained the context of all the input words.

Let's think of a natural language translation task where we want to convert sentences from English into French. As an example, let's pick the sentence, *Learning Natural Language Processing* and see what the encoder does to convert it into its French equivalent:

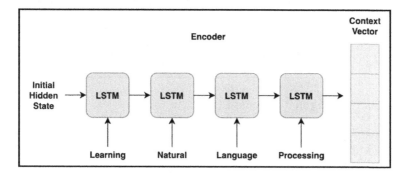

The preceding diagram illustrates an encoder built using LSTM that develops a context vector for the English sentence, *Learning Natural Language Processing*. The output from the encoder is the context vector, which contains two parts:

- The hidden state from the last timestep of the encoder
- The memory state of the LSTM for the input sentence

The `return_state` parameter in Keras' LSTM implementation allows us to include the last hidden state in our output.

Now that we have successfully built a context vector of our input sentence, the next step is to decode this context vector and build our French sentence using it. Let's do that next.

Decoders

We got an embedding of our input sentence, *Learning Natural Language Processing,* using the encoder. The next part is to decode this context vector and build its French representation, *Apprendre le traitement du langage naturel*. The following diagram shows how a decoder, built using LSTM, gets trained to do this:

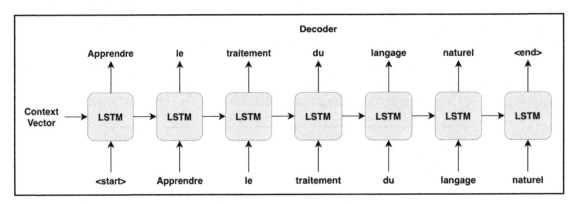

Let's understand its working in depth next.

Up to now, we have seen that the initial hidden state for any RNN-based architecture is a randomly initialized vector. However, with decoders, the input is the context vector that we received as output from the encoder.

Okay, we have now understood that the initial hidden state should not be a randomly initialized vector, but rather, the context vector. However, we still don't understand what the input to the decoder should be.

The input to the decoder at the first timestep is a token that indicates the start of the sentence, <start>. Using this <start> token, the decoder now has the task of learning to predict the first token of the target sentence. However, the working of the decoder is a little different for the learning and inferencing phases explained next. Let's understand that now.

The training phase

During the training phase, the decoder has passed the target sequence as input along with the context vector. The input to the decoder at timestep *0* is the <start> token. At timestep *1* the input to the decoder is the predicted token or the first token of the target sequence, and so on. The decoder's job here is to learn that when provided a context vector and an initial <start> token, it should be capable of producing a set of tokens.

The inference phase

During the inference stage, we don't know what the target sequence should be and it is the decoder's job to predict this target sequence. The decoder will receive the context vector and the initial token using which it should be able to predict the first token. Thereon, it should be able to predict the second token, using the first predicted token and the hidden state from the first timestep, and this should continue as such. Essentially, the input at timestep *t* is the predicted output of the previous timestep *t-1*, as shown in the diagram in the *Decoders* section. The input at timestep *1* is Apprendre, which is actually the predicted output from the previous timestep. The same pattern follows for the rest of the decoder's work.

Okay, we've got a fair idea of the initial hidden state and also how the decoder learns and predicts, but we need to stop sending outputs at the point when predictions occur. How do we do that?

Whenever the output from a decoder state is a token indicating the end of the sentence, <end>, or we have reached a pre-defined maximum length of output or target sequence, we get a signal that the decoder has completed its job of building the output sequence and we need to stop here.

Simple LSTMs on both ends enabled us to convert one sequence of data to another using just a context vector in between them. This approach for Seq2Seq generation can be used to build chatbots, speech recognition systems, natural language translation systems, and so on. Now that we have a sound theoretical understanding of Seq2Seq generation systems, let's try and do some practical stuff with it in the next section.

Translating between languages using Seq2Seq modeling

English is the most spoken language in the world and French is an official language in 29 countries. As part of this exercise, we will build a French-to-English translator. Let's begin:

The dataset used here is sourced from http://www.manythings.org/anki/

1. As with any other exercise, we begin by importing the libraries that we need to build our French-to-English translator:

```
import pandas as pd
import string
import re
import io
import numpy as np
from unicodedata import normalize
import keras, tensorflow
from keras.models import Model
from keras.layers import Input, LSTM, Dense
```

2. Now that we have imported our libraries, let's read the dataset using the following code block:

```
def read_data(file):
    data = []
    with io.open(file, 'r') as file:
        for entry in file:
            entry = entry.strip()
            data.append(entry)
    return data
data = read_data('dataset/bilingual_pairs.txt')
```

3. Let's figure out some basics of our data.

We can see some of the data points using the following code block:

```
data[139990:140000]
```

Here's the output:

```
['Never choose a vocation just because the hours are short.\tNe
choisissez jamais une profession juste parce que les heures y sont
courtes.',
 "No other mountain in the world is so high as Mt. Everest.\tAucune
montagne au monde n'atteint la hauteur du Mont Everest.",
 "No sooner had he met his family than he burst into tears.\tÀ
peine avait-il rencontré sa famille qu'il éclata en sanglots.",
 "Nothing is more disappointing than to lose in the finals.\tRien
n'est plus décevant que de perdre en finale.",
 "Now that he is old, it is your duty to go look after him.\tÀ
présent qu'il est vieux, c'est ton devoir de veiller sur lui.",
 "Now that you've decided to quit your job, you look
happy.\tMaintenant que vous avez décidé de quitter votre emploi,
vous avez l'air heureux.",
 "Now that you've decided to quit your job, you look
happy.\tMaintenant que tu as décidé de quitter ton emploi, tu as
l'air heureux.",
 "Now that you've decided to quit your job, you look
happy.\tMaintenant que vous avez décidé de quitter votre emploi,
vous avez l'air heureuse.",
 "Now that you've decided to quit your job, you look
happy.\tMaintenant que tu as décidé de quitter ton emploi, tu as
l'air heureuse.",
 'Please drop in when you happen to be in the
neighborhood.\tVeuillez donc passer quand vous êtes dans le coin
!']
```

The output shows that our data consists of tab-separated English-French sentence pairs.

Let's see the size of our dataset next:

```
len(data)
```

The size of our data is as follows:

```
145437
```

We use the first 140,000 English-French sentence pairs for this exercise:

```
data = data[:140000]
```

4. We saw that our dataset contains tabs that separate the English-French sentence pairs, so we need to split them into different English and French lists:

```
def build_english_french_sentences(data):
    english_sentences = []
    french_sentences = []
    for data_point in data:
        english_sentences.append(data_point.split("\t")[0])
        french_sentences.append(data_point.split("\t")[1])
    return english_sentences, french_sentences
english_sentences, french_sentences = 
build_english_french_sentences(data)
```

5. Now that we have different lists holding our English and French sentences, let's clean our data next.

The `clean_sentence` method defined in the following code block takes care of processing individual sentences:

```
def clean_sentences(sentence):
    # prepare regex for char filtering
    re_print = re.compile('[^%s]' % re.escape(string.printable))
    # prepare translation table for removing punctuation
    table = str.maketrans('', '', string.punctuation)
    cleaned_sent = normalize('NFD', sentence).encode('ascii', \
                                                'ignore')
    cleaned_sent = cleaned_sent.decode('UTF-8')
    cleaned_sent = cleaned_sent.split()
    cleaned_sent = [word.lower() for word in cleaned_sent]
    cleaned_sent = [word.translate(table) for word in cleaned_sent]
    cleaned_sent = [re_print.sub('', w) for w in cleaned_sent]
    cleaned_sent = [word for word in cleaned_sent if \
                    word.isalpha()]
    return ' '.join(cleaned_sent)
```

The previous function does the following:

- Normalizes characters
- Removes punctuation
- Performs case-folding
- Removes non-printable characters
- Keeps only alphabetic words

Next, we will build a function, `build_clean_english_french_sentences()`, and get it to clean our English and French sentences by calling the function we defined in the previous code block on individual sentences:

```
def build_clean_english_french_sentences(english_sentences,
french_sentences):
    french_sentences_cleaned = []
    english_sentences_cleaned = []
    for sent in french_sentences:
        french_sentences_cleaned.append(clean_sentences(sent))
    for sent in english_sentences:
        english_sentences_cleaned.append(clean_sentences(sent))
    return english_sentences_cleaned, french_sentences_cleaned

english_sentences_cleaned, french_sentences_cleaned =
build_clean_english_french_sentences(english_sentences,
french_sentences)
```

6. We cleaned our data in the previous step. The following steps are where we build our vocabulary and also add tokens that convey the start and end of a sequence, as required by our decoder.

In Chapter 10, *Capturing Temporal Relationships in Text*, when we had built a text generator, we used words as our vocabulary. However, we will go down to the character level in order to build our vocabulary in this exercise, as defined in the following code block:

```
def build_data(english_sentences_cleaned,
french_sentences_cleaned):
    input_dataset = []
    target_dataset = []
    input_characters = set()
    target_characters = set()
    for french_sentence in french_sentences_cleaned:
        input_datapoint = french_sentence
        input_dataset.append(input_datapoint)
        for char in input_datapoint:
            input_characters.add(char)
    for english_sentence in english_sentences_cleaned:
        target_datapoint = "\t" + english_sentence + "\n"
        target_dataset.append(target_datapoint)
        for char in target_datapoint:
            target_characters.add(char)
    return input_dataset, target_dataset, \
            sorted(list(input_characters)), \
            sorted(list(target_characters))
```

```
input_dataset, target_dataset, input_characters, target_characters
= build_data(english_sentences_cleaned, french_sentences_cleaned)
```

The method defined in the previous code block helped us to do the following:

- Add \t to our target data to convey the start of a sentence to our decoder.
- Add \n to our target data to convey the end of a sentence to our decoder.
- Prepare a list of unique input and output characters. Our model will try and predict at the character level for this exercise.

7. We developed our input and target vocabularies in the previous step. Let's see what unique input and output characters are in store for us with the following command:

```
print(input_characters)
```

Here's our set of input characters:

```
[' ', 'a', 'b', 'c', 'd', 'e', 'f', 'g', 'h', 'i', 'j', 'k', 'l',
'm', 'n', 'o', 'p', 'q', 'r', 's', 't', 'u', 'v', 'w', 'x', 'y',
'z']
```

Next, let's see our target characters with the following command:

```
print(target_characters)
```

Here's our set of target characters:

```
['\t', '\n', ' ', 'a', 'b', 'c', 'd', 'e', 'f', 'g', 'h', 'i', 'j',
'k', 'l', 'm', 'n', 'o', 'p', 'q', 'r', 's', 't', 'u', 'v', 'w',
'x', 'y', 'z']
```

Notice that in addition to our input characters, the target character dataset has \t and \n tokens, which help the decoder to understand the start and end of a target sequence.

8. Our input and output vocabulary may not be the same for tasks such as natural language translation. In fact, at times, our character set may not be the same either. For example, we might be trying to translate between English and Hindi, which have different character sets altogether.

Apart from the difference in vocabulary, we should also be aware that our input sequence and target sequence may not be of the same size.

The English sentence *how are you today, dear?* is written in French as *comment tu vas aujourd'hui mon cher.*

The number of words in the preceding sentences is different. If we go to the character level, then we can see that the number of characters in both sentences is very different as well.

Let's take another very similar English sentence, *how are you today?* which is written in French as *comment vas-tu aujourd'hui?* Now, if we make a comparison between the two examples we discussed, their English and French counterparts have differing lengths.

We next want to find out some metadata about our data, in terms of the following:

- The size of the input and target vocabularies (basically, the size of the input and target character sets)
- The maximum length of input and output character sequences

The following code block helps us to do that:

```
def build_metadata(input_dataset, target_dataset, \
                   input_characters, target_characters):
    num_Encoder_tokens = len(input_characters)
    num_Decoder_tokens = len(target_characters)
    max_Encoder_seq_length = max([len(data_point) for data_point \
                                  in input_dataset])
    max_Decoder_seq_length = max([len(data_point) for data_point \
                                  in target_dataset])
    print('Number of data points:', len(input_dataset))
    print('Number of unique input tokens:', num_Encoder_tokens)
    print('Number of unique output tokens:', num_Decoder_tokens)
    print('Maximum sequence length for inputs:', \
          max_Encoder_seq_length)
    print('Maximum sequence length for outputs:', \
          max_Decoder_seq_length)
    return num_Encoder_tokens, num_Decoder_tokens, \
           max_Encoder_seq_length, max_Decoder_seq_length

num_Encoder_tokens, num_Decoder_tokens, max_Encoder_seq_length,
max_Decoder_seq_length = build_metadata(input_dataset,
target_dataset, input_characters, target_characters)
```

Here's the metadata we acquired using the previous code block:

```
Number of data points: 140000
Number of unique input tokens: 27
Number of unique output tokens: 29
Maximum sequence length for inputs: 117
Maximum sequence length for outputs: 58
```

Here's what we get from the metadata:

- We have 140,000 unique English-French sentence pairs in our dataset.
- The number of unique input tokens/characters is 27.
- The number of unique target tokens/characters that we'll try and predict is 29.
- Our longest input character sequence is 117 characters long.
- Our longest target character sequence is 58 characters long.

9. A very important step is to build mappings from characters to indices and vice versa. This will help us to do the following:

- Represent our input characters using their corresponding indices
- Convert our predicted indices into their corresponding characters when making predictions

The following code block helps us with this:

```
def build_indices(input_characters, target_characters):
    input_char_to_idx = {}
    input_idx_to_char = {}
    target_char_to_idx = {}
    target_idx_to_char = {}
    for i, char in enumerate(input_characters):
        input_char_to_idx[char] = i
        input_idx_to_char[i] = char
    for i, char in enumerate(target_characters):
        target_char_to_idx[char] = i
        target_idx_to_char[i] = char
    return input_char_to_idx, input_idx_to_char, \
           target_char_to_idx, target_idx_to_char

input_char_to_idx, input_idx_to_char, target_char_to_idx,
target_idx_to_char = build_indices(input_characters,
target_characters)
```

10. Next, we build our data structure based on the metadata we obtained in *step 8* using the following code block:

```
def build_data_structures(length_input_dataset,
max_Encoder_seq_length, max_Decoder_seq_length, num_Encoder_tokens,
num_Decoder_tokens):
    Encoder_input_data = np.zeros((length_input_dataset, \
        max_Encoder_seq_length, num_Encoder_tokens), dtype='float32')
    Decoder_input_data = np.zeros((length_input_dataset, \
```

```
    max_Decoder_seq_length, num_Decoder_tokens), dtype='float32')
    Decoder_target_data = np.zeros((length_input_dataset, \
    max_Decoder_seq_length, num_Decoder_tokens), dtype='float32')
    print("Dimensionality of Encoder input data is : ", \
        Encoder_input_data.shape)
    print("Dimensionality of Decoder input data is : ", \
        Decoder_input_data.shape)
    print("Dimensionality of Decoder target data is : ", \
        Decoder_target_data.shape)
    return Encoder_input_data, Decoder_input_data, \
        Decoder_target_data

Encoder_input_data, Decoder_input_data, Decoder_target_data =
build_data_structures(len(input_dataset), max_Encoder_seq_length,
max_Decoder_seq_length, num_Encoder_tokens, num_Decoder_tokens)
```

Here's the output that shows the shape of the data structures we built:

- The dimensionality of the encoder input data is `(140000, 117, 27)`.
- The dimensionality of the decoder input data is `(140000, 58, 29)`.
- The dimensionality of the decoder target data is `(140000, 58, 29)`.

Note the following points:

- The dimensionality of the input data is `(140000, 117, 27)`:
  - The first dimension caters to the number of data points we have: 140,000.
  - The second dimension caters to the maximum length of our input sequence: 117.
  - The third dimension caters to the number of unique inputs we can have or the size of our input character set: 27.
- The dimensionality of the decoder input and decoder target data is `(140000, 58, 29)`:
  - The first dimension caters to the number of data points we have: 140,000.
  - The second dimension caters to the maximum length of our target sequence: 58.
  - The third dimension caters to the number of unique inputs we can have or the size of our target character set: 29.

11. Now that we have our data structure ready, it is time to add some data to it:

```
def add_data_to_data_structures(input_dataset, target_dataset,
Encoder_input_data, Decoder_input_data, Decoder_target_data):
    for i, (input_data_point, target_data_point) in \
            enumerate(zip(input_dataset, target_dataset)):
        for t, char in enumerate(input_data_point):
            Encoder_input_data[i, t, input_char_to_idx[char]] = 1.
        for t, char in enumerate(target_data_point):
            # Decoder_target_data is ahead of Decoder_input_data by
            # one timestep
            Decoder_input_data[i, t, target_char_to_idx[char]] = 1.
            if t > 0:
                # Decoder_target_data will be ahead by one timestep
                # and will not include the start character.
                Decoder_target_data[i, t - 1, \
                                target_char_to_idx[char]] = 1.
    return Encoder_input_data, Decoder_input_data, \
            Decoder_target_data

Encoder_input_data, Decoder_input_data, Decoder_target_data =
add_data_to_data_structures(input_dataset, target_dataset,
Encoder_input_data, Decoder_input_data, Decoder_target_data)
```

We have used the character-to-indices mapping and converted some entries in our data structure to 1, which indicates the presence of a particular character at a specific position in each of the sentences.

If you carefully examine our work so far, notice that the last dimension (27 in the encoder input data structure and 29 in the decoder input or decoder target) is a one-hot vector, which indicates which entry is present for that particular position in our data.

One final thing to note is that when building the decoder target data, we do not include anything for the <start> token, and it is also ahead by one timestep for the same reasons that we discussed when talking about decoders in the previous section.

Our decoder target data is the same as the decoder input data, except that it is offset by one timestep.

12. We are ready with our data, so let's define the hyperparameters for our model:

```
batch_size = 256
epochs = 100
latent_dim = 256
```

13. It's time we bring our encoder into existence using the following code block:

```
Encoder_inputs = Input(shape=(None, num_Encoder_tokens))
Encoder = LSTM(latent_dim, return_state=True)
Encoder_outputs, state_h, state_c = Encoder(Encoder_inputs)
Encoder_states = [state_h, state_c]
```

We have set `return_ state` as `True` so that the decoder returns us the last hidden state and memory, which will form the context vector.

`state_h` and `state_c` represent our last hidden state and memory cell, respectively.

However, how does our encoder learn?

The encoder's job is to provide a context vector where it captures the context or thought in the input sentence. However, we do not have any explicit target context vector defined against which to compare the encoder's performance. The encoder learns from the performance of the decoder, which happens further down the line. The decoder's error flows back and that's how the backpropagation in the encoder works and it learns.

14. Let's define the second part of our architecture, the decoder, using the following code block:

```
Decoder_inputs = Input(shape=(None, num_Decoder_tokens))
Decoder_lstm = LSTM(latent_dim, return_sequences=True, \
                    return_state=True)
Decoder_outputs, _, _ = Decoder_lstm(Decoder_inputs, \
                        initial_state=Encoder_states)
Decoder_dense = Dense(num_Decoder_tokens, activation='softmax')
Decoder_outputs = Decoder_dense(Decoder_outputs)
```

As we discussed, during training, the decoder is provided both the input data and the target data and is asked to predict the input data with an offset of 1. This helps the decoder to understand, given a context vector from the encoder, what it should be predicting. This method of learning is referred to as **teacher forcing**.

The initial state for the decoder is `Encoder_states`, which is our context vector retrieved from the encoder in *step 13*.

A dense layer is part of the decoder where the number of neurons is equal to the number of tokens (characters in our case) present in the decoder's target character set. The dense layer is coupled with the softmax output that helps us to get the normalized probabilities for every target character. It predicts the target character with the highest probability.

The `return_sequences` parameter in the decoder LSTM helps us to retrieve the entire output sequence from the decoder. We want an output from the decoder at every timestep and that is why we set this parameter to `True`. Since we used the dense layer along with the softmax output, we get a probability distribution over our target characters for every timestep, and as mentioned already, we pick the character with the highest probability. We judge the performance of our decoder by comparing its output produced at every timestep.

15. We have defined our encoder and decoder, but how do they come together to build our model? The way we define our model here will be a little different from what we had in our previous examples. We use the Keras Model API to define the various inputs and outputs we will use at various stages. The Model API is provided by `Encoder_input_data; Decoder_input_data` is the input to our model, which will be used as the encoder and decoder inputs; and `Decoder_target_data` is used as the decoder output. The model will try to convert `Encoder_input_data` and `Decoder_input_data` into `Decoder_target_data`:

```
model = Model(inputs=[Encoder_inputs, Decoder_inputs],
outputs=Decoder_outputs)
```

Let's compile and train our model next:

```
model.compile(optimizer='rmsprop', loss='categorical_crossentropy')
model.summary()
```

Here's the summary of our model:

```
Model: "model_1"
```

Layer (type) Connected to	Output Shape	Param #
input_1 (InputLayer)	(None, None, 27)	0
input_2 (InputLayer)	(None, None, 29)	0

```
lstm_1 (LSTM)                        [(None, 256), (None, 290816
input_1[0][0]

lstm_2 (LSTM)                        [(None, None, 256),  292864
input_2[0][0]
lstm_1[0][1]
lstm_1[0][2]

dense_1 (Dense)                      (None, None, 29)     7453
lstm_2[0][0]
================================================================
================================
Total params: 591,133
Trainable params: 591,133
Non-trainable params: 0
```

Let's train our model now:

```
model.fit([Encoder_input_data, Decoder_input_data],
          Decoder_target_data,
          batch_size=batch_size,
          epochs=epochs,
          validation_split=0.2)
```

We train on 80% of our data and validate on the remaining 20% of the data.

Here's some sample output from our model training:

```
Train on 112000 samples, validate on 28000 samples
Epoch 1/100
112000/112000 [==============================] - 114s 1ms/step -
loss: 0.9022 - val_loss: 1.5125
Epoch 2/100
112000/112000 [==============================] - 115s 1ms/step -
loss: 0.7103 - val_loss: 1.3070
Epoch 3/100
112000/112000 [==============================] - 115s 1ms/step -
loss: 0.6220 - val_loss: 1.2398
Epoch 4/100
112000/112000 [==============================] - 116s 1ms/step -
loss: 0.5705 - val_loss: 1.1785
Epoch 5/100
112000/112000 [==============================] - 116s 1ms/step -
loss: 0.5368 - val_loss: 1.1203
```

```
Epoch 6/100
112000/112000 [==============================] - 116s 1ms/step -
loss: 0.5117 - val_loss: 1.1075
Epoch 7/100
112000/112000 [==============================] - 115s 1ms/step -
loss: 0.4921 - val_loss: 1.1037
Epoch 8/100
112000/112000 [==============================] - 114s 1ms/step -
loss: 0.4780 - val_loss: 1.0276
```

16. We save our model next using the following code:

```
model.save('Output
Files/neural_machine_translation_french_to_english.h5')
```

17. Hey! Are we done? We trained our model to convert a French sentence into English. However, we did not figure out how we would infer from the model we built.

We do this with the following code block. This performs the following steps:

1. We send the input sequence to the encoder and retrieve the initial decoder state.
2. After this, we send the start token (\t in our case) and the initial decoder state to the decoder to get the next target character as the output.
3. We then add the predicted target character to the sequence.
4. Repeat from *step 2* until we obtain the end token or reach the maximum number of predicted characters:

```
Encoder_model = Model(Encoder_inputs, Encoder_states)

Decoder_state_input_c = Input(shape=(latent_dim,))
Decoder_state_input_h = Input(shape=(latent_dim,))
Decoder_states_inputs = [Decoder_state_input_h, \
                         Decoder_state_input_c]

Decoder_outputs, state_h, state_c = Decoder_lstm(Decoder_inputs, \
initial_state=Decoder_states_inputs)
Decoder_states = [state_h, state_c]
Decoder_outputs = Decoder_dense(Decoder_outputs)

Decoder_model = Model([Decoder_inputs] + Decoder_states_inputs,
                      [Decoder_outputs] + Decoder_states)
```

Let's define the `decode_sequence()` method that uses the encoder-decoder model we built:

```
def decode_sequence(input_seq):

    states_value = Encoder_model.predict(input_seq)

    target_seq = np.zeros((1, 1, num_Decoder_tokens))
    target_seq[0, 0, target_char_to_idx['\t']] = 1.

    stop_condition = False
    decoded_sentence = ''
    while not stop_condition:
        output_tokens, h, c = Decoder_model.predict([target_seq]+ \
                                                    states_value)
        sampled_token_index = np.argmax(output_tokens[0, -1, :])
        sampled_char = target_idx_to_char[sampled_token_index]
        decoded_sentence += sampled_char

        if (sampled_char == '\n' or len(decoded_sentence) > \
            max_Decoder_seq_length):
                stop_condition = True

        target_seq = np.zeros((1, 1, num_Decoder_tokens))
        target_seq[0, 0, sampled_token_index] = 1.
        states_value = [h, c]
    return decoded_sentence
```

A simple call to the `decode_ sequence()` method defined in the preceding code will help us with our inference.

18. Let's translate some French to English now:

```
def decode(seq_index):
    input_seq = Encoder_input_data[seq_index: seq_index + 1]
    decoded_sentence = decode_sequence(input_seq)
    print('-')
    print('Input sentence:', input_dataset[seq_index])
    print('Decoded sentence:', decoded_sentence)
```

Let's make a few calls to the `decode` method to perform our translations. The `decode` method takes in the index of a French data point and converts it into English.

Let's decode the 55,000[th] French sentence from our data first:

```
decode(55000)
```

Here's the output:

```
Input sentence: hier etait une bonne journee
Decoded sentence: yesterday was a little too far
```

The next call will decode the 10,000th sentence:

```
decode(10000)
```

Here's the output:

```
Input sentence: jen ai ras le bol
Decoded sentence: im still not sure
```

The next method call decodes the 200th sentence:

```
decode(200)
```

Here's the output:

```
Input sentence: soyez calmes
Decoded sentence: be careful
```

Let's decode the 3,000th sentence next:

```
decode(3000)
```

Here's the output:

```
Input sentence: je me sens affreusement mal
Decoded sentence: i feel like such an idiot
```

We will decode the 40,884th sentence next:

```
decode(40884)
```

Here's the output:

```
Input sentence: je pense que je peux arranger ca
Decoded sentence: i think i can do it
```

Comparisons with Google Translate results showed that our model performs a decent job. Also, the output contains proper English words. However, we have only tried to decode sentences from the input data.

The model can further be built at the word level instead of training it at the character level, as we did in this exercise.

We can try tuning our hyperparameters and see if we make improvements with our translation results.

Now that we have successfully built a Seq2Seq model, in the upcoming sections, let's understand some more architectures that were developed in the recent past.

Let's pay some attention

The encoder-decoder architecture that we studied in the previous section for neural machine translation converted our source text into a fixed-length context vector and sent it to the decoder. The last hidden state was used by our decoder to build the target sequence.

Research has shown that this approach of sending the last hidden state turns out to be a bottleneck for long sentences, especially where the length of the sentence is longer than the sentences used for training. The context vector is not able to capture the meaning of the entire sentence. The performance of the model is not good and keeps deteriorating in such cases.

A new mechanism called the **attention mechanism**, shown in the following diagram, evolved to solve this problem of dealing with long sentences. Instead of sending only the last hidden state to the decoder, all the hidden states are passed on to the decoder. This approach provides the ability to encode an input sequence into a sequence of vectors without being constrained to a single fixed-length vector as was the case earlier. The network is now freed from having to use a single vector to represent all the information in the source sequence. During the decoding stage, these sequences of vectors are weighted at every timestep to figure out the relevance of each input for predicting a particular output. This does not mean a one-to-one mapping between the input token and output token. The target word is predicted during the decoding stage using the sum of the weighted context hidden states along with the previous target words:

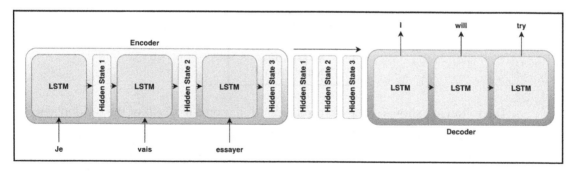

Let's understand in depth how the attention mechanism works. The computation of the context vector is performed using the following steps:

1. The first step is to obtain the hidden states, as shown in the following diagram:

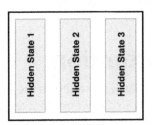

2. Now we have the decoder hidden state vector d. Each of the encoder's hidden state vectors, along with the decoder hidden state vector, are passed to a function such as a dot product, as shown in the following diagram. The function returns a score for each of these input hidden states for that particular timestep t. This score reflects the importance of the various input tokens toward the prediction of the token at timestep t:

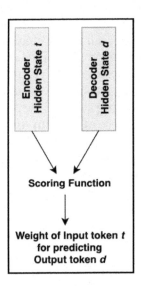

The following shows some example attention scores for each of the hidden states:

11	5	5

The scores represent the importance of each hidden state for that particular timestep.

3. Scores obtained are normalized using the softmax function:

$$a_{ij} = \frac{exp(b_{ij})}{\sum_{k=1}^{T_x} exp(b_{ik})}$$

In the preceding equation, the following is the case:

- T_x represents the length of the input.
- b_{ij} is the influence of input token j in the prediction of the output i. We get this value in the previous step.

The softmax score, a_{ij}, is nothing but the probability of the output token y_i being aligned to the input x_j.

The softmax scores for each of the hidden states are as follows:

0.995	0.0025	0.0025

4. The input hidden state vectors are multiplied by their corresponding softmax scores:

$$a_{ij} \times h_j$$

5. The weighted input hidden state vectors are summed up, and this summed vector represents our context vector for timestep t, as shown in the following diagram:

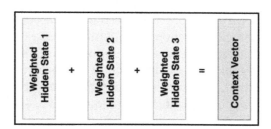

The formula for the summed vectors that represent our context vector for timestep t can be written as follows:

$$contextVector_i = \sum_{j=1}^{T_x} a_{ij} \times h_j$$

The context vector at timestep i carries the overall weight of each of the input tokens in determining the output at timestep i.

The aforementioned steps are repeated for each timestep at the decoder end. Also, this approach does not perform a one-to-one mapping between the encoder input at timestep t and the decoder output at timestep t. Instead, the learning involved allows the architecture to align tokens in the input sequence at various positions to tokens in the output sequence, possibly at different positions.

 The paper *Neural Machine Translation by Jointly Learning to Align and Translate (Bahdanau et al.)* discussed the concept of the attention mechanism, and is available at https://arxiv.org/pdf/1409.0473.pdf.

The attention mechanism has significantly improved the ability of neural machine translation models.

Do we stop at attention?

No, let's take this forward and understand how Transformers came into existence and how we can use them to advance even further.

Transformers

The encoders and decoders we built up to now used RNN-based architectures. Even while discussing attention in the previous section, the attention-based mechanism was used in conjunction with RNN architecture-based encoders and decoders. Transformers approach the problem differently and build the encoders and decoders by using the attention mechanism, doing away with the RNN-based architectural backbones. Transformers have shown themselves to be more parallelizable and require a lot less time for training, thus having multiple benefits over the previous architectures.

Let's try and understand the complex architecture of Transformers next.

Understanding the architecture of Transformers

As in the previous section, Transformer modeling is based on converting a set of input sequences into a bunch of hidden states, which are then further decoded into a set of output sequences. However, the way these encoders and decoders are built is changed when using a Transformer. The following diagram shows a simplistic view of a Transformer:

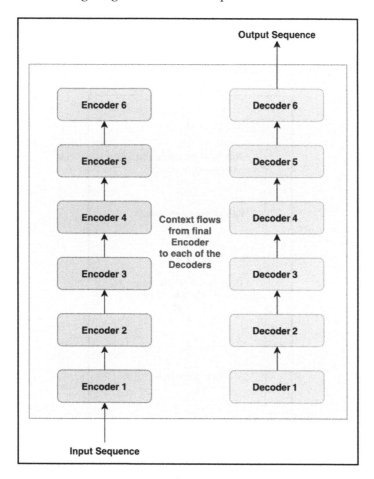

Let's now look at the various components involved.

Encoders

Transformers are composed of six encoders stacked on top of each other. All these encoders are identical but do not share weights between them. Each encoder is composed of two components: a self-attention layer that allows the encoder to look into other tokens in the input sequence as it tries to encode a specific input token, and a position-wise feedforward neural network.

A residual connection is applied to the output of each of these aforementioned components, followed by layer normalization. We will look at residuals and layer normalization in the upcoming sections. The input flowing into the first encoder is an embedding for the input sequence. The embeddings can be as simple as one-hot vectors, or other forms such as Word2Vec embeddings, and so on. The input to the other encoders is the output of the previous encoder, as shown in the following diagram:

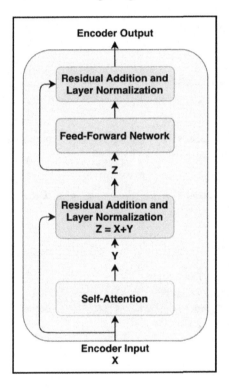

The preceding diagram shows a detailed flow of the signal into the encoder and out from it.

Decoders

Like the encoder, the Transformer architecture has six identical decoders stacked on top of each other. The following diagram shows the architecture of one of these stacked decoders. In addition to the self-attention and feedforward neural network present in the encoder, the decoder has an additional attention layer, which allows it to pay attention to the relevant parts in the output of the encoder stack.

The self-attention layer in the decoder is modified to allow positions to only attend to previous positions and not attend to subsequent positions. This is referred to as masked attention. Also, from the previous sections of this chapter, we remember that output embeddings are offset by 1 position in the decoder. This offsetting, along with the masked attention, ensures that while predicting for a particular position, we only have outputs from the previous positions available to us.

Like encoders, the output from each sub-layer here is applied with residual connects and layer normalization:

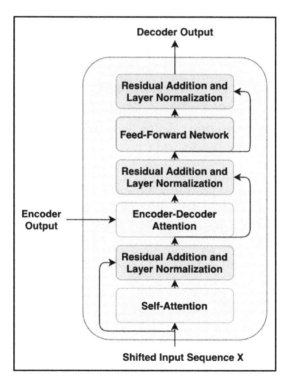

Now that we have understood the architecture for the Encoder and Decoder, let's look into the attention mechanism used in the Transformer architecture.

Self-attention

When trying to build a representation for a position in an input sequence, the self-attention mechanism allows the model to look at other positions/input tokens in the same sequence, which can help the model to build a better representation for this input position. This helps the model to infuse information about other tokens in the sequence that are relevant for a particular token when building the representation for this token.

Let's consider an example to understand this:

> *The man is eating a lot of mangoes and they seem to be his favorite fruit.*

In this sentence, when the embedding of the word *they* is being built, the self-attention mechanism allows the representation of *they* to be highly influenced by the word *mangoes* and associates *they* with *mangoes*. Similarly, when the embedding for *his* is built, self-attention allows it to be associated with the word *man*.

How does self-attention work mathematically?

Self-attention tries to find the embedding of a token based on the other tokens in the sequence. For this purpose, it uses three abstractions, namely the key, query, and value vectors. Let's understand all of this now:

1. In the first step, the input embedding is multiplied by three matrices, Wk, Wq and Wv. This multiplication produces three embeddings, namely the *key*, *query*, and *value* embeddings. The model learns the three matrices, Wk, Wq, and Wv, during the training process as a result of backpropagation. The dimensionality of each of these embeddings is the same:

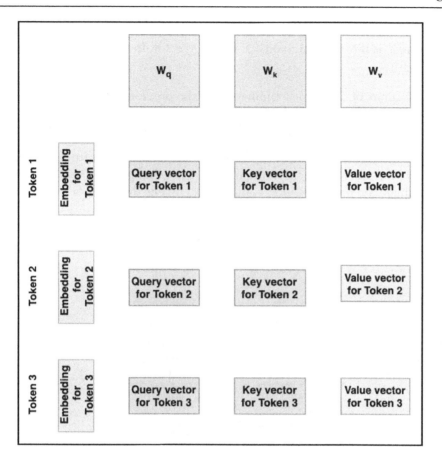

2. The second step is to understand how important the other tokens are for every individual token in the sequence. Let's say that we are computing the embedding for the second token. Our job is to figure out how important each token in the sequence is for the second token. This is found by performing the dot product between the query vector of the second token with the key vector of all tokens individually. This process can be thought of as the second token asking other tokens how important they are to it by sending the tokens its query vector, and the other tokens responding with their key vectors, and finally the dot product between them, giving the importance. Since the key and query vectors are of the same dimension, the output of this is a single number. Let's refer it as the *score*.

3. In the third step, the scores obtained for each word are divided by root $\sqrt{d_k}$, where d_k is the dimensionality of the key vector. In the standard Transformer, this is 64.

    The softmax of the scores obtained from the previous step is performed next. This leads to stable gradients. The intuition here is that the higher the score for a token, the more important it is for the token whose representation is being computed.

4. Next, the value vector of each token is multiplied by its softmax score. As a result, the tokens that are more important for that position will have their values dominate the representation compared to tokens that are not that relevant for that specific position:

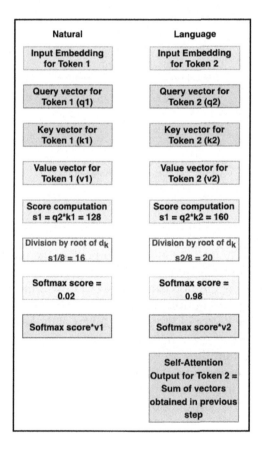

5. Finally, the obtained value vectors from the previous step are summed up to obtain the new representation for the token under consideration. The preceding diagram shows how the self-attention representation of the token *Language* is constructed for the input sequence *Natural Language*.

However, the Transformer doesn't just use a single attention head. The model uses multiple attention heads, which allows the model to focus on multiple different positions, instead of just one. The outputs from the multiple attention heads are concatenated and projected to provide the final values.

A small note on masked self-attention

Another important thing to understand is that inside the decoder, the multi-head attention mechanism is masked, meaning that it is only allowed to use representations from positions toward the left. This is because, while predicting the token for a particular position, only tokens from the left side would be available. As a result, all embeddings from the right are multiplied with 0 to mask them and the representations created can only be influenced by the tokens on the left.

Before we move on, let's quickly look into the encoder-decoder attention layer. This layer allows the decoder to capture contextual and positional information coming in from the encoder; basically, the information contained in the input sequence.

Now that we have discussed attention in detail, let's understand the rest of the components in the Transformer architecture shown in the following diagram:

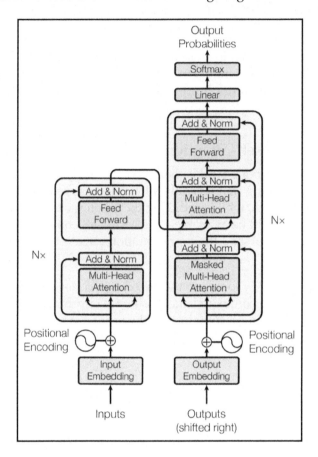

 The Transformer model from the original paper Attention is all you need (available at https://arxiv.org/pdf/1706.03762.pdf)

Feedforward neural networks

Each encoder and decoder in the Transformer stack has a fully connected two-layer feedforward neural network with a ReLU activation function in between them. This feedforward neural network maps embeddings from one space to another space and the dimensionality of the inputs and outputs to these networks are the same.

Residuals and layer normalization

Residuals are applied to the output of each layer in a Transformer, thus enabling it to retain some information present in the previous layer. After the application of the residuals, the output is fed into layer normalization, which applies normalization across the features. The values calculated as a result are independent of the other examples.

Positional embeddings

Another interesting feature that we should try and capture is the sequential order of tokens in terms of the absolute position of the tokens, as well as features such as the relative distance between tokens. The Transformer architecture achieves this by using a positional embedding vector, which is added to the input embeddings. This model learns a pattern for this vector, which enables it to understand the aforementioned features.

How the decoder works

We have already seen the decoder's architecture and discussed the working of its internal components. Let's quickly try and throw light on the inputs to the decoder and the outputs from it. The output from the final encoder is transformed into a set of attention vectors represented by K and V. These outputs are received by the encoder-decoder attention layer in each of the decoders. Also, the decoder receives the embeddings for the tokens of the output sequence shifted by one, as happens in normal decoder operation. The decoder keeps producing outputs until it reaches the <end> token.

The linear layer and the softmax function

The decoder produces a vector of values as its output. Now, these values are projected to our vocabulary using the linear layer whose dimensionality is the same as the size of our vocabulary. The obtained values are normalized and a probability distribution is produced over the vocabulary using the softmax function, and the highest value is taken to be the output for that timestep. The index for the highest value is mapped to the vocabulary to obtain the predicted token.

The error computation happens in a similar way and the loss is backpropagated to the network for it to learn.

Transformer model summary

So, to summarize the architecture and training that we've looked at so far, the encoder receives an input embedding along with a position embedding, which are summed together and passed to a series of stacked encoders composed of self-attention and feedforward neural networks. The output from the last encoder is passed to the decoder, which itself contains the self-attention and feedforward neural network layers. In addition, the decoder contains an encoder-decoder attention layer, which helps it to understand the information coming in from the encoder. The decoder produces a vector as output, which is applied to a dense layer followed by softmax, and the word with the highest probability is taken as output for the given timestep. The error is computed based on the performance of the Transformer in predicting the output and the result is backpropagated for the network to learn.

BERT

The embeddings that we created when discussing Word2vec and fastText were static in the sense that no matter what context a word was being used in, its embedding would be the same.

Let's consider an example to understand this:

> *Apple is a fruit*
>
> *Apple is a company*

In both these sentences, no matter what context *Apple* is being used in, the embeddings for the word would be the same. Instead, we should work on building techniques that can provide representations of a word based on the current context it is being used in.

Moreover, we need to build semi-supervised models that could be pre-trained on a broader task and later be fine-tuned to a specific task. The knowledge built while solving the broader task could be applied to solve a different but related task. This is referred to as **transfer learning**.

BERT catered to both our aforementioned problems in its own unique way. Researchers at Google developed BERT and made the methodology that they used to build BERT open source, along with the pre-trained weights.

Let's look into the architecture for BERT next.

The BERT architecture

We read about Transformers in the previous section. BERT was built using the encoder component of the Transformer architecture. BERT is nothing but a set of stacked encoders, as we saw in the previous section. The researchers built two variants of the BERT model, as summarized in the following table:

	BERTBASE	BERTLARGE
Number of encoder blocks	12	24
Hidden layer size	768	1024
Self-attention heads	12	16
Total parameters	110M	340M

The Transformer architecture upon which BERT was built had six stacked encoders. The hidden layer size (that is, the number of hidden units in the feedforward layers) was 512 and it had 8 self-attention heads. The details of the various layers in BERT are the same as what we discussed while talking about Transformers.

The BERT model input and output

Since the BERT model was built such that it could be fine-tuned to a wide variety of tasks, its inputs and outputs needed to be designed carefully such that they could handle single-sentence tasks such as text classification, along with two-sentence tasks such as question answering. The BERT model was built with a vocabulary of 30,000 words and used the WordPiece tokenizer for tokenization.

The BERT model input is explained in the following diagram. Let's try and understand each of the input components in the diagram.

The first input token to the BERT model is the [CLS] token, where CLS stands for **Classification**. It is a special token and the final hidden state output from the BERT model corresponding to this token is used for classification tasks. The [CLS] token carries the output for single-sentence classification tasks.

For two-sentence tasks, the sentences are brought in together and separated by a special [SEP] token, which helps to differentiate between the sentences. In addition to the [SEP] token, an additional learned embedding is added to the token to represent whether it belongs to the first sentence or the second.

As with Transformers, a positional embedding is added to the tokens for the same reason we discussed regarding Transformers.

Hence, the input for every token to the BERT model is a sum of the *token embeddings, positional embeddings,* and *segment embeddings:*

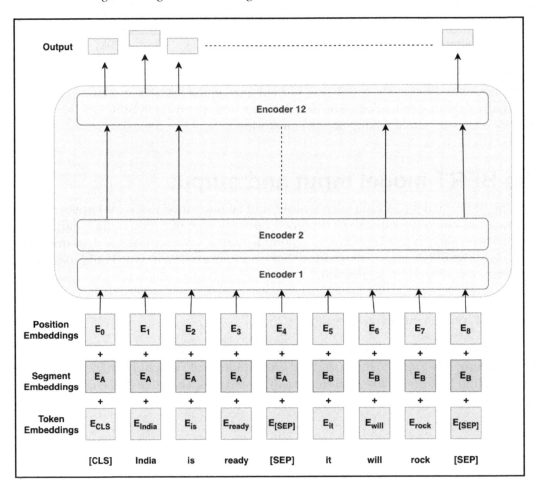

Now that we have talked about the inputs, let's briefly discuss the outputs. The BERT model at every position on a vector of size 768 is BERT$_{BASE}$ and a vector of size 1024 is the BERT$_{LARGE}$ model. These output vectors can be used differently depending on the fine-tuning task to be solved.

So, we've understood that BERT is such a cool thing, along with its architecture and the inputs and outputs for the model. One thing that we haven't got a sense of yet is how it was trained. Let's investigate this now.

How did BERT the pre-training happen?

The BERT model was pre-trained using two unsupervised tasks, namely the **masked language model** and **next-sentence prediction**. Let's look at the details of these next.

The masked language model

Conditional language models prior to BERT were built using either the left-to-right approach or the right-to-left approach. We know that a bidirectional approach that can look both backward and forward would be more powerful than a unidirectional model. However, since with Transformers we have a multilayered context, the bidirectional approach would allow each token to indirectly see itself.

How do we build a model that can be conditioned using both the left and right contexts?

The developers of BERT decided to use masks to allow bidirectional conditioning. The BERT model picks 15% of the tokens at random and masks them. Next, it tries to predict these masked tokens. This process is referred to as **Masked Language Modeling (MLM)**.

However, there is a problem with this approach: the [MASK] token will not be present during fine-tuning. In order to resolve this, among the 15% of the tokens chosen at random, let's say if the *ith* token is chosen, then the following would happen:

- It would be replaced with the [MASK] token 80% of the time (80% of 15% = 125 of the times).
- It will be replaced with a random token 10% of the time (10% of 15% = 1.5% of the time).
- It is kept unchanged for the remaining 10% of the time (10% of 15% = 1.5% of the time).

Next-sentence prediction

During the MLM task, we did not really work with multiple sentences. However, with BERT, the thought process was to accommodate the possibility of tasks involving a pair of sentences, as often happens in question answering tasks, where the relationships between multiple sentences need to be captured. In order to do this, BERT resorted to working with a next-sentence prediction task. A pair of sentences, *A* and *B*, are input to the model such that 50% of the time, sentence *B* would actually be the next sentence in the corpus after sentence *A* where the labeling used would be *IsNext*, and it would not be the next sentence 50% of the time, where the labeling would be *NotNext*. In the next-sentence prediction task, the model would be asked to predict whether sentence *B* is actually the next sentence following sentence *A* or not.

Now we know how the BERT pre-training worked, let's look into the fine-tuning of BERT next and understand how its outputs can be utilized.

For the purpose of pre-training, we used as our datasets the Book Corpus, comprising 800 million words, and English Wikipedia, comprising 2.5 billion words.

BERT fine-tuning

The pre-trained weights developed using the ways we've discussed can now be fine-tuned to cater to a number of tasks. Let's look at those next.

For single classification tasks, the output for position 1 carries information about the classification label. The vector from the first position is sent across to a feedforward neural network, followed by the application of the softmax function, which returns the probability distribution for the number of classes involved in the task, as shown in the following diagram:

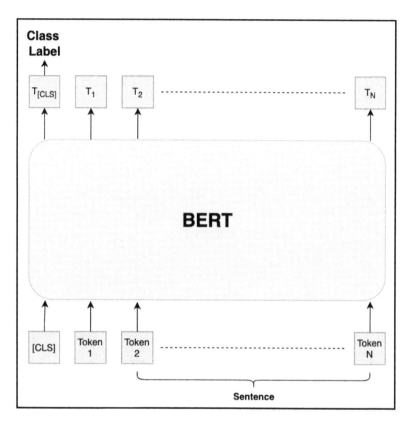

Similarly, for sentence-pair text classification tasks, such as whether the second sentence follows the first sentence in a corpus or the second sentence is the answer to the first sentence (a question), these are classification tasks where we need to respond with a *Yes* or *No* answer. Such tasks can also make use of the first output vector to determine the results, as shown in the following diagram:

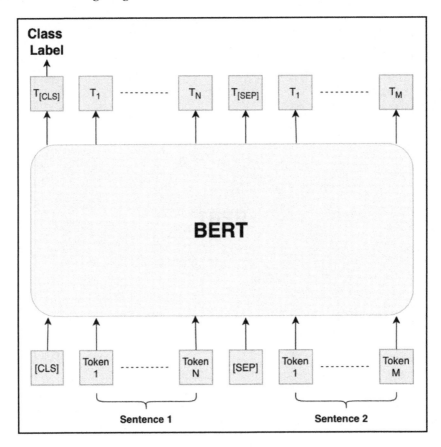

Named Entity Recognition (**NER**)-like tasks want an output for each input token. For example, in an NER task, we may require the model to figure out whether the tokens in a sentence refer to a person, location, date, and so on. Each token must say which entity it is catering to from the ones we've mentioned. This is a Seq2Seq task where the size of the input should be equal to the size of the output. The BERT model outputs a vector for each position. Now, each of these position outputs can be fed to a neural network to figure out the named entity for a particular token. This is illustrated in the following diagram:

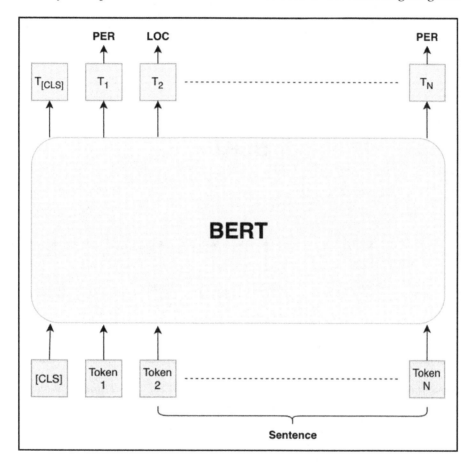

Similarly, the BERT model can be fine-tuned for other tasks such as question answering, as shown in the following diagram:

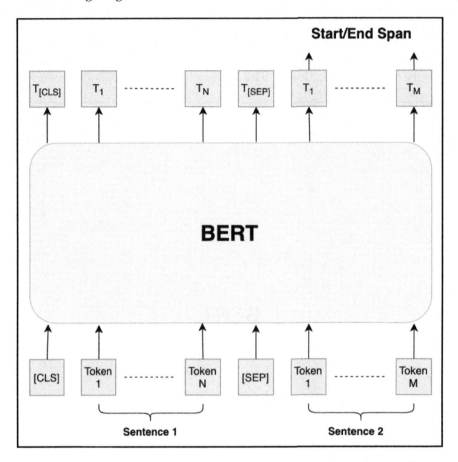

Ideas for these have been sourced original BERT paper, *BERT: Pre-Training of Deep Bidirectional Transformers for Language Understanding* by *Delvin et al.*, available at `https:// arxiv.org/pdf/1810.04805.pdf`.

The rise of BERT revolutionized the domain of NLP and great improvements were achieved in solving numerous tasks. BERT even outperformed all the previous benchmark results for certain tasks.

The open source code for BERT is available on GitHub at `https://github.com/google-research/bert`.

An approach to fine-tune the BERT model for the question classification task we tried solving in `Chapter 8`, *From Human Neurons to Artificial Neurons for Text Understanding*, was made, and the code has been posted at `https://github.com/amankedia/Question-Classification-using-BERT`, along with the results.

Similarly, BERT can be applied to numerous tasks such as part-of-speech tagging, building chatbots, and so on.

Summary

In this chapter, we had a look at some of the recent advancements in the field of NLP, encompassing Seq2Seq modeling, the attention mechanism, the Transformer model, and BERT, all of which have revolutionized the way NLP problems are approached today. We began with a discussion on Seq2Seq modeling where we looked at its core components, the encoder and decoder. Based on the knowledge garnered, we built a French-to-English translator using the encoder-decoder stack. After that, we had a detailed discussion on the attention mechanism, which has allowed great parallelization leading to fast NLP training, and has also improved upon the results from the existing architectures. Next, we looked at Transformers and discussed every component inside the encoder-decoder stack of the Transformers. We also saw how the attention mechanism can be used as the core building block of such architectures, and can possibly provide a replacement for the existing RNN-based architectures. Finally, we had an in-depth discussion on BERT, which is a very recent development that has paved the way for building highly efficient, fine-tuned NLP models for a wide variety of tasks.

Throughout this book, attempts were made to understand multiple NLP techniques and how they could be applied to solve a plethora of problems related to NLP. We built numerous applications such as a chatbot, a spell-checker, a sentiment analyzer, a question classifier, a sarcasm detector, a language generator, and a language translator, among many others throughout the course of this book. As a result, along with the theoretical knowledge we've acquired, we've had plenty of necessary hands-on experience in solving NLP problems as well.

Other Books You May Enjoy

If you enjoyed this book, you may be interested in these other books by Packt:

Natural Language Processing with Python Quick Start Guide
Nirant Kasliwal

ISBN: 978-1-78913-038-6

- Understand classical linguistics in using English grammar for automatically generating questions and answers from a free text corpus
- Work with text embedding models for dense number representations of words, subwords, and characters in the English language for exploring document clustering
- Deep Learning in NLP using PyTorch with a code-driven introduction to PyTorch
- Using an NLP project management Framework for estimating timelines and organizing your project into stages
- Hack and build a simple chatbot application in 30 minutes
- Deploy an NLP or machine learning application using Flask as RESTFUL APIs

Deep Learning for Natural Language Processing
Karthiek Reddy Bokka, Shubhangi Hora, Et al

ISBN: 978-1-83855-029-5

- Understand various preprocessing techniques for solving deep learning problems
- Build a vector representation of text using word2vec and GloVe
- Create a named entity recognizer and parts-of-speech tagger with Apache OpenNLP
- Build a machine translation model in Keras
- Develop a text generation application using LSTM
- Build a trigger word detection application using an attention model

Leave a review - let other readers know what you think

Please share your thoughts on this book with others by leaving a review on the site that you bought it from. If you purchased the book from Amazon, please leave us an honest review on this book's Amazon page. This is vital so that other potential readers can see and use your unbiased opinion to make purchasing decisions, we can understand what our customers think about our products, and our authors can see your feedback on the title that they have worked with Packt to create. It will only take a few minutes of your time, but is valuable to other potential customers, our authors, and Packt. Thank you!

Index

Universal Sentence Encoders (USE) 150
unstructured data 21
unsupervised learning 106
update gate 246

V

Valence Aware Dictionary and sEntiment Reasoner
    (VADER) 36
vanishing and exploding gradients problem 224
vanishing gradient problem 224
vectors 78, 79

W

web scraping 37, 39, 41, 42
word embeddings 104
Word Mover's Distance (WMD) 124, 125, 126,
    148
word normalization
    about 63
    case folding 71, 72
    lemmatization 65

n-grams 72, 73
stemming 63
stopword removal 69, 70
Word2vec architecture
    about 109
    CBOW method 116
    Skip-gram method 110
Word2vec model
    applications 123
    building 118, 119
    configurable parameters 122, 123
    min_count parameter, modifying 120, 121
    training 118
    vector size 121
Word2vec
    demystifying 105
    limitations 123
WordNet lemmatizer 66, 67, 68
WordPunct tokenizer 60

Z

Z-score standardization 161, 162

Made in the USA
Coppell, TX
22 March 2021